The Asbury Theological Seminary Series in Christian Revitalization Studies

This volume is published in collaboration with the Center for the Study of World Christian Revitalization Movements, a cooperative initiative of Asbury Theological Seminary faculty. Building on the work of the previous Wesleyan/Holiness Studies Center at the Seminary, the Center provides a focus for research in the Wesleyan Holiness and other related Christian renewal movements, including Pietism and Pentecostal movements, which have had a world impact. The research seeks to develop analytical models of these movements, including their biblical and theological assessment. Using an interdisciplinary approach, the Center bridges relevant discourses in several areas in order to gain insights for effective Christian mission globally. It recognizes the need for conducting research that combines insights from the history of evangelical renewal and revival movements with anthropological and religious studies literature on revitalization movements. It also networks with similar or related research and study centers around the world, in addition to sponsoring its own research projects.

In this volume, Samuel Law presents an interdisciplinary and intercultural study, engaging mission theory with social realities and complex systems analysis of the twenty first century, and doing so in a manner which revisits and supersedes the classical model for the study of revitalization within society developed in the twentieth century by Anthony Wallace. This study actually develops a model for the study of Christian revitalization and revitalization movements for the contemporary world, which comprehensively engages theory and practice from the standpoint of a hermeneutics of Christian revitalization.

J. Steven O'Malley, PhD
General Editor
The Asbury Theological Seminary Studies in World Christian Revitalization

Sub-Series Foreword
Intercultural Studies

Change happens, whether we want it to nor not. Too often we propose change, perhaps a different style of leadership or a different form of organization, and the proposal is not adopted. In both cases, natural change or directed change, it usually turns out that the situation was more complex than we thought at first. That is why we have theoretical models.

In the study of mission, our models have lagged behind those of the social sciences and physical sciences, dramatically in this age of unprecedented rapid global change. In the face of complexity, there is a tendency to search for single causes for complex phenomena. Why does it appear that the spread of Christianity in this county never took off, while in another country, without heavy missionary presence, 40% of the population has become believers? Why is it that this particular denomination that grew like wildfire in the last decade now seems to have plateaued out? Attempts to get at "the" reason often fail, as do the proposed solutions based on those studies.

Perhaps that is because, in the area of Christian revitalization studies, we rarely get a scholar who has been trained first in the social sciences, let alone trained in the hard sciences. Our scholars most often are a church worker or missionary who then has to be trained in research methods as well as social and cultural theory. This book is a welcome exception to that trend.

In this book, Sam Law, who already had a doctorate in material sciences, pushes us to consider the complexity of emerging systems. He began with what seemed like a simple question: Why did leadership conflict seem to be the norm in multi-generational Chinese churches in America? After pursuing some seemingly obvious but simple potential causes, and then rejecting them, Dr. Law began to draw on Complex Systems Theory to frame the issues. This book is an account of Dr. Law's journey to understand complex systemic change in a way that helps the church understand what is happening while staying true to its mandate and mission.

Michael Rynkiewich, PhD
Sub-Series Editor

Revitalizing Missions on the Cusp of Change

Complex Systems Science Mazeways for
Mission Theory amid
Twenty-First Century Realities

The Asbury Theological Seminary Series in World Christian Revitalization Movements in Intercultural Studies

Samuel K. Law

EMETH PRESS
www.emethpress.com

*Revitalizing Missions on the Cusp
of Change: Complex Systems
Science Mazeways for Mission
Theory amid Twenty-First
Century Realities*

Copyright © 2016 Samuel K. Law
Printed in the United States of America on acid-free paper

All rights reserved. No part of this book may be reproduced, or stored in a retrieval system or transmitted in any form or by any means, electronic, mechanical, photocopying, recording, scanning or otherwise, except as permitted by the 1976 United States Copyright Act, or with the prior written permission of Emeth Press. Requests for permission should be addressed to: Emeth Press, P. O. Box 23961, Lexington, KY 40523-3961. http://www.emethpress.com.

Library of Congress Cataloging-in-Publication Data

Names: Law, Samuel K., author.
Title: Revitalizing missions on the cusp of change : complex systems science mazeways for mission theory amid twenty-first century realities / Samuel K. Law.
Description: Lexington : Emeth Press, 2016. | Series: Asbury Theological Seminary series in world Christian revitalization movements in intercultural studies | Includes bibliographical references.
Identifiers: LCCN 2015049482 | ISBN 9781609470975 (alk. paper)
Subjects: LCSH: Missions--Theory. | Change--Religious aspects--Christianity.
Classification: LCC BV2063 .L316 2016 | DDC 266.001/1--dc23
LC record available at http://lccn.loc.gov/2015049482

Table of Contents

List of Figures / ix

List of Tables / xi

Acknowledgement / xiii

Chapter 1: Mission on the Cusp of Change / 1

    1.1 Introduction: The New Twenty-first Century Context and the Necessity for More Appropriate Research Approaches to Understand the New Realities / 1
    1.2 A Personal Narrative of a Church in Complex Change / 8
    1.3 A Summary of Wallace's Model of Revitalization / 11
    1.4 Inadequacies in Wallace's Revitalization Model in Responding to Twenty-first Century Realities / 15
    1.5 Research Aim: In Search of New Mazeways Through Complex Change / 24
    1.6 Research Case Study: Multicultural Churches of the Chinese Diaspora in North America / 29
    1.7 Significance of the Dissertation – Charting the Trajectory through Complex Change / 30
    1.8 Dissertation Outline / 31
    1.9 Chapter Summary / 33

Chapter 2: A Failure of Existing Mazeways / 35

    2.1 Introduction / 35
    2.2 The Illusion of Simple Social Models / 37
    2.3 Recognizing the Reality of Cultures in Complex, Continuous Change / 39
    2.4 Chapter Summary / 42

Chapter 3: An Emerging Mazeway for Missiological Revitalization / 43

    3.1 From Simple to Complex in the Hard Sciences / 43
    3.2 Emerging Metaphors and Mazeways from Complexity / 48
    3.3 From Simple to Complex in the Soft Sciences / 52

- 3.4 Visualizing Complexity in Social Systems, Organizations and Leadership / 55
- 3.5 Visualizing Complexity Missiology and Revitalization / 66
- 3.6 Complex Systems Science and Social Movement Theory / 74
- 3.7 Using Complexity Theory to Visualize Mazeways through Complex Change / 76
- 3.8 Chapter Summary / 79

Chapter 4: Developing a Complex Systems Model / 81

- 4.1 Theoretical Framework Delimitations: / 81
  - 4.1.1 Complex Systems Science, Chaos Theory, and Complexity Theory / 82
  - 4.1.2 Stability, Chaos, and the Cusp of Change / 83
  - 4.1.3 Emergence Theory in the Strong / 84
- 4.2 Study Population / 85
  - 4.2.1 The Heterogeneous Nature of the Chinese Diaspora / 85
  - 4.2.2 Study Population Delimitations / 91
- 4.3 An Overview of the Churches Studied / 92
- 4.4 Methodology for Data Collection / 93
  - 4.4.1 Subpopulation Differentiation and Interaction (2006-2007) / 94
  - 4.4.2 Evaluating Change over Time (2013) / 94
- 4.5 Confidentiality of Participants / 94
- 4.6 Data Analysis and Model Development / 95
- 4.7 Chapter Summary / 97

Chapter 5: Data Presentation and Analysis: An Emerging Gestalt / 99

- 5.1 Overview of Church Contexts / 99
- 5.2 Summary of Church Distinctiveness and Ministry Characteristics / 101
- 5.3 Overview of Church Leadership and Structure / 103
- 5.4 Summary of Cultural and Generational Issues / 106
- 5.5 Summary of Reported Changes between 2006-7 and 2013-14 / 109
- 5.6 Selection of Primary Variables for Investigation / 112
  - 5.6.1 Immigration Patterns / 112
  - 5.6.2 Leadership Flexibility in Adapting to Change / 113
  - 5.6.3 Level of Systemic Comprehension or Unity / 114

    5.6.4 Level of Transcultural Identity / 114
    5.6.5 Intentional Spiritual Formation / 115
  5.7 The Gestalt Process: Capturing the Variables into an Integrated Model / 116
    5.7.1 Meso-level Model / 117
    5.7.2 Micro-level Agent-based Model / 119
  5.8 Chapter Summary / 121
    5.8.1 Observations / 121
    5.8.2 Model Development / 122
    5.8.3 Normative Insights from the Complex Systems Science-framed Cusp of Change model / 123

Chapter 6: Discussion – A Tale of Two Paradigms / 125

  6.1 Analysis 1.0 – The Linear Approach / 127
  6.2 Analysis 2.0 – The Complex Systems Approach / 130
    6.2.1 Historicity: The Dynamic Nature of Complex Systems / 130
    6.2.2 Networks: The Relational Nature of Complex Systems / 134
    6.2.3 Dimensional Integration: The Nature of Scale in Complex Systems / 137
      6.2.3.1 Micro-level Agency: The Emergent Roles of Individuals / 139
      6.2.3.2 Meso-Level: The Role of Leaders and a new 21st Century Definition for Revitalization / 147
      6.2.3.3 Macro-Level: The Role of the Holy Spirit / 152
  6.3 Defining Christian Revitalization: A Psychological Sickness or the Cusp of Change? / 154
    6.3.1 Source of Christian Revitalization / 154
    6.3.2 Historicity of Christian Revitalization / 156
    6.3.3 Locus of Revitalization / 157
    6.3.4 Christian Revitalization as a Spirit-imbued, Continuous, Systemic Process / 161
  6.4 The Critical Importance of a More Complex Model / 168
  6.5 Chapter Summary / 169

Chapter 7: Developing Complex Systems Mazeways for 21st Century Multicultural Contexts / 173

  7.1 Gestalting Historicity / 173
  7.2 Gestalting the Networks / 178

7.3 Gestalting Dimensional Integration / 183
   7.3.1 Micro-level Agency / 183
   7.3.2 Meso-level Role of Leadership / 185
7.4 Model Integration / 189
7.5 Chapter Summary: Formulating a New Mazeway Through Rapid, Complex Change / 192

Chapter 8: Missiology on the Cusp of Change – The Creation of New Mazeways to Shalom Via Complex Systems Science / 195

8.1 Physician, Heal Thyself / 195
8.2 Integrating Complex Systems Analysis into Existing Missiological Mazeways / 207
8.3 The Role of Missiologists in the Twenty-First Century Context of Globally Networked, Rapid, Complex Change / 211

Bibliography / 213

Appendix 1: Definition of Terms / 231

Definition of Terms / 231
Systems / 231
Complex Systems Subdisciplines and Characteristics / 232
Modeling / 233

Appendix 2: Lilly Endowment Interview Questions / 235

Appendix 3: Second Time Point Follow Up Survey / 237

List of Figures

Figure 1 - Domain of Complex Systems and the Subdomain of "General Linear Reality" / 5
Figure 2 - Limitations of Wallace's model from a Systemic Perspective / 18
Figure 3 - Comparison between a Complicated and a Complex Network / 21
Figure 4 - Serial Processing of Codes (Shaw 2010, 209) / 25
Figure 5 - Parallel Distributive Processing Ideas (Shaw 2010, 210) / 26
Figure 6 - Contrasting Models of Mission (Shaw 2010, 211) / 27
Figure 7 - Evoked Potential Recordings (Law 1991, 144) / 44
Figure 8 - Topographic Maps of Brain Activity (Law et al, 1993:145) / 46
Figure 9 - Time evolution of x, y, and z from the Lorenz system (Flake 1998, 171) / 60
Figure 10 - Two time evolutions of x with an infinitesimal initial difference (Flake 1998, 169) / 61
Figure 11 - An illustration of a Lorenz Attractor (Flake 1998, 172) / 61
Figure 12 - Emergence of a New Attractor (Goldstein et al 2010, 62) / 62
Figure 13 - Representative Pathways for Attractor Change (Goldstein et al 2010, 70) / 63
Figure 14 - Stylized Model of an attractor in an organization with multiple individuals (Goldstein et al 2010, 59) / 64
Figure 15 - The Emergence of Dissipative Systems Complemented with the Dual Function of Organizational Communication (Aula and Siira 2007) / 65
Figure 16 - from Hiebert et al, 1999:349 / 69
Figure 17 - Illustration of Cultural Homeostasis (Hofstede et al 2010, 467) / 70

Figure 18 - Lorenz Attractor with application to missiology / 71
Figure 19 - Scientific and Mathematical Fields Making Up Complexity Science (Goldstein et al 2010, 7) / 83
Figure 20 - Immigration Numbers with Historical Timeline of Key Events (from 2013 Immigration Statistics Yearbook; X. Yin 2007, 125) / 87
Figure 21 - Chinese Immigration plotted with number of Chinese churches / 88
Figure 22 - Co-existence of Multiple Identities to form an Adhesive Identity - from Yang (1999, 184) / 91
Figure 23 - Complex Description of a CIC Church / 118
Figure 24 - Micro-agent Model depicting changes in Adhesive Identity over time / 20
Figure 25 - Expansion of Church Networks over Time / 179
Figure 26 - CIC Church on the Cusp of Change / 190
Figure 27 - Visual Signatures and Contribution of Complexity Research (from Ramalingam 2013, 232) / 201
Figure 28 - The Missional Helix (Van Rheenan 2004, 188) / 208
Figure 29 - Nonaka SECI model of Knowledge Creation (Wierzbicki and Nakamori 2006, 69) / 209

List of Tables

Table 1 - Matrix of Generational and subcultural diaspora Chinese study populations / 90
Table 2 - Overview of Churches Studied / 100
Table 3 - Church Distinctives and Characteristics / 102
Table 4 - Characterization of Church Leadership and Structure 104
Table 5 - Cultural and Generational Issues / 107
Table 6- Changes in the Churches between 2006-7 and 2013-14 / 110
Table 7 - Comparison of complexity and conventional views on conflict management, communication and leadership (Aula & Siira 2007, 380) / 136
Table 8 - Comparison of Properties of Christian Revitalization / 169
Table 9 - Conventional and Alternative Approaches to Aid (from Ramalingam 2013, 142) / 200
Table 10 - Tabulation by Category of Missiology Journals from 2010 – 2014 / 204

Aknowledgments

I came to Asbury burned out after nearly two decades of mediating conflicts. It left me nearly empty of grace, short-tempered, and cynical. The five years at Asbury has enabled me to renew my strength and my hope for the last trimester of life (I'm writing this at the ripe old age of fifty-two!). I am indebted to many who have helped me in this journey, more that these pages could possibly hold (please know that though you are nameless here, the Lord knows your role in my life).

The first group I'd like to thank is my family. Though my mother passed away in 2007 to be with the Lord, in many ways, she is the one who encouraged me to pursue my calling. When I was troubled at church, I would often go over to her house, about a mile away, for lunch. She'd listen to my complaints, provide perspective, comforted me, and, oftentimes, rebuked me. But she always encouraged me to press ahead. I'm thankful for my wife, Esther, who has supported and stood by me through the many years of ministry, and to make the move from Seattle to Lexington. Without her, I do not think I would have the courage to undertake this endeavor. I'm also thankful to my children, Jeremiah, Josephine, Jason, and Julia, who willingly gave up their father to mounds of books and a computer screen. They rarely complained.

The second group I'd like to thank is my dissertation committee. This dissertation would not have been possible without their mentorship. I'm thankful to Dr. Rynkiewich for teaching me never to accept the *status quo* and to continually challenge preconceptions; his meticulous nature and breadth of knowledge made sure I had "turned over every stone" in the research process. Though he graciously removed himself from the committee (due to a change in the doctoral program from three to two serving members), I'm thankful to Dr. Kima's (Lalsangkima Pachau) contributions for always offering new rabbit trails to follow, and for encouraging me to try to integrate my previous and present vocations. I'm thankful to Dr. Offutt for pointing me in the direction of quantitative analysis. True, it meant re-working the proposal and taking a different path; but ultimately, it proved a most satisfying journey. Thanks also to Dr. Art McPhee for his willingness and effort to serve as my examiner.

The third group is the two churches that have supported me in this endeavor. I'm thankful to the Evangelical Chinese Church of Seattle for their willingness to call a wet-behind-the-ears seminary graduate to serve in the church I have been a part of since age ten, and for the many brothers and sisters who mentored and co-labored with me to grow and mature in ministry. I'm also thankful to the Lexington Chinese Christian Church which has become my "home away from home." I have learned much about being a "Chinese Ministry pastor" (as opposed to an English Ministry pastor) through their patient co-laboring.

I would also like to express my sincere gratitude to Dr. Steven O'Malley and Mr. Larry Wood for their willingness to publish this work through Emeth Press.

Last and most importantly, all praise and glory belong to my heavenly Father, my Lord, and the Holy Spirit, who has been my constant companion these many years. In my weakness, His grace has always proved sufficient. I am thankful that He has called this wretched sinner into His service, and even though I almost lost hope, God never gave up on me. In my weariness, He renewed my strength. This dissertation is a testament of His faithfulness.

Chapter 1

Mission on the Cusp of Change

1.1 Introduction: The Twenty-first Century Context and the Necessity for More Appropriate Research Approaches to Understand the New Realities

The recognition of complexity and change has been present since the creation of the world. One need only look passages such as Genesis 1, Psalm 139, Isaiah 55, and 2 Corinthians 5:17 to understand that complexity and change are part of the biblical narrative.

But toward the end of the twentieth century, humanity has entered an unprecedented period of change (Snyder 1995, 13). The twenty-first century is an era of perceived constant change (Guder 1998, 29); *even change is changing* (Hofstede *et al* 2010, 475; Law 2012, 8). These changes are fundamental and require us to change not only the way we live, but require us to continuously adapt our worldviews in order to stay afloat in the turbulent seas of change (Hiebert 1999, 1).

Furthermore, the processes of change are no longer local; its sweep is broader and more diverse than ever before. What defines our twenty-first century context is that these change processes are now networked across a global communication system that ceaselessly transmits changes nearly instantaneously, and rapidly permeates the whole of the global human sociocultural system at levels not experienced in previous epochs (Kluger 2008, 12). Change has become *more systemic.* Whether it be a tribe in the remotest jungles of the Amazon or an inner city church in one of the busiest cities in China, a store owner in Lagos, Nigeria or a farmer in rural Iowa, as a consequence of global factors such as climate change, the competition for ever decreasing resources among nations, the electronic speed of information dissemination, and the interaction across an ever increasing number of overlapping, intertwining boundaries, every culture or society on our planet is now impacted by such changes at such a fast frequency that change is perceived as pervasive and continuous (Roxburgh and Regele 2000, 18; King 2011, 87).

Moreover, as every part of our world becomes networked for instantaneous communication and interaction, as every constituent element is being assimilated into "the internet of everything," change *has become more complex.* The magnitude and diversity of complexity and change – and the effort to collect, process, and analyze the data – continue to exponentially increase, far beyond what human cognition and senses are able to absorb and comprehend – even increasingly beyond what traditional, simple and linear approaches can analyze. Hence, compared to previous epochs, change processes in the twenty-first century context are *more continuous, systemic, and complex.*

Alan Roxburgh and Mike Regele, recognizing that the patterns of change had changed, realized the impact this was having on churches. They wrote that

> Leaders of congregations or denominations are in the midst of massive destabilizing change. We have to address, in ourselves and with our people, these inner responses to massive changes. How do we learn to lead people through the transitions we are all experiencing when the photographs in our hearts no longer correlate with the images of the world we are in today? (2000, 12)

In the last sentence, Roxburgh and Regele allude to the fact that changes are now on a scale so rapid and systemic that the "photographs in our hearts," that is, one's worldview, and later to be defined as a "mazeway," are no longer able to provide adequate guidance through one's life time as in the past epochs. Hence, if churches are to remain relevant and vital, that is, to be able to respond and adapt to changing realities, in the twenty-first century, then they must find ways to update continuously, to revitalize, "heart photographs" that accurately represent twenty-first century realities and contexts that are vastly different from previous epochs as a consequence of the exponentially widening networks that transmit complex change.

How then can Christian communities respond to such systemic, continuous, and complex change to avoid ending up with obsolete "heart photographs?"

The answer is a mental video camera, for only an instrument designed to record motion can record such rapid change; and not just a single camera, but a host of video cameras recording from multiple angles and integrated into a single framework that is processed and analyzed through sufficiently robust metaphors and models that visualize the data such that they can serve as "heart *videos*." Only such a system can record and analyze the global network of diverse and complex change, and distill the legion of data into a comprehensible, efficacious form.

In order to develop the appropriate systems that will empower churches to generate such "heart videos," rapidly adapting worldviews to navigate continuously changing realities, church leaders and members, and academicians and practitioners alike, all must take up the mantle of missiologists. Missiology,[1] being a discipline that aids the Church to cross geographic and cultural boundaries, is best able to develop the metaphors, metaphors, and models to analyze, predict, and navigate the moving temporal boundaries of change. *This book describes how the field of missiology can develop helpful and appropriate analytical tools for the twenty-first century realities of continuous, systemic, and complex change.* Specifically, missiology must harness the metaphors, models, and methodologies of the emerging science of Complex Systems if it is thrive and navigate the new realities.

Complex Systems Science benefits missiology because by nature, missiology is itself complex, historically contested, and contingent. Following Alan Tippett and Louis J. Luzbetak, Stanley Skreslet defines missiology not as

> "a *mere conglomeration* of disciplines, but a network of disciplines that systematically interact with one another" ... missiology is a field rather than a discipline, where all the dimensions of mission demand to be examined carefully. (2012, 14) ... [missiology] properly encompasses every kind of scholarly inquiry performed on the subject of mission without necessarily subordinating any group of studies to any other. (2012, 15)

Missiology as a complex system thus benefits directly from Complex Systems Science-framed approaches.

---

[1] Operatively, this book defines "the field of missiology" to encompass those who contribute and read the three journals reviewed (to be detailed later) among others (see Bonk *et al* (2013) and the discussion by Robert Priest in his blog: http://www.missiologymatters.com/2012/03/13/topjournal/. accessed November 7, 2014)

Complex Systems Science[2] is considered by many to be the "science of the twenty-first century," (Waldrop 1992, 13) and the paradigm shift from a traditional to a Complex Systems Science framework is already occurring across a multitude of fields. One may wonder why this shift is so significant, so at this juncture, it may be helpful define what *traditional* science is in order to understand why Complex Systems Science is so critical.

For the purposes of this book, *traditional* science is defined as research approaches that are positivist, and, consequently, working from a reductionist and linear framework. It is a framework that some call *logical empiricism,* that which can be deduced and materially measured. Traditional science can also be termed *modern* science, birthed during the Enlightenment, as both positivism and logical empiricism are "widely used as a label for the general epistemological foundations underlying much of modern scientific thought." (Hiebert 1999, 3) According to Paul Hiebert (1999), in such a mindset, reality is objective and material (4) and thus without a sense of mystery (13). Reality is reduced to basic components because knowledge is additive (11); that is, it is linear. Unfortunately, this represented reality is then considered a "closed" system, that is, disconnected and confined to an "ideal case." Consequently, this pseudo-reality is resigned to being mechanically causal without reflecting natural causality, in other words, lacking a systems metanarrative and without teleology (6).

Prior to the assimilation of Complex Systems-framed paradigms, the majority of the social sciences dwelt in what Andrew Abbott terms *general linear reality*. In this paradigm, most theories in the social sciences, missiology included, rely on traditional, linear approaches. According to Abbott, the dominance of linear models leads social scientists,

> ... to construe the social world in terms of a "general linear reality." This reality assumes (1) that the social world consists of fixed entities with variable attributes, (2) that cause cannot flow from "small" to "large" attributes/events, (3) that causal attributes have only one causal pattern at one, (4) that the sequence of events does not influence their outcome, (5) that the "careers" of entities are largely independent, and (6) that causal attributes are generally independent of each other." (1988, 169)

---

[2] To delineate terminology in the new paradigm of Complex Systems Science from the more common usage of words, this dissertation will follow Russ Marion's convention to capitalize Chaos Theory and Complexity Theory. (Marion 1999, 13)

consequently, complexity and change are, as a matter of fact, dismissed in the formulations and representations of reality.

But beginning at the turn of the twentieth century, with the ability to expand the scales of study, from the subatomic level in quantum mechanics to the exponential broadening of the bounds of astronomy and astrophysics, there was a growing realization that the simple laws of *traditional* science were valid only in the middle scale, the range of human cognition and human senses. Outside of this middle scale, quantum mechanics revealed that things were "fuzzy," and astrophysics revealed that assumed inviolable physical laws such as gravity could be "bent." The more the scales expanded in both directions, the more the traditional science framework was shaken and began to crumble.

Consequently, reality can no longer be perceived as simple, ordered, and mechanically causal. The realities above and below the middle scales are complex, chaotic, and unpredictable. This expansion of scales increasingly forces traditional science to acknowledge what humans already know in their hearts, that reality is an "open system."

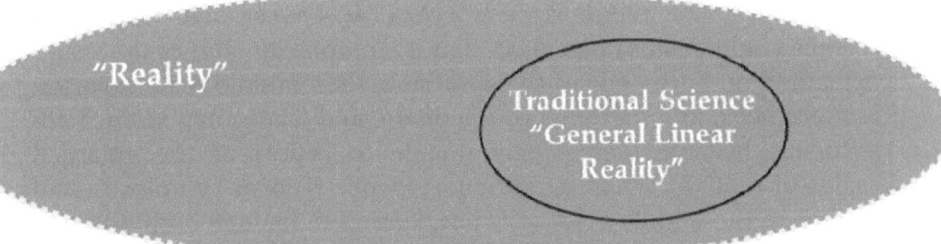

Figure 1 - Domain of Complex Systems and the Subdomain of "General Linear Reality"

The relationship between traditional and Complex Systems Science is thus essentially one of scale and boundedness. From a systems perspective, the traditional science system occupies only a small corner of Complex Systems Science, a subset of simple, linear, middle scale, contexts and realities (see Figure 1). Traditional science itself setsits own rigid, impermeable boundaries of validity to what can be reduced to constituent elements (positivist), what can be deduced, what can be materially measured (logical empiricism), and how it can act (general linear reality). In contrast, Complex Systems Science is left unbounded, recognizing that what is observed does not represent reality completely, and, as such, reality is inherently "fuzzy." Consequently, Complex Systems Science is inductive and inferential and, as such, metaphorical, recognizing that the physical and material are mere representations of true reality, limited by the extent of human and technological abilities.

A useful analogy to compare the boundedness of traditional science and the boundlessness of Complex Systems Science involves looking at the characters of printed material (Hiebert 1999, 79). The human eye sees the edges of the characters as sharp and distinct. But on the microscopic level, the edges become "fuzzy." If one were to look at the print material from a hundred feet away; it would again be a "fuzzy" dot.

The same can be said of the increased diversity as the boundaries are expanded. What is visible to the eye is one color, but magnifying the print, what is perceived as one color is in actuality three on printed media. And if the analogy is a computer screen, from the first monochrome monitor screens to contemporary screens, the diversity of colors has increased by several orders of magnitude. As scales expand, so the diversity of observations increases.

As long as the middle scale is all that was observable, traditional science could dismiss fuzziness, that is, complexity. But as the scales expanded on both ends of the spectrum, then middle scale theories, models, laws, and methods broke down, and traditional science approaches became increasingly unable to represent the enlarged scales of reality. Where traditional science ignores complexity and change in the middle scale, it is now forced to include both if it is to provide some semblance of reality in the micro and macro levels.

Hence, the adaptation to Complex Systems Science was out of a desperate need to be able to comprehend the exponential increase of systemic scale, and as well, an increase in the number of variables and their related data that are associated with the expansion of networked relationships. As will be detailed in Chapter 3, the adaptation to Complex Systems Science only accelerated toward the end of the twentieth century as computers that empowered humanity to process, analyze and visualize complex data in a comprehensible fashion became accessible and normative in daily life.

Andrew Abbott thus summarizes the daunting challenges that social scientists, missiologists included, face at the beginning of the twentieth-first century:

The single most important challenge facing the empirical social sciences in the next 50 years is the problem of finding patterns in such monumentally detailed data. And the blunt fact is that sociology is woefully unprepared to deal with this problem: We have neither the analytical tools nor the conceptual imagination necessary. Our stock-in-trade analytic methods were designed for investigating relations between small numbers of variables and are useless for large-scale pattern-recognition or, as we have pejoratively labeled it, data dredging....

Nor is it just a matter of ramping existing methods. We have to rethink data analysis from the ground up. In the short run, we are going to have to jettison the idea of causality that has lead us to denigrate precisely the analytic tools necessary to address the problems of huge data sets. We have to give up the futile quest for effects "net of other variables" and wall in the endless multiplexity of data. We have to enter a world of iterative pattern-recognition, of simulation, of Monte Carlo optimization. It is a methodological world that will draw heavily on computer science, on algorithmic and aleatory approach to knowledge. And it is a world completely foreign to our methods courses. We have in the past simply ignored the vastness of data. We talk about "finding the right variable," but in reality we have always had thousands of variables to choose from and no sensible way to make the choice. There results in our literature the amusing spectacle of one indicator being used to indicate dozens of different things in dozens of different articles. In 50 years, people will view these activities the way we now view the people who paged through sheaves of two-way crosstabs. (2000, 299)

The adaptation to Complex Systems Science first occurred in the hard sciences of mathematics and engineering toward the latter third of the twentieth century (Kellert 1993, 137), but at the advent of the twenty-first century, is increasingly being adapted for anthropological (Mosko and Damon, 2005; Reyna 2002), sociological (Eve et al 1997, Marion 1999; Wilensky 1999; Johnson 2001; Walby 2007; Kluger 2008), and for religious studies (Spickard 2004; Purzycki et al 2014).

There have also been several publications using principles from Complexity Leadership Theory for ecclesiological and missiological practice (Bandy 1999, Roxburgh and Regele 2000, Herrington et al 2000, Hirsch 2006, Thompson 2007, Hall 2010). However, these take Complex Systems Science as a metaphor for leadership and change, and thus mine a few insights; none are a serious call to do research from a Complex Systems Science-framed paradigm.

In fact, the adaptation to Complex Systems Science remains at the conception stage in missiology. In reviewing three major missiological journals (please see Chapter 8 for a fuller discussion. The journals are: *Missiology* of the American Society of Missiologists, *Mission Studies* of the International Association of Mission Studies, and the

International Bulletin of Missionary Research of the Overseas Ministry Study Center) of the last five years, from 2010 – 2014, while more than two-thirds, 189 of 284, of the articles recognize and qualitatively attempt to describe complexity, *only two*, less than one percent, applied metaphors, terminology, or research methodology directly from Complex Systems Science (e.g. Shaw 2010, Van Gelder 2014). Of these two, only R. Daniel Shaw uses Complex Systems Science as a methodology; Van Gelder only uses the term "adaptive leadership" as a call for the American Society of Missiology to respond to the changing realities of the twenty-first century. As such, *with only one study*, the paradigm shift to Complex Systems has yet to even reach the mitotic (where the fertilized egg finally splits into two cells) stage missiologically to look at the ever increasing and complex interactions in and across multicultural systems (confirmed in personal communication with Philip Clayton, March 2012).

This book is then an exercise in applying Complex Systems Science metaphors, models, and methodology to the field of missiology to address the growing, networked complexity and continuous change that are the characteristics of the twenty-first century context. Anthony F.C. Wallace's model of religious revitalization and the Complex Systems Science-framed Cusp of Change model are compared to evaluate which model is more efficacious in representing diverse, twenty-first century realities. The models are compared by applying both models to the case study of multicultural, multicongregational, multilingual churches of the North American Chinese diaspora.

The following sections provide the rationale for the book in the form of a personal background narrative, a review of Wallace's model of revitalization and a consideration of why linear approaches are increasingly unable to reflect the twenty-first century context, and an introduction to the benefits of Complex Systems Science to existing mission theory and methods. These will be expanded in greater detail in Chapters 2 and 3. Finally, an overview of the book and its significance are provided.

1.2 A Personal Narrative of a Church in Complex Change

As a pastor for fourteen years, and Elder Board Chair (functionally senior pastor) for ten of those years, at a large Chinese church in the Pacific Northwest of the United States, I was a witness to dramatic and continuous change - but it was not all good. On the one hand, as the urban population grew and became more diverse, our church by God's grace benefited. From 1999 to 2009, we grew from a church of 600 with two language congregations (Mandarin/Cantonese and English) and two pastors to a church of 1200 with five congregations (one stand-alone Mandarin, one stand-alone Cantonese, one Mandarin/Cantonese and two stand-alone English) on two campuses and a staff of nine. By all accounts, I should have been overjoyed at God's blessings; but I wasn't. Instead, I became more and more frustrated because of increasing inter-personal conflicts I needed to mediate. These were not because of moral, theological or even administrative issues. Rather, these issues were personal conflicts among respected leaders in the church.

So, as I sought to lead God's people on the mission that God had given, our mission was being blocked by relational rifts among leaders who had known each other for years, some for decades. What was the cause of such change in directions that seemed detrimental to the church?

At first, I assumed this was a result of growing pains of a church's life cycle (Saarinen 2001) and institutionalization (Hiebert *et al* 2009, 333). So I applied for and received a Lilly Endowment Clergy Renewal Grant (Grant number 2005 0931-000) in 2005 to visit ten Chinese churches of similar size in the US and in Taiwan hoping to find answers to my problems.

What I discovered from my visits was that this rise in conflict seemed endemic as all the churches visited were facing similar issues regardless of whether the church was in North America or Taiwan. My grant report concluded that "conflict was the ministry" as every church faced similar changes and issues (Wan 2003) and, unfortunately, most pastors and leaders were at a loss to know how to respond. Some churches, despite continuing population growth locally, were stagnating, others even declining. Clearly, a far larger change process was occurring across the Chinese Diaspora church community, and not merely as a consequence of local community factors.

The similarities discovered across the churches did not mean that there was no response to the changes all the churches seemed to be experiencing. In fact, most of those interviewed recognized that change, similar to the detrimental, conflictual change I was observing, was occurring. Church leaders and members alike generally recognized the broad systemic changes that were enveloping them.

These changes included phenomena such as changing immigration patterns, dissimilar worldviews of new immigrants compared to previous immigrants, social and cultural shifts in the North American context, and technological impacts on life-styles and communication patterns among others. These changes were not self-initiated, singular events, but spontaneous, systemic, continuous, and complex changes, impacting every aspect of daily life, individually and organizationally.

But the responses were varied. Much of this variation, in my opinion, was cultural, as was the perception by church leaders of how significant the change process was. Yet the variability of the responses only created more questions that begged further investigation as to why some made the paradigm shift in response to change and others did not. These observations are similar to what Roxburgh and Regele note, writing that

> Understanding is a crucial element in this process [i.e., response to change]. Without the appropriate frameworks that help us interpret our experience personally and within our church systems, we may become disoriented in our leadership. Indeed, many will revert to what we have known – the tried and true – for resources in coping with what we do not know. Unfortunately, if what we have known does not work in the unknown, our responses prove ineffective, if not harmful. (2000, 12)

This was very similar to what I was facing. I was at a loss to know how to lead my church forward in such a context of change.

So in 2009, I decided to resign as pastor and go back to school to try and understand what was happening and to seek a "new way" to mitigate the swath of conflicts created by the turbulence of change; I sought a means of revitalization that would create a new mazeway to navigate through the systemic changes observed across the Chinese Diaspora Church community and consequently, it was hoped that my dissertation would be a journey of discovery.

As a pastor, my main question was: *"In such an environment of unprecedented change, what will be defined later as complex change, how should Christian communities understand, respond and adapt to, and even mediate this change, yet maintain their biblical identity, mandate and mission?"* Put more succinctly, *"How can Christian communities revitalize[3]- that is, the dialectic process of adaptation*

---

[3] For the purposes of this dissertation, "revitalization" is to be understood in the context of Christianity, that is, "Christian revitalization." Although many of the concepts most likely can be transferred to the broader definition of cultural or social revitalization, the dissertation delimits "revitalization" to "Christian revitalization." These terms will be defined in the following section.

while maintaining one's root identity - in the context of rapid, complex change?"

But as I trained to become a missiologist, a pathfinder to help the Church traverse new boundaries (Skreslet 2012, 13) - geographic, cultural, *and now, temporal* – as will be described in the following section, I realized that the metaphor and model "maps" I was provided, specifically, Wallace's model of revitalization, were outdated. The contextual landscape has changed so radically that the mazeways forward are no longer the simple, linear routes indicated by the original map. As well, just because there was a route did not mean that it was best path as the "traffic" of change across 21st century global communication and transportation networks and pathways has now exponentially increased to an extent that one now needs to take into account "traffic jams."

Hence, my dissertation, and the basis of this book, became primarily a "map-making" endeavor to discern a more relevant methodology to translate the 21st century realities of complex change into models and metaphors that will enhance the abilities of missiologists to map mazeways forward through new and constantly changing future landscapes. Metaphorically, this book seeks to build a "missiological GPS (Global Positioning System) device" that will enable missiologists to dynamically and predictively alter their contextual mazeways in response to the systemic, continuous, and complex changes of 21st century realities. My journey of discovery remains, but is now a secondary concern until I can develop the appropriate tools to navigate the new landscape of change.

1.3 A Summary of Wallace's Model of Revitalization

For major cultural-system innovation, the model of revitalization movements proposed by Anthony FC Wallace in his 1956 article, entitled simply "Revitalization Movements," is one of the most frequently cited articles in anthropological circles (Grumet 2003, vii), and considered the normative yardstick of analysis for how societies respond to change. Further, Wallace's influence extends well beyond anthropology and his work is cited in fields ranging from history to psychology. This is particularly true in the field of missiology to describe Christian revitalization (Rynkiewich 2011, 40; Irwin 2011, 231).

In a compendium of essays to mark the fiftieth anniversary of Wallace's seminal work, editor Robert S. Grumet writes that Wallace's "most lasting legacy lies in his vision of culture as an organizer of diversity rather than as a replication of uniformity." (2003, viii). According to Grumet, Wallace's article came at a time when uniformitarian and generalizing principles were on the ascendency in anthropology.

> Culture was variously seen as a unitary phenomenon spreading from originating places (a central tenet of Fritz Graebner's diffusionism), a reflection of human mental architecture (as in Freudian psychology and various structuralisms of Emile Durkheim, A.R. Radcliffe-Brown, and Claude Levi-Strauss), or of quasi organic processes in general (as in the functionalism of Bronislaw Malinowski and his followers). Departures from patterns in these normative paradigms generally were interpreted as deviant, abnormal, and in many cases, needful of cure, castigation, or something more drastic. (Grumet 2003, viii)

In this context, Wallace argued that "culture was best viewed as providing a diverse range of choices to individuals rather than a single set of rules to which all members must conform." (Grumet 2003, x) Hence, Wallace's revitalization paradigm argues for discontinuity over and against the uniformitarian *status quo*. He was, in a sense, one of the first to recognize "complexity." His willingness to break from the normative paradigm enabled others to do the same, birthing new mazeways not only in anthropology, but throughout the social, and even hard (specifically psychology), sciences. As such, one should not underestimate Wallace's contributions.

By way of review, revitalization, as defined by Wallace, is

> a deliberate, organized, conscious effort by members of a society to construct a more satisfying culture. Revitalization is thus, from a cultural standpoint, a special kind of culture change phenomenon: the persons involved in the process of revitalization must perceive their culture, or some major areas of it, as a system (whether accurately or not); they must feel that this cultural systems is unsatisfactory; and they must innovate not merely discrete items, but a new cultural system, specifying new relationships as well as, in some cases, new traits." (1956, 265)

For Wallace, several characteristics are mandatory; there must be *intentionality*, and revitalization must be *systemically discontinuous*. To counter the then pervasive attitude of passive uniformitarianism, Wallace does not consider evolution, drift, diffusion, historical change, or acculturation as revitalization because they are neither intentional nor systemically discontinuous (1956, 265).

The foundation of Wallace's model of revitalization is organic and based on psychological theory. Revitalization is grounded in the principle of *homeostasis*, "that a society will work, by means, to preserve its own integrity by maintaining a minimally fluctuating, life-supporting matrix for its individual members, and will, under stress, take emergency measures to preserve the constancy of this matrix" (1956, 265). Wallace defines stress as the "condition in which some part, or the whole, of the social organism is threatened with more or less serious damage." (1956, 265)

Wallace calls the ability of an organism to respond to stress and return to homeostasis a *mazeway*. He defines a *mazeway* as the "perceptions of both the maze of physical objects of the environment (internal and external, human and nonhuman) and also of the ways in which this maze can be manipulated by the self and others in order to minimize stress." (1956, 266) A mazeway is grounded in an individual's understanding of the system, "the ability of constituent units autonomously to perceive the system of which they are a part, to receive and transmit information, and to act in accordance with the necessities of the system, than on any all-embracing central administration which stimulates specialized parts to perform their function." (1956, 266) In missiological terms, mazeway is similar to the term *worldview* (Kraft 1979, 53; Hiebert 1999, 84), and in Roxburgh and Regele's analogy of "photographs of the heart."

Wallace defines a revitalization movement as a five-stage process that is initiated when stress is introduced, and a culture's mazeway is inadequate to enable its constituent individuals to return to homeostasis. The five stages are: 1) Steady State (that is, homeostasis); 2. Period of Individual Stress; 3. Period of Cultural Distortion; 4. Period of Revitalization; and 5. New Steady State (a new homeostasis). The period of revitalization incurs the functions of mazeway reformulation, communication, organization, adaptation, cultural transformation and routinization.

To be considered a revitalization movement, readers are reminded that Wallace mandates that it be *systemically discontinuous*. "Gradual modification or even rapid substitution of techniques for satisfying some needs may occur without disturbing the steady state." (1956, 268) Hence, revitalization involves

> the *Gestalt* of his image of self, society, and culture, of nature and body, and ways of action. It may also be necessary to make changes in the "real" system in order to bring mazeway and "reality" into congruence. The effort to work a change in mazeway and "real" system together so as to permit more effective stress reduction is the effort at revitalization; and the collaboration of a number of persons in such an effort is called a revitalization movement. (1956, 267)

The term *Gestalt* is the German word for "form, shape, or figure" and is understood as the ability to grasp the totality of a system and how all the constituent elements are integrated into the whole.

(Reese 1996, 257) Hence, only a systemic, discontinuous response can be considered a revitalization movement. "The culture of this [new steady] state will probably be different, organization or *Gestalt*, as well as in traits, from the earlier steady state; it will be different from that of the period of cultural distortion." (Wallace 1956, 275)

It should be noted that Wallace's discontinuity does not mean that everything in the old mazeway is discarded. Certain elements of traditional material remain. But "for some reason, each movement tends to profess either no identification at all, a traditional orientation, or foreign orientation." (1956, 276) Hence, there is componential continuity, but no identity continuity.

Lastly, to highlight the place of individuals in contrast to the inevitability of uniformitarianism, Wallace qualifies that revitalization generally occurs in a single person who will become the prophet or leader. "With a few exceptions, every religious revitalization movement with which I am acquainted has been originally conceived in one or several hallucinatory visions by a single individual." (1956, 270) In fact, Wallace dismisses Max Weber's broader understanding of revitalization as a social movement involving leaders and followers, arguing that Weber's "generalizations do not deal with the revitalization formula itself, but rather with the nature of the relationship of the early adherents to their prophet." (1956, 275) Hence, in the vessel of a single leader, revitalization is "a synthesizing and often therapeutic process performed under extreme stress by individuals already sick." (Wallace 1956, 273)

In summary, Wallace contends that "the historical origin of a great proportion of religious phenomena has been in revitalization movements," (1956, 279) defined by stress such that an existing homeostatic mazeway is no longer able to address, thereby requiring a *gestalt* of a new mazeway, and defining a new steady state. The process of revitalization takes place in an individual sickened by untenable stress to the extent that s/he has a vision, a *gestalt* of a new mazeway, that leads to a new culturally systemic and discontinuous, steady state.

Although some have argued that this definition of revitalization may still be too simplistic, even for monolithic societies (Leach 1954; Roth 1992, 214), and others have questioned its validity in globalized, urban contexts (Rynkiewich 2011, 41), nevertheless, despite such concerns, Wallace's original 1956 model is generally deemed to be the normative framework for the analysis of revitalization. Anthropologists and sociologists continue to measure and fit their ethnographies to conform to Wallace's theory of revitalization movements (Harkin 2004, xxxiv), despite the growing realization that "revitalization seems a concept whose time has come and gone. It dates to the 1950s and 1960s, an era when social thought tended toward the creation of formal, rule-driven constructs that attempted to account for the entire range of human behavior with reference to one or two driving principles." (Harkin 2004, xviii)

Similarly, Wallace's model of revitalization remains the predominant model of interpretation for Christian revitalization (Shaw 2008, 770). In a recent consultation on revitalization, many still

> ... assumed Anthony Wallace's definition of revitalization as the standard or norm for understanding Christian revitalization movements, a definition that, though perhaps true for some forms of cultural change, did not correspond with many examples and dimensions of revitalization illustrated in the consultation case studies. ... it was clear from the discussions that perspectives of several participants had been shaped or influenced by the work of Wallace. (Johnson-Miller 2013, 168-169)

Hence, despite the recognition that Wallace's paradigm could not consistently model all the case studies of Christian revitalization, the paradigm still casts a considerable shadow on current terminology, metaphors, and methodology in missiology.

Unfortunately, this lethargy to change has left many researchers unprepared to adequately address the twenty-first century context of continuous, systemic, and complex change. "Our empirical and quantitative models of process [continue to] remain rooted almost exclusively in the mechanical worldview of the seventeenth century and in the organic worldview of the nineteenth century" (Roth 1992, 200). Sadly, this rut of analysis is even more entrenched in the discipline of missiology (Henry 2002, 237). Consequently, reliance on traditional approaches may prevent researchers from seeing the changing contexts of twenty-first century realities (Abbott 1988, Kuhn 1996), the contention discussed in the following section.

1.4 Inadequacies in Wallace's Revitalization Model in Responding to Twenty-first Century Realities

When one observes the continuous changes in cultures and societies in the modern, globalizing age of technology and interlacing communication networks, and understands the twenty-first century realities to be one of continuous, systemic, and complex change, one must seriously question whether or not Wallace's model of revitalization should be the normative yardstick for Christian revitalization. As

Beverly Johnson-Miller notes in the previous section, Wallace's model of revitalization may be adequate for *some*, but *not for many* of the case studies presented in the consultations on Christian revitalization. For the majority of the case studies presented, Wallace's model of revitalization was inadequate as a model to explain the observed phenomena.

Indeed, Wallace's model of revitalization could not explain my case studies of sixteen churches I visited in Taiwan, Canada, and the United States. In my preliminary interviews gathered during the sabbatical study, response to change was occurring, some sufficiently significant that one could suggest "revitalization," a change in mazeway or *Gestalt,* was occurring in certain churches. But it seemed that such revitalization processes were not a result of a single individual experiencing a "religious vision," (Wallace 1956, 273), but rather a collective group of leaders from different congregations, with different cultural perspectives, working together to make sense of the change process - unity in diversity creating a new mutually-created composite *"Gestalt"* of competing, yet interlacing, visions.

In other church communities, revitalization appeared not to be moving from one steady state to another steady state; rather, these church communities seemed to be revitalizing in a continuous process of transformation; that is, they were in constant flux, yet they appeared to be stable rather than in discontinuity.

Further, my observations revealed that these multicultural communities were not moving toward a uniform mazeway, but were moving between multiple mazeways, using whatever mazeway worked at the appropriate time. These churches were able to navigate through conflict and use it to their advantage instead of enduring conflicts which disrupted their social structure.

If these processes are indeed revitalization movements, then one might also ask the questions, "In such an environment of continuous change and complexity, what if revitalization occurs through the steady state via the aggregate interactions of a social network by the majority of the social group instead of the *Gestalt* of a single visionary leader?" and "what if revitalization was in fact not a state but in actuality a stable, continuous, embraced process?" That is, can an institution thrive in an atmosphere of continuous, systemic change?

If these observations are correct, then at no point can revitalization be reduced to a two steady-state, linear, and discrete and discontinuous system. The real contexts are an infinite series of possible states, nonlinear (that is non-additive), and continuously dynamic.

For example, in urban settings where more than half of the world's currently population resides, social systems are continuously influenced by a complex number of multi-dimensional, multi-directional, interlacing variables of cultural change (Costa 2010, 12). For Diaspora communities, particularly with a history of long-term, continuous migration, their cultures are not monolithic nor independent, but are composed of members from multiple waves of immigration, each with a different initial entry parameters of their immigration story and a dissimilar similar journey of response and adaptation (Lewellyn 2002; Rynkiewich 2002). And for transnational communities which are defined by multiple sociocultural loci, individuals maintain multiple identities which co-exist concurrently in response to constant change (Yang 1999, Grant 2011, Lewellyn 2002, 154; Walby 2007). Such individuals cannot be defined by a single mazeway, for transnationals can draw from a number of mazeways and alternate across them depending on their specific contexts.

Hence, without invalidating Wallace's revitalization model, one must question whether or not it should be applied to every emerging context of the twenty-first century realities of systemic, continuous and complex change. Consider the following: What if a social system is continuously inundated with an ever increasing number of diachronic change events (i.e., derivative or change across time) and multicultural influences? What if a community is comprised of multiple oftentimes competing cultural entities that must co-exist simultaneously? What if the change agent is not an individual, but the aggregate response of the system network to change? (Johnson 2001, 66; Law 2012, 16) If so, what if revitalization is through intentional transformation of the network?

Consider Figure 2. The upper left diagram is a mathematical representation, an analogue step function, of Wallace's model of revitalization. One can consider the first phase of the plot as the first steady state. The oscillations may represent homeostatic phenomena as the system responds to stress and returns to its initial state. The plot then undergoes a revitalization process moving it to the second level, a second steady state. One may conclude that this is a reasonable explanation for an observed revitalization by Wallace's definition.

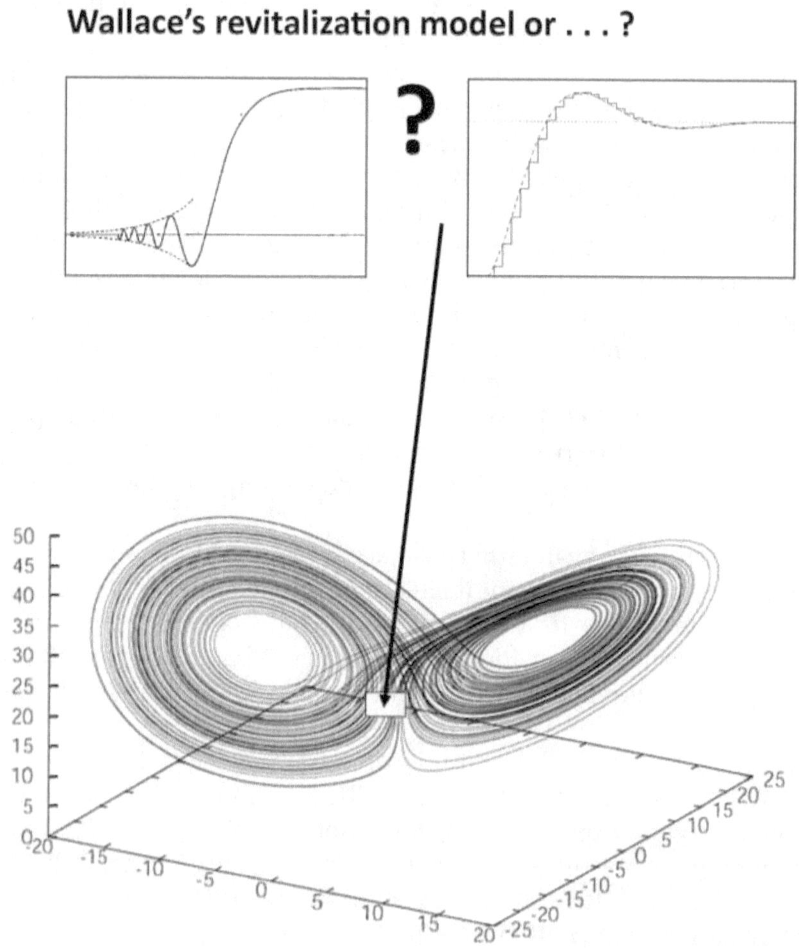

Figure 2 - Limitations of Wallace's model from a Systemic Perspective

But if one considers the upper right diagram, one notes exactly the same beginning and end points. Instead of an analog step function, the plot is that of a multiple number of incremental steps. In other words, an incremental process can equally explain how one goes from the first level to the second level.

If one enlarges the perspective and places the diagram within a larger reality as illustrated in the bottom diagram by the Lorenz attractor (which will be elaborated in Chapter 3) that describes shared trajectories of a complex, multicultural system, one realizes that the process of Wallace's revitalization model is, in reality, only one of a multitude of infinite possible trajectories that could explain the same revitalization phenomenon. Wallace's model can explain some trajectories, but not all trajectories.

Frederick Barth recognized the same problem in 1966. He writes,

> Because of our general unwillingness to abandon well-established routines, studies explicitly addressed to the investigation of change have been prone to contain descriptions of a social system at two points in time – or even at *one* point in time! – and then to rely on *extrapolation* between these two states, or from the one state, to indicate the course of change. (1967, 661)

Barth uses a fish and a crab to illustrate the deficiencies in existing methodology, and then calls for a new paradigm to research change.

> Imagine a situation where you stand looking into an aquarium and you observe a fish. A moment later you find yourself looking at a crab in the same place where the fish was. If you ask yourself how it got claws instead of fins, you are implying a certain kind of continuity: this is the same body, and it has changed its shape. If, one the other hand, you say to yourself that this is the same aquarium, you are specifying another kind of continuity, implying a set of constraints that leads you to formulate other hypotheses about the dynamics of change in this instance. Different specifications of the nature of the continuity that ties two situations together in a sequence of change give rise to very different hypotheses about the mechanisms and processes of change. (664)

In other words, we should not be asking how a fish became a crab, but rather: What are the conditions (environment, resources, limitations) that allow a fish to exist at one point in time and a crab to exist in another in the same place?

In light of this quandary, Barth thus concludes, ". . . we must recast our very description of social systems in order to accommodate these data about the events of change[;] that makes our task more difficult but also more interesting." (661) Hence, in a complex, multicultural environment, while a linear model may be valid for some cases, it is impossible to contend that Wallace's revitalization model should remain the only normative model in the larger and increasingly diverse global context of the twenty-first century.

Wallace's revitalization model becomes even more problematic when one considers the social connections across the expanding networks of a globalizing, urban, multicultural context. Randolph Roth points out that Wallace presents only

> a simplified model [as opposed to a complex model] that lacks adequate feedback mechanisms and reflexivity. Wallace's model, like most social science models, draws from outmoded classical mechanical and scientific theory.... [in reality], such systems may exist in several different states of equilibrium, as well as chaotic states of "excitability." (Harkin 2007, xxx-xxxi)

The lack of adequate feedback mechanisms in traditional, linear approaches makes it difficult, if not impossible, to account for the expansion in scale of globally networked influences. Consider Figure 3. These diagrams represent a "complicated" (more than two constituent elements, but still additive) and a "complex" network (nonlinearity introduced through multiple feedback connections). In the complicated diagram, one may be able to "isolate" a group as pictured by the square. A linear *may* model be adequate to describe the "closed" system. Using Barth's analogy, one can look at the pathway to see whether or not a crab crawls into the picture.

Illustration courtesy of: https://www.apsense.com/

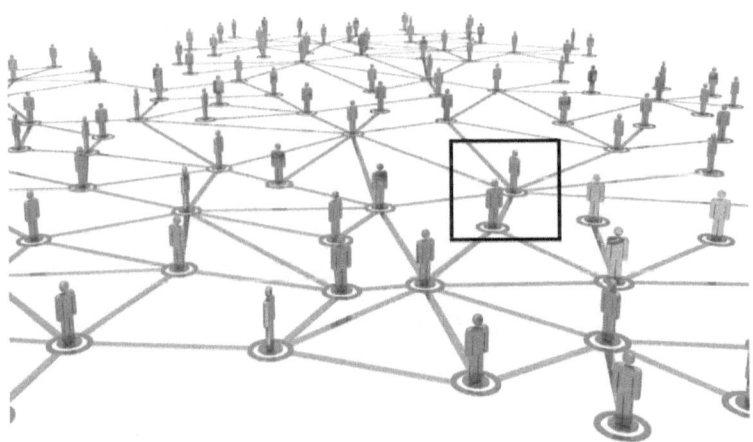

Illustration courtesy of:
https://mexicoinstitute.files.wordpress.com/2013/08/people-network.jpg

Figure 3 - Comparison between a Complicated and a Complex Network

But in the complex model, because of multiple pathways, while an observer is looking at one pathway, the crab can crawl in through any number of pathways. In network theory, the addition of one feedback loop exponential increases by a factor of two (to account for bi-directionality) the number of variables necessary to describe the system. Such a system is no longer linear; it is complex. The complexity of the issue is further exacerbated because Wallace's model is homeostatic, and as such, accounts for only negative feedback. There is no means to account for positive feedback, increasingly observed across social networks, which enables incremental change to result in a paradigm shift (Walby 2007). Stephen Reyna thus concludes "The fact that the social monism is *continually* in motion means that it is dynamic . . . The preceding means that the old distinction between statics and dynamics . . . is not very useful." (Reyna 2002, 175)

Hence, I came to realize that Wallace's model of revitalization that continues to be widely used in missiology to evaluate Christian revitalization is inadequate for multicultural systems such as my own case study. Indiscriminately forcing my data through the lens of the Wallacian model would unwittingly create "blind spots" in research. Two apparent ones come to mind.

First, Wallace's linear model of revitalization does not take into account the change process occurring via social groups or movements, for as mentioned before, Wallace discounts Weber's more systematic framework. Wallace's model only looks for a "revitalization event" and for a "prophet or new leader" (1956, 27); it does not, as Abbott (2000, 299) noted earlier, look for emerging patterns of relationships of a social network in change, consequently introducing a bias toward single, discrete variables. What results is akin to a set of epistemological blinders placed on researchers to see only a narrow set of variables, thereby potentially preventing them from noticing a larger set of variables which, while incremental and disperse and of themselves may not account for the change, when evaluated in the aggregate, reveals a larger process that is generating the change (see also Reyna 2002, 179; Clayton and Davies 2009, 8).

Second, because Wallace's linear model of revitalization is designed to look for dramatic paradigm shifts, what may be described as *phase change* (a sudden shift from a previous pattern to a new pattern) or a *catastrophic change* (the destruction of the system altogether), it dismisses *incremental changes* and considers them to be part of the "steady state" condition (1956, 265).

But with the development of Chaos Theory, sociologists now posit that, by positive feedback, a bifurcation process can occur, such that incremental changes can precipitate into rapid, significant changes that mimic the "revitalization" phenomenon, much like the incremental step function shown earlier (Walby 2007, 455). As such, the process of incremental change may be the true etiology of change and the "paradigm shift" merely the symptom. Hence, the existing model once again biases researchers to consider only phenomena that may fit the model, and blinds researchers from considering other phenomena that may be the true source of change, in this case those with a history of long-term progression through incremental change (Abbott 1988, 172).

As such, Roth writes that Wallace's theory is

> ... open to criticism on nonlinear terms. It assumes that the response of a social system to disruptive and ordering forces is additive, proportional, and univocal. In fact, feedback loops and competing effects can amplify the consequences of minor events and dampen the consequences of major events in surprising and unpredictable ways. Revitalization theory also assumes that order cannot produce disorder spontaneously or vice versa. In fact, order and disorder can emerge suddenly from their opposites in nonlinear processes. (Roth 1992, 220)

Reyna thus aptly concludes with four observations about what was misleading about the traditional model:

> The first was that reality was treated as linear, when it was anything but. The second was that reality was believed to be predictable, when it often was not. The third was that reality was treated as if it were a closed system, when it was actually open to a huge number of systems. The fourth was that reality was treated as static, when it was dynamic. . . . I had mistaken social realities in this latter manner, seeing photographs, when what was going on around me was a movie. (2002, 170)

Indeed, in later years, Wallace himself recognized the changes in twenty-first century social and cultural contexts and recommended ". . . a more nuanced approach seeking change in indirect subtle conjunctions of trivialities and seeming irrelevancies as well as more widely recognized directly linked causal factors." (Grumet 2003, x-xi)

It should be noted that these observations do not obviate Wallace's linear model of revitalization, but in expanding the universe of realities, one realizes that Wallace's model cannot explain revitalization in all contexts and may only remain adequate for middle scale, relatively confined, and minimally networked contexts. Most likely, these marginal, cultural systems *may* be described with simple, linear and with discretized change functions, the kind that anthropologists sought out to study before 1980 (Grumet 2003, viii, comments this is the reason why anthropologists tend toward isolated, primitive regions for study – they wanted a "pure test tube"). However, as more of the human cultural and social system becomes globalized, urbanized, and interconnected, we are hard pressed for more robust models that are more reflective of complex, networked, continuously changing systems (Clayton and Davies 2009, 166; Page 2011, 8; Purzycki *et al* 2014). Indeed, the complex nature of globalizing, urbanized social systems has left many social scientists and historiographers at a loss for a metanarrative and hermeneutic to explain emerging global history (Postman 1992, 173; Iggers *et al* 2008, 365).

Complex Systems Science removes the boundaries of reality required by traditional science and allows researchers to consider new mazeways to explain the new expanse of twenty-first century realities. It allows for nonlinear processes, interdisciplinary approaches, and multi-dimensional theoretical frameworks. One no longer needs to be reductionist, subscribe to general linear realities, and choose just one mazeway. In fact, because everything is now seen as networked, multiple mazeways can be concurrently valid.

Hence, the Complex Systems Science-framed paradigm does not invalidate the traditional science paradigm. Rather, "elements of the old paradigm can be incorporated in the new, but because they are part of a new configuration, they take on new meanings." (Hiebert 1999, 79) Abbott agrees, writing, that "The general linear model (GLM) is a formidable and effective method. But I argue that the model has come to influence our actual construing of social reality, blinding us to important phenomena that can be rediscovered only by diversifying our formal techniques." (1988, 169) As such, in the larger universe of realities, new ways of visualizing this new expanse are needed.

1.5 In Search of New Mazeways through Complex Change

In response to this dilemma, echoing Roth's call to improve Wallace's theory and imagery (Roth 1992, 235), Rynkiewich's challenge to expand the model ". . . to account for the degree of urbanization and globalization in the world today" (Rynkiewich 2011:43), and even Wallace's own call for a more nuanced approach (Grumet 2003, x), in order to better visualize and analyze data, and eliminate biases which may lead to inaccurate and misleading conclusions, **this book 1) evaluates Complex Systems Science approaches for the twenty-first century contexts by comparing Wallace's model of revitalization with the Complex Systems Science Cusp of Change model for**

Christian revitalization in order to understand Complex System's Science's ability to represent, respond, and adapt to change using the case study of multicultural Christian diaspora communities in globalizing, urban settings; 2) concludes that the Complex Systems Science Cusp of Change model is indeed more robust, and efficacious and proposes that the Cusp of Change model for Christian revitalization is fundamentally more representative of twenty-first century realities as observed by the contemporary consultations by the Center for the Study of World Christian Revitalization Movements; and 3) develops a Complex Systems Science-framed maze way for mission theory and the missiological contextualization of twenty-first century realities.

This comparative study confirms the benefits found in the solitary article from the journal review that draws directly from Complex Systems Science. It is the article written by R. Daniel Shaw and entitled "Beyond Contextualization: Toward a Twenty-first Century Model for Enabling Mission."

Like Abbott, Shaw recognized the deficiencies of existing, even normative, traditional models in the context of the increased complexities of twenty-first century realities and argued new approaches needed to be developed. In Shaw's case, it is Eugene Nida's normative, traditional model for contextualization (see Figure 4) that was proving to be inadequate for the new realities. Shaw argued that Nida's model assumed a realist perspective and, as such, "despite having 'dynamic equivalence' in its name, the model was relatively static and product oriented." (2010, 209)

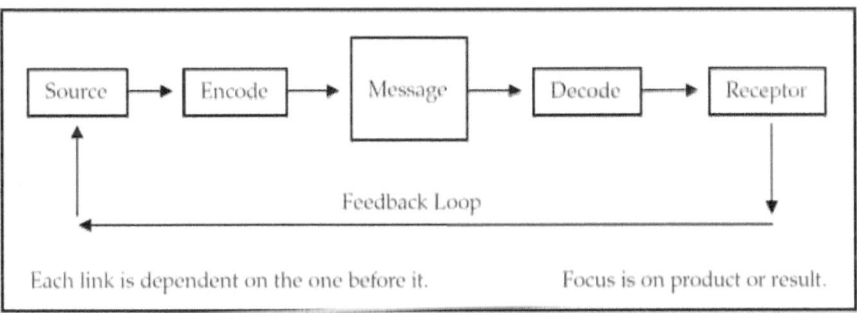

Figure 4 - Serial Processing of Codes (Shaw 2010, 209)

Shaw then describes how he developed a new mazeway that takes into the account the networked, complex, and nonlinear nature of communication that defines twenty-first century realities. It is a multi-layered, networked model that incorporates multiple theories across a variety of disciplines (see Figure 5). It is a Complex Systems Science-framed model. Shaw writes that

> The implications of this approach are vast. The S-M-R, or code, model is linear and focused on the result, that is, the delivery, in as intact a fashion as possible, of a prepackaged product. Connectionist network theory, by contrast, directs attention to the processes by which recipients construct meaning in their contexts.... The complex process shown in the diagram is actually slower than the serial processing of earlier linear models, but it more clearly represents how human beings process information. (2010, 210)

The new model incorporates a variety of theories and integrates models from several disciplines. This allows the model to be express realities on multiple dimensions via different modalities. The multiple mazeways also allow for the system to be dynamic with different basins of stable equilibria.

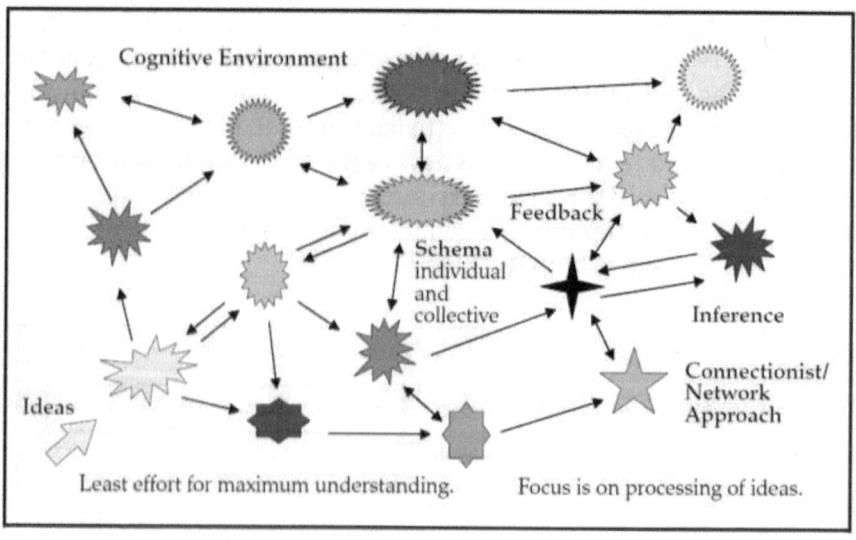

Figure 5 - Parallel Distributive Processing Ideas (Shaw 2010, 210)

The direct benefit of this new Complex Systems Science-framed model allowed Shaw to develop a new model for enabling mission (Figure 6). Shaw concludes that

> The new missional model reflects God's intention for people "from every race, tribe, nation, and language." (Rev 7:9, CEV). As a statement of purpose,

that wording may not seem new, but the emphasis the model places on the relevance of every context is quite different from the twentieth-century approaches to mission. . . . the new model for mission accents a both/and approach rather than an either/or perspective. It seeks to be interactive, modeled on God's communication with human beings. It is relational, with a focus on being rather than doing. It is primarily enabling and encouraging rather than static and knowledge-focused. It envisions a biblical theology in context rather than a contextual theology (2010, 212)

Descriptive— *Delivery* *(Doing)*	◄——*Mission*——►	*Cognitive—* *Discover Meaning* *(Being)*
• Great Commission Mission (McGavran) • Largely Individual • Static and Largely External (telling) • Contextualization (make Christianity like culture) • Local Theology • Church Growth (numbers)	Shift from Product Orientation to Process Orientation (from Doing to Being)	• Relationship and Transformation (Lingenfelter) • Increasingly Group Oriented (teamwork) • Dynamic and Largely Internal (enabling) • Beyond Contextualization (knowledge transforms—focus on knowing God) • Biblical Theology in Context • Interactive Hermeneutical Community (discipleship—missional/emerging church)

Figure 6 - Contrasting Models of Mission (Shaw 2010, 211)

Hence, Shaw's example suggests that the adaptation of Complex System Science-framed approaches can provide metaphors, models, and methods that can aid missiology to more broadly – and accurately – represent and analyze the new realities of the twenty-first century context, and consequently, form dynamic, heuristic mazeways with which to respond to change.

This book takes a similar approach to evaluate the benefits of a Complex Systems-framed approach. In this book, I compare Wallace's traditional revitalization model with the Complex Systems Science-framed Cusp of Change model and find four primary benefits.

First, where the current revitalization model is primarily a local, anthropocentric, psychological, behavioral model that is simple, linear, static and discrete or discontinuous, Complex Systems Science provides a complex, systemic, network-oriented, multi-dimensional analysis that is that is nonlinear, dynamic, and historical.

For example, Emergence Theory, a key element of Complex Systems Science, forces researchers to move away from the present bias toward reductionism such that processes would no longer need to be defined as the mere sum of constituent parts. Rather, Emergence Theory would allow consideration of the possibility of macroscopic phenomena (not yet visible) which may be in fact the constituent basis of the system's response. Hence, with both micro- (local) and macro- (global) level processes equally weighted, the inherent bias toward simplicity and linearity in Wallace's model would be removed.

Second, the book explains how the Complex Systems Science Cusp of Change model allows for a more interdisciplinary and dynamic approach to missiology. One is now be able to integrate Wallace's "constituent units" and "mazeway" (1956, 266) with more macroscopic and theological concepts such as *missio Dei* and missiological concepts such as Andrew Wall's "indigenizing" and "pilgrim" Hegelian dialectic.

For example, the nonlinear, multivariate nature of Chaos Theory allows for multiple "attractors" that can co-exist even in a dynamically, changing environment. One does not need a simple, closed-looped solution to be valid. As such, revitalization viewed through the lens of Complex Systems Science allows for mutually supporting equilibrium states, that is, parallel mazeways, between dialectic positions such as "local with the global," "centrifugal and centripetal," "indigenizing and pilgrim," among others even as the change process continues to occur.

Third, a Complex Systems revitalization model provides a framework for the discussion and analysis of multiple, concurrent cultural identities and processes, a necessary element in globalization research (Lewellyn 2002, 147; Hofstede *et al* 2010, 468; Rynkiewich 2002, Walby 2007). Wallace's linear model looks for a singular hybridized mazeway of realism as the end of the revitalization process. But in so doing, the linear model implies an inability to consider that cultural identity, such as the case of transnationals, may have two or more concurrent, even contested and contingent, mazeways. In contrast, a Complex Systems-famed revitalization model allows for the construction and discussion of multiple co-existent cultural identities (Walby 2007, 454).

Fourth, because Complex Systems Science is dynamic and focuses on trends rather than static states, it can also be used for trend analysis to predict forward. Agent-based models have already been used in a variety of applications to predict traffic patterns, global conflicts, economic and market systems, and living systems (Flake 1999, Epstein 2006, Miller and Page 2007, Railsback and Grimm 2012). Hence, the trajectories Complex Systems Science-framed models provide religious communities to anticipate, participate, and even mediate future change.

Thus, as missiological research increasingly seeks to understand the relationship between the complex and changing, global understanding of *imago Dei* and the ever diversifying local or transnational understandings of *imago anthropos* within the context of *missio Dei*, Christian revitalization viewed through the lens of Complex Systems Science can serve as an integrative and corrective research tool for the evaluation, analysis, and visualization of revitalization processes. The new holistic metaphors provided may help multicultural religious communities discern a biblical response to change through revitalization via "unity in diversity," and through intentional, incremental, systemic transformation into a biblical *ecclesia* (Ephesians 2:14) instead of divisive conflict as a consequence of an overly static and discrete world view.

1.6 Case Study: Multicultural Churches of the Chinese Diaspora in North America

For model conceptualization, development, and validation, I use the case studies of multicultural communities of the Chinese Diaspora. Six case studies in North America are the focus of analyses. The data will be used to identify how change changes over time, and to identify variables with which to develop a Complex Systems Science-framed model that reflects these communities. The Chinese Diaspora population provides a suitable test case to highlight the benefit of the model in that it is both complex in nature due to its lengthy history and geographic breadth of successive immigrant waves and their response and adaptation to change on the one hand, while on the other hand, as a consequence of differences in external appearance and by social and/or cultural choice, remains relatively distinct from local, majority, non-Chinese populations (Zhou 2009, 52). In other words, one has sufficient complexity while retaining a discernible systemic boundary.

1.7 Significance — Charting the Trajectory through Complex Change

The anticipated significance of the book is two-fold. The book endeavors to help missiologists, particularly those on the social science side, who have a history of lagging their academic colleagues in adopting new paradigms, some by decades, to more readily adapt to the paradigm shift of Complex Systems science, and to introduce potential research tools that may be used to understand the complex nature of twenty-first century missiology.

The primary objective seeks to effectively argue that models from Complex Systems Science can serve as new and better metaphors and communication tools to perceive and understand the new realities of the global complexities of twenty-first century realities that are defined by rapid, complex change. As Russ Marion writes, "In many ways, humans don't have a grasp on reality.... we really don't know what reality is. Our perceptions of reality are just that: perceptions. We call them models or theories. They are our best shot at explaining reality. Models can explain a broad variety of behaviors and can help us predict what will happen in similar future circumstances." (1999, 11) As has been introduced and as will be argued, many current missiological methodologies and models, including that of Wallace's linear model of revitalization, are increasingly inadequate to provide accurate models of reality in modern, globalized contexts. As such, it is hoped that the metaphors, models, and methodologies presented in this book will help missiologists better understand present and future realities.

And more practically speaking, it is hoped that this book will enable multicultural religious communities to *gestalt* the revitalization process, and provide guidance in illuminating new "mazeways" in the twenty-first century contexts. For unlike the linear model of revitalization movements, which looks for a charismatic leader and a discrete point in time, revitalizations in the twenty-first century context will most likely emerge from intentional, incremental, and systemic transformation where the social network is the change agent. The hope is that multicultural communities can recognize that they are to become the "new humanity in Christ" (Ephesians 2:14). Rather than looking for a visionary leader or singular mazeway for revitalization, we should recognize that the Spirit's work is cosmopolitan, with every member contributing their "piece of the puzzle" to create new mutually-created composite mazeways through change.

It is hoped that the findings of this book will make it possible to visualize and as such, "... identify a wide range of active forces, and how they potentially intersect, evolve, and coincide with particular forms of revitalization. While the Holy Spirit is *the* catalytic force, many other Spirit empowered forces exist." (Johnson-Miller 2011, 13)

The secondary objective, to address the personal narrative, seeks to provide a conceptual model to better understand the Christian revitalization process in multicultural contexts that can also subsequently serve the basis for the development of a complex adaptive system computational model for visualization and analysis of cross-cultural interaction in multicultural communities. Beverly Johnson-Miller writes,

> Searching to identify forces of revitalization begs the question: *Can revitalization be initiated in a test-tube?* If we gather all key ingredients identified in the history of Christian revitalization movements, can we manufacture revitalization, or create a controlled *greenhouse* environment for cultivation growth? Could that be the point of revitalization research? Who controls the forces at work in revitalization? If *greenhouse revitalization* is not possible or a good idea, why? What are the forces of revitalization that, even though we cannot or perhaps should not attempt to control, invite and guide meaningful participation? Is there a mechanism of revitalization available to us? How do we discern what is really at play in the birth and growth of Christian revitalization? (2011, 13)

Such a model would provide just that, a "test-tube" by which to better study and understand revitalization movements in the complex contexts of the twenty-first century. In fact, such models are already being developed in other social science disciplines (particularly organization theory) to study complex urban systems such a traffic patterns, economic systems and epidemiology with much benefit (Wilensky 1999, Spickard 2004, Miller and Page 2007, Mitchell 2009, Purzycki *et al*). Of particular relevance to missiology are the agent-based models (ABM) that have been developed in the field of economics which study organizations (Tesfatsion and Judd 2006, Hazy *et al* 2007, Ulh-Bien and Marion 2008, Goldstein *et al* 2010). Such models, however, should not be seen as an end in themselves – for that would only repeat the errors of positivist and reductionist paradigms of general linear reality.

1.8 Book Outline

This book is divided into eight chapters. The following chapter, Chapter 2, reviews the author's personal journey that establishes the need for this research. It also serves as the Literature Review, exploring the various traditional approaches of looking at ethnographies and the subsequent weaknesses of focusing on simple, linear, and discrete closed-loop solutions.

Chapter 3 provides a summary of Complex Systems Science and its development in the area of social science as relevant to its application to missiology; it serves as the development of the Theoretical Framework for the book. Consequently, the chapter lays out frameworks for model development with respect to missiological concerns.

Chapter 4 outlines the parameters of research for the case study of Chinese Diaspora churches, the Delimitations, and Data Analysis Methodology and Model Development of the book.

Chapter 5 presents the data to ascertain likely variables with which to develop the proposed model. A metaphor model to reflect the multiethnic, multicongregational immigrant Chinese congregations in the North American Diaspora is presented and its benefits discussed.

Chapter 6 compares the differences between the traditional Wallacian model of Christian revitalization and the Complex Systems Science Cusp of Change model. The chapter argues that the Cusp of Change model is both more conceptually and practically robust to explain the questions and observations of the contemporary consultations on Christian revitalization of the Center for the Study of World Christian Revitalization movements.

Chapter 7 applies the Complex Systems Science Cusp of Change model of Christian revitalization to analyze the case study of multicultural, multicongregational churches of the Chinese Diaspora in North America, highlighting its benefits in missiological research.

The final chapter, Chapter 8, concludes with recommendations for how Complex Systems Science can be used to develop new mazeways for mission theory and the missiological contextualization of multicultural, 21st century realities of systemic, continuous, and complex change. It describes the potential of Complex Systems Science-framed models, methodology and metaphors for applications in missiology. The chapter suggests that Complex Systems Science-framed approaches not only provide tools to understand the social and cultural systems missiologists study, but have the potential to integrate the nebulous host of other missiological theories and disciplines from the theology and history or mission to inter-religious dialogue to contextual theology, to holistically inform mission praxis.

1.9 Chapter Summary

1. As a consequence of globalization, particularly in the aspect of instantaneous, electronic networks, change has changed. In the twenty-first century context, change is continues, rapid, and complex

2. I am seeing increased conflicts in churches that are not necessary related to theological or moral issues. These conflicts appear to be result of the change of change.

3. Probative Question: How can Christian communities revitalize in the context of continuous, rapid, complex change?

4. After considering Wallace's theory of revitalization as a model to study the problem, I realized that the model was insufficient for the twenty-first century context. Biased toward linearity (historical and relational) and static analysis, the traditional model of revitalization was severely limited in a networked, rapid, complex change context.

5. Research Question: *Using the comparison of the existing Wallacian model of Christian revitalization with the Cusp of Change model, how does the emerging paradigm shift to Complex Systems Science enhance missiological research approaches to understand better the processes of response and adaptation to change of multicultural Christian communities in globalizing, urban settings?*

6. Research Aim: Develop a more robust model of Christian revitalization through integrating analytical methodology from Complex Systems Science that can properly study twenty-first century contexts. Data from multicultural, multicongregational Chinese churches in the North American Diaspora will be used as the case study.

Chapter 2

A Failure of Existing Mazeways

2.1 Introduction

The purpose of this section is to highlight the need for a more robust approach to study cultural change above and beyond the traditional scientific approach, using my personal research journey in the Diaspora Chinese Church community in North America as an example. This chapter considers, and then rejects Wallace's model of religious revitalization as a normative model on the grounds that it is static (synchronic), linear (discrete and additive), and thus not sufficiently dynamic (diachronic) to account for continuous change and not sufficiently flexible to account for all the observed trajectories of the case study. The chapter sets the stage for a Complex Systems Science-framed model of culture change that is not discrete, that is, looking statically only at a specific point or period in time and with a fixed pattern, but is heuristic, that is, with the ability to adapt to change and to various contexts by learning from experience. While the traditional approach would most likely have resulted in some valid conclusions, nevertheless, the conclusions most likely would have become irrelevant and obsolete by the time the project was concluded as the context would have already changed; as well, the conclusions would not be valid for all observed realities of the case study. Metaphorically, the normative Wallacian model provides only a snapshot in time; it cannot record nor analyze, nor inform about the complex and diverse trajectories of change.

When I began my journey to understand what I was experiencing as a pastor, I was introduced to a variety of models and methods to try and make sense of the theological, social, and cultural contexts of my experiential reality. What I had learned over the initial two years of coursework resulted in two outcomes: first, that there is a growing sense of the increased complexity and rate of change in the twenty-first century contexts; and second, many of the current approaches appeared unable to properly describe or represent the new contexts. There is a sense of ambiguity in missiological research, such as terms like "from everywhere to everywhere," "reverse mission" (but what is the frame of reference?), and "dialectic tension."

On the one hand, the methods and examples offered sought to reduce case studies into specific behavioral, sociological, or anthropological parameters, then to seek a dyadic, causal relationship. It was essentially a methodology grounded in logical empiricism. Even though there were many hints of greater complexity in studying trends in Christianity (Van Engen 1996; Walls 1996, Tennent 2007), the methods I was taught were to try to describe our observations in a simple, cause-and-effect (linear) fashion (Hiebert et al 1999, 348). Therefore, if I wanted to understand how to "revitalize" my church, it was suggested that I should look to a single theoretical framework such as revitalization movements (Wallace 1956) or the life cycles of churches (Saarinen 2001).

On the other hand, it seemed that missiology itself was in the process of undergoing a paradigm shift and had yet to arrive at a clear understanding of what was changing. Issues such as Christendom and post-Christendom, modernism and postmodernism, colonial and post-colonial, and Western and global South Christianity were creating chaos in theories and models that had been around for centuries. Worse, with concepts of missions "from everywhere to everywhere," the impact of global migrations and diasporas, and new terms such as transnationalism, even the definitions of long held vocabularies were changing. In the midst of this chaotic change, we are tasked to accept and hold things in tension, between the "global and the local," the "indigenizing and the pilgrim," and even multiple explanations that are equally valid at the same time (Bosch 1999; Walls 2002; Bevins and Schroeder 2004). While it may be that the gospel is a "mystery," this vagueness seems conflicted with the methodology.

These two polar factors collided in the midst of my research and placed me at the galactic boundary of traditional science and the universe of Complex Systems Science; it placed me at the edge of chaos. On the one hand were the traditional approaches I had been taught. On the other hand, the twenty-first century realities were threatening to alter the fundamental elements and even the definitions undergirding these approaches. The dilemma is described in the following section.

2.2 The Illusion of Simple Social Models

As I began my research, Wallace's model of revitalization was the natural framework with which to center my research problem. I proposed that stress was created when traditional cultures, such as a Confucianist-constructed culture, with its emphasis on maintaining the *status quo (harmony)* through hierarchical and fixed social structures, are enveloped by the twenty-first century's continuous waves of change. If Confucianism was the mazeway for Chinese culture to maintain homeostasis, then change as a result of immigrant acculturation and continuous waves of new immigrant groups were the stressors and the source of cultural distortion. When mazeways are no longer able to restore homeostasis, a seedbed for conflict is created (Hiebert et al 1999, 348). For according to Wallace's revitalization model, in the period of cultural distortion, the natural response is resistance and, consequently, conflict. In Wallace's model, conflict is seen as an impediment to revitalization, that is, the formation of what Wallace calls a new "mazeway" to a new steady state condition.

Hence, as I began my search for understanding, I sought to find one or two parameters that could help me measure why conflict seemed to be developing in Chinese churches. It was my hypothesis that altering these parameters would lead to the mitigation of conflict and open the doors for revitalization of my church community. In short, if the problem was conflict, then the solution to the problem would be to remove any hindrance to revitalization.

My initial research led me to look at the influence of Chinese culture on the Christian faith as previous studies indicated that there is an inherent propensity for conflict in Asian cultures compared to other cultures, particularly in Confucian-based societies (Jandt and Pederson 1996, 7). In my mind, my question was "what elements are preventing the revitalization *Gestalt?*"

As I reflected on who were involved in the conflicts, it seemed that the more a culture conformed to classic Confucian values and social structure, the greater the proclivity for conflict. This perception is supported by my discussions with fellow Korean seminarians who mutually concurred that the situation was worse in Korean churches as the Korean context is more monocultural and possesses a stronger Confucian cultural system. The consensus is that because Confucianism is based on a rigid hierarchical and ritualistic social framework, Confucian-based cultures lack the flexibility to efficiently resolve conflicts (Wang 2003, 32).

It has been argued that because Confucian-based cultural identity is heavily defined by one's place in the social structure, as a consequence, the pressure to avoid losing "face," a redefinition of one's position, even if it is temporary, hinders the acknowledgment of responsibility one has in a conflict (Ho 1976, 873). It is interesting to note, perhaps critically, that the act of confession is not found at all in Confucianism (Konior 2010, 98).

As such, conflict resolution is almost nonexistent in the early phases of conflict in traditional Asian cultures. When "resolution" occurs, it is indirect through third parties or merely "swept under the table" over the course of a meal. But such superficial reconciliation more often than not results in explosive interactions that destroy relationships rather than strengthening them which one would expect if conflict resolution is handled appropriately (Ho 1974, 95).

For Chinese Christians, while one would expect that conflict resolution should follow biblical principles of mutual submission and the concept of "unity in diversity," it nevertheless is not the case. For the Chinese church in diaspora, conflicts still remain common in families and church boards alike. While research shows that Chinese Christians are more forgiving when compared to adherents of other Chinese religions (Paz et al 2007), nevertheless research continues to suggest that the influence of Confucianism remains extant in Chinese Christianity and continues to negatively impact conflict resolution in the Chinese church (Wang 2003, 141).

This particular narrative dominated the literature. Surely, I thought, this cultural influence was the reason behind a failure to revitalize. By seeking to hold onto the Confucianist worldview and social structure, Chinese churches could not revitalize because the culture inherently maintains the existing mazeway. I asked myself, "What then might cause this dialectic between Christianity and Confucianism?"

Paul Hiebert offered a model for conversion and observed that oftentimes, conversion can be inhibited by ongoing resistance from one's cultural origins. In Hiebert's model of conversion (Hiebert 2008, 316), one might conclude that the Chinese church is "stuck" at the first level, being outwardly Christian but not yet able to confess and undergo the work of genuine inner transformation (second level) that results in a paradigm shift in world view (third level).

Beyond this, I had thought to argue that this transformational resistance was further heightened as a result of the identification of Christianity with Confucianism by certain missionaries in order to build a bridge for evangelism. For example, early missionaries from Matteo Ricci to Hudson Taylor actually made great effort to identify Christianity with Confucianism (Muck 2009, 140). Additionally, on the other end of the historical spectrum, in North American Chinese churches of the early twenty-first century, Christianity has been used as a means of preserving Confucianism as one aspect of Chinese culture (Yang 1999, 153).

Perhaps, I reasoned, the conflicts I observed were not merely cultural, but due to a missiological misstep. It wasn't merely a cultural issue, but an issue of failed contextualization.

As such, I wanted to explore the relationship between the missiological identification of Christianity with Confucianism as the reason for an inhibited Christian identity formation in the Chinese context, and to see if I could find an alternative within Chinese culture as corrective thereby mitigating conflict, and removing the Confucian propensity toward intransigence with a more balanced worldview that includes a higher level of reconciliation whose characteristics are, for example, expressed in the Kohlberg scale as a measure of moral development (Kohlberg 1984).

Consequently, it was my belief that here was the "magic bullet" that would mitigate conflict in the Chinese Church. If I could somehow determine how to better incorporate the act of confession into Chinese Church culture and identity, surely this would be the means of mitigating conflict.

But as I reflected on my pastoral experiences of the past few years, and reviewing my initial research data, I began to realize that such an approach may be too simplistic and the conclusions I reach could be obsolete by the time I submit my dissertation.

Why? Because the influence of Confucianism is waning in Chinese culture in general, certainly in China itself, and also in Chinese churches in diaspora.

2.3 Recognizing the Reality of Cultures in Complex, Continuous Change

Recent research supports my observation that the traditional Confucian world view may already be passing. Yeo argues that the "museumization" of traditional Confucianism is well along the way (Yeo 2008, 404) because its emphasis on an external, rigid hierarchical structure prevents its adherents from responding to the increasingly globalized, modern, multicultural world. A rigid hierarchical system is incompatible with a world of diversity in continuous flux. Hence, while Confucianism is so ingrained and its influence is so pervasive throughout, not just Chinese, but many Asian cultures and even among American-born Asians, that it can never be fully eradicated from the Asian identity, nevertheless, many scholars believe that Confucianism in its present form is becoming "obsolete" (Tamney and Chiang 2002, 212).

Further, as I delved deeper into the multicultural landscape of the North American Chinese church, I began to realize that shifts were already occurring in the Chinese psychological framework. The propensity toward conflict is no longer true of all Chinese and differences are now visible between cultural subgroups with regard to the ability to resolve conflicts. I found that young Chinese born after 1980, whether Christian or non-Christian, are much more able to resolve conflicts, a finding confirmed by Su and Hwang. (2003, 308). This is generally true regardless of whether they grew up in the US, Taiwan, Hong Kong, or mainland China. As a consequence, younger Chinese Christians in North America are increasingly dissatisfied at the intransigence of their predecessors and have left their immigrant church nests to form their own worshipping communities (Fong 1999, 94).

As well, I have found that Hong Kong Chinese of all age groups also appear to be more able to resolve conflicts and more often than not are the intermediaries between opposing parties in many Chinese churches. On the flip side, mainland Chinese who settled in Taiwan after the Chinese civil war tend to be those who are the responsible for conflicts and tend to hinder the conflict resolution process in many churches. These observations were confirmed by several of the pastors that I interviewed in the course of the Clergy renewal grant (see Tables 4 and 5).

What I came to understand was that while certain populations within the North American Chinese Church were in conflict, others were not. In fact, the influence of their cultural journeys had already mitigated conflict by enhancing conflict resolution. *New mazeways were being formed in front of my eyes!*

What does this suggest? *Changes were occurring simultaneously and spontaneously.* There is no single identifiable revitalization process, as defined by the Wallacian model, that one could point to. If so, revitalization as modeled by Wallace may no longer be a very helpful lens through which to examine the complex, changing realities of the churches of the Chinese diaspora. The North American

Chinese Church "system" was not conforming to Wallace's model of revitalization because the system was in itself changing, not linearly and sequentially, but incrementally and in parallel. Using Reyna's analogy, *I realized I was looking at a movie, not a photograph* (2002, 170), and thus neither the actors nor the scenes stood still long enough for me to study what was happening.

Rynkiewich has argued previously that "culture is contingent, culture is constructed and culture is contested." (2002, 301). If so, culture is spontaneous, constantly in flux, and constantly being redefined. Contrary to Wallace, culture change need not be "deliberate, organized, or conscious." (1956, 265) Additionally, if change is constant, then one can no longer assume that a "steady state" can ever be achieved (Rynkiewich 2011, 41). A "steady state" is the anthropologist's fiction, stopping the frame in order to describe a moment in time that never had more than a fleeting existence. When considering the Chinese in diaspora, Rynkiewich writes "Within the diaspora community, the processes of selection, discernment, resistance, acceptance, modification, construction, and adaptation *are all going on at the same time."* (my italics, 2012, 211)

In globalizing, urbanizing realities of the early twenty-first century, under the influence of multiple cultural changes, *inter*cultural analysis is now the necessity as relying solely on *intra*cultural analysis is no longer valid (Rynkiewich 2002, 2012). Arjun Appadurai (1996) argues that "the dilemmas of perspective and representation," and "the changing social, territorial, and cultural reproduction of group identity." (48), as well as the "deconstructions of the idea of self, person, and agency in philosophy, sociology, and anthropology" (52) now "imply for ethnography... that ethnographers can no longer simply be content with the thickness they bring to the local and the particular, nor can they assume that as they approach the local, they approach something more elementary, more contingent, and thus more real than life seen in larger-scale perspectives." (54) Lewellen similarly argues that because of globalization, one's identity is no longer static and monolithic, but a patchwork of multiple cultural influences and identities (2002, 147, see also Walby 2007, Grant 2011). Russ Marion concludes that ". . . relatively few social events are the result of simple one-way causation; rather they result from complex interactions among a number of variables." (1999, 41)

As such, had I followed Wallace's linear model of revitalization as I was taught to do, my findings would not have been very helpful since they would not have accurately considered all the influences of change. And from a practical perspective, my findings would be irrelevant by the time they are published because the context would have already changed because new immigrant groups were entering the system.

As a consequence of my initial research, it became clear that a new model which more appropriately reflects constantly changing, complex social and cultural systems is necessary. The search for that model is the driving force behind my research. Additionally, I had to face concerns about the long term viability of traditional approaches in the face of the systemic, continuous, and complex changes that are the characteristics of twenty-first century realities; it is what ultimately led me to consider Complex Systems Science-framed approaches for more robust models. It is a journey which many others have already traveled in other fields as part of a major paradigm shift in science, a journey which will be chronicled in the next chapter.

2.4 Chapter Summary

1. The research methodology I was taught to use were twentieth-century reductionist, general linear reality approaches.
2. My original proposal was to look at the effect of culture (Confucianism) in the context of Chinese churches as the possible root cause of increasing conflict.
3. In the process of collecting research data, I realized that culture was changing even as I watched. This would have made my findings obsolete even before the dissertation was completed.
4. Conclusion: a more robust approach is necessary in a multicultural, network context in systemic, continuous, and complex change that are the characteristics of twenty-first century realities.

Chapter 3

An Emerging Mazeway for Missiological Revitalization

This chapter is an expansion of my historical record to help readers understand the locus of this book in the context at the beginning of the twenty-first century. The intent of this chapter is to help readers understand that Complex Systems Science is not a novel, optional approach, but a paradigm shift that is well in emergence and permeating across all fields of study. If so, the shift to Complex Systems Science-framed approaches is not an option for missiology; to stay relevant with the rest of the academy, and remain effective in its role as pathfinder for the Church, it is mandatory.

As I shared my journey as a pastor to the point of being a missiologist in the last chapter, I now extend the perspective into the historical past to the late 1980s, the period where the adaptation to Complex Systems Science began to accelerate, to frame why the trajectory of research has led me to this approach.

3.1 From Simple to Complex in the Hard Sciences

The focus of my doctoral studies in Biomedical Engineering in the late 1980s and early 1990s was to better understand how the brain functions through developing new methods to measure and visualize electrical activity. At that time, due to the limits of technology, data were collected in the form of one-dimensional electroencephalograms (EEGs) recorded from electrodes placed at multiple locations over the skull (see Figure 7). The understanding at that time was that the location of the largest recorded signal was where the source of the electrical activity could be found.

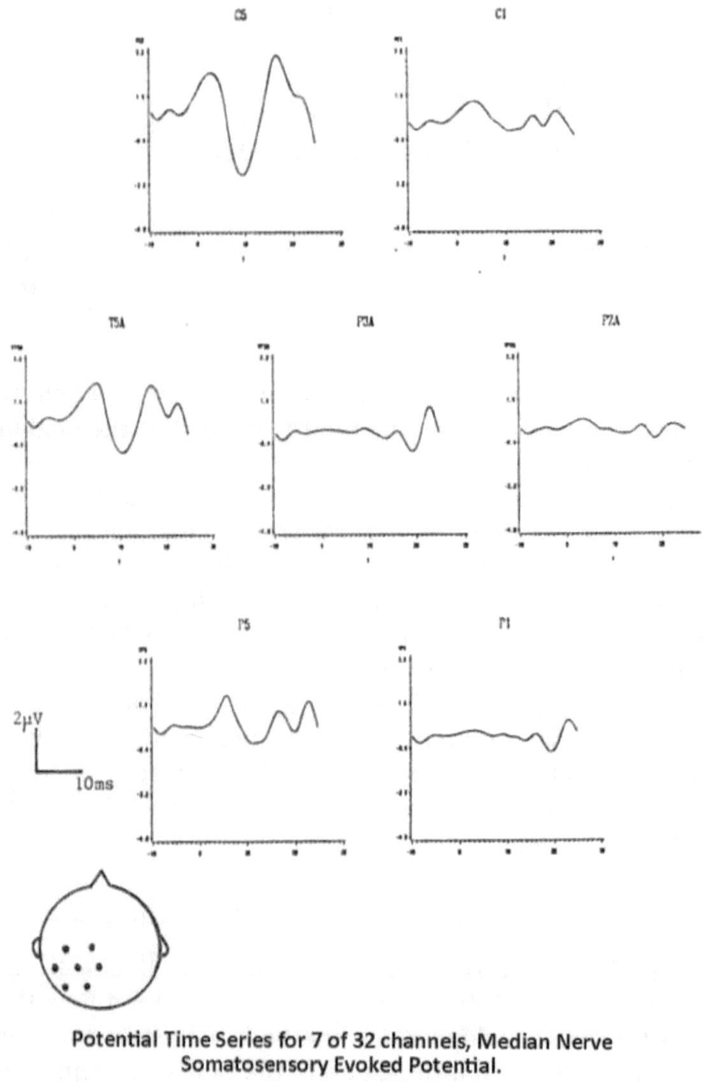

Potential Time Series for 7 of 32 channels, Median Nerve Somatosensory Evoked Potential.

Figure 7 - Evoked Potential Recordings (Law 1991, 144)

The relationship between recorded data and presumed source was based on a simple linear model that assumed that what was recorded on the surface of the head was directly related to a source immediately underneath. But in truth, it was only an assumption since there could be an infinite number of ways to generate such a signal. For example, in addition to a single source, multiple sources, like throwing several rocks in a pond could generate a large wave as if one large rock was thrown with exactly the same amplitude, shape, and characteristics.

But without a more complex model or an easy means to collect and analyze the large quantity of complex data, it was impossible to determine realistically how the signal was actually generated. In the absence of an adequate method to collect, model, and a means to analyze complex data, the simple linear model of brain activity was, in the 1980s, the generally accepted basis of diagnosis.

With the advent of the personal computer and its increasing accessibility by the average researcher, brain research changed radically. I began my research in 1987, only three years after the personal computer (pc) was introduced in 1984 powered by an 8088 Intel processor. Its ability to analyze the interactions from the various recording sites was still severely limited at that time, and any fruitful analysis still required access to a room-sized mainframe computer.

But by the time I was graduated in 1991, the personal computer was in its fourth generation, powered by an 80486 Intel processor. Though the computational power was small compared to contemporary personal computers, its computational power was nearly a hundred times more powerful[4] than the 8088 and opened the door to more complex analysis. Through table-top Sun Corporation work stations that ran multiple 80486 processors in parallel, our lab was instrumental in creating the algorithms and software to generate two and three-dimensional maps of EEGs (see Figure 8), allowing doctors and neurologists to understand not just where the sources of electrical activity occurred, but how the various sources were generated and interacted with one another.

In Figure 8, the map on the left is a model of thousands of columnar sources (2-3 mm in diameter) which more accurately represent real brain activity as a network of interacting sources rather than a few monolithic sources. The maps model the single motion of lifting one's index finger. The study helped neuroscientists understand that even a simple motion is not necessarily controlled by a single inch-sized patch of neocortex that traditional science approaches seemed to imply, but of thousands, even millions, of microscopic cells throughout the brain, working across a concerted network to sense,

---

[4] this is why its designation has five digits instead of four digits; it is one order of magnitude more powerful

control and provide feedback to and from the finger's nerves and muscles and intermediary neural connections to the brain. The middle and right maps are of algorithms that process the simulated data from the model of the electrical activity across the network of the millions of cells in the brain required to move a finger. This was considered "state of the art" in 1993.

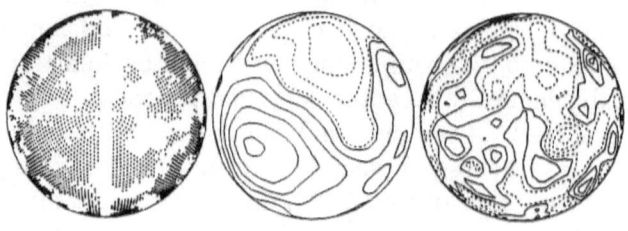

Figure 8 - Topographic Maps of Brain Activity (Law *et al*, 1993:145)

One may note however that the maps are circular rather than in the shape of an actual human head. Although equations were developed for an ellipsoid, in the absence of access to a supercomputer, the computational power available to the average researcher in the early 1990s could not reproduce data in any form beyond that of a simple sphere. Additionally, one notes that the maps are static, not dynamic. While it was possible to generate a video of activity over time using still-action graphs, it was extremely tedious and required days, even weeks, of intensive computational processing. Again, without an adequate means of analysis, the model was restricted to simple geometries.

At the time of my writing this paragraph in 2014, computer processors are now more than 1000 times more powerful than those in 1991. In fact, in the interim period, the Intel Corporation gave up the numerical designation with the Pentium chip (80586) and just started to use names because basing the name on the increasing power of each chip would have become tedious. Any contemporary neighborhood neurologist's office can now easily generate beautiful, colored multi-dimensional videos on their laptop pc of a patient's brain activity onto more anatomically correct representations of the human head.

Additionally, brain activity can now be modeled through simulation using Complex Systems Theory, enabling researchers to explore via simulation how activity patterns might change as various parameters are altered. Scientists can now use computers to mimic signals generated by millions, even billions, of simulated brain cells, in an attempt to simulated observed patterns of brain activity.

And while it is not yet viable for routine use, researchers are now moving toward being able to refine topographic brain maps to account for the realistic, nonlinear nature of the human head such as the unique and local variations in skull thickness, shape of the brain convolutions (specific to each individual much like a fingerprint), among other unique characteristics for each individual patient. Such improvements serve to improve visual resolution of the data such that one no longer needs to rely on general algorithm to estimate brain activity; rather, researchers are able to develop individualized algorithms derived from each individual's head shape and brain activity.

With the aid of more powerful computers, we are now able to move away from a simple, linear, static model to a complex, multidimensional, dynamic model of the brain; and as a result of these developments in brain mapping and computational models, all the brain science disciplines such as brain physics, neuroscience, psychology and psychiatry, and cognitive science have been "revitalized." While the data, the electrical activity of the brain, remain the same, and while there are still a number of uncertainties, nevertheless a paradigm shift in thinking has resulted because complex data are now visualized through a medium that is able to generate a clearer *Gestalt* of the activity.

Thomas Kuhn would call this a paradigm shift in *world view*, like "'scales falling from the eyes,' or the "lightning flash,' that 'inundates' a previously obscure puzzle, enabling its components to be seen in a new way that for the first time permits its solution" (Kuhn, 1996: 122). Gerald Edelman agrees, arguing that "the 'neuro-scientific revolution' might be a 'prelude to the largest possible scientific revolution, one with inevitable and important social consequences' (1992, xiii), quoted from Reyna 2002, 183). This change of perspective is not unlike Wallace's new vision or "mazeway" that leads to a discontinuous, paradigm shift in approach; hence the term "revitalization" would be appropriate for what has happened in the field of brain sciences.

3.2 Emerging Metaphors and Mazeways from Complexity

I share this narrative because it illustrates a major paradigm shift that is occurring in the sciences that is being driven by the availability of increasing power and abilities of contemporary computing devices to the average scientist, and how the paradigm shift has resulted in new metaphors and a new *Gestalt* that has led to an expanded understanding of physical phenomena. The advent of this new tool has provided humans with new lenses to expand the dimensional limits of understanding on both sides for the spectrum, from the microscopic to the macroscopic and develop increasingly complex models that more realistically represent reality compared to the simple, linear, and discrete models of the pre-computer age that were based primarily on Newtonian mechanics and empirical data. "Computational models allow us to consider rich environments with greater fidelity than existing techniques permit, ultimately enlarging the set of questions that we can productively explore. They allow us to keep a broad perspective on the multiple, interconnecting factors that are needed to understand social life fully." (Miller and Page 2007, 26)

These new dimensions of perception have in turn given rise to new methodologies and new sciences that allow us to travel outside the middle scale domain of simple, linear, Newtonian models into the broader expanse of Complex Systems Science and its complex and more realistic models of the physical world. This new trajectory from simple to complex, as relevant to this book, can be characterized by four primary shifts, from 1) reductionism to holism; 2) linear to nonlinear analysis; 3) static to dynamic; and 4) empirical to metaphor.

The first shift in the new sciences is not to rely solely on the methodology of reductionism, but to step back and consider the larger, holistic context; in other words, it is not merely to study the tree, but to recognize that the tree is part of a forest ecosystem. Reductionism, the dominant approach to science since the 1600s, is helpful in explaining phenomena in the intermediate dimensional range that can be observed by the human senses and perception. But in the 20th century, beginning with the development of quantum physics and later systems theory, it became increasingly clear that reductionism was limited in explaining phenomena in the extreme ranges of the subatomic and the macroscopic respectively. Mitchell

Feigenbaum writes "you know the right equations but they're just not helpful. You add up all the microscopic pieces and you find that you cannot extend them to the long term. They're not what's important in the problem. It completely changes what it means to *know* something" (Gleick 1987, 174-75).

What resulted was the formation of an epistemological chasm between the assumption of certainty of a "clockwork universe" to the realization of uncertainty. A scientific "crisis of faith" was created because "When a scientist faces a complicated world, traditional tools that rely on reducing the system to its atomic elements allow us to gain insight. Unfortunately, using these same tools to understand complex worlds fails, because it becomes impossible to reduce the system without killing it." (Miller and Page 2007, 10).

As a consequence, a scientific paradigm shift took place through the twentieth century that is increasingly enveloping all disciplines and moving them from reductionism to holism. Melanie Mitchell writes that scientific reductionism has been

> . . . noticeably mute in explaining the complex phenomena closest to our human-scale concerns. Many phenomena have stymied the reductionist program: the seemingly irreducible unpredictability of weather and climate; the intricacies and adaptive nature of living organisms and the diseases that threaten them; the economic, political, and cultural behavior of societies; the growth and effects of modern technology and communication networks; and the nature of intelligence and the prospect for creating it in computers. The antireductionist catch-phrase, "the whole is more than the sum of its parts," takes on increasing significance as new sciences such as chaos, systems biology, evolutionary economics, and network theory move beyond reductionism to explain how complex behavior can arise from large collections of simpler components. By the mid-twentieth century, many scientists realized that such phenomena cannot be pigeonholed into any single discipline but require an interdisciplinary understanding based on scientific foundations that have not yet been invented. Several attempts at building those foundations included (among others) the fields of cybernetics, synergetics, systems science, and more recently, the science of Complex Systems (Mitchell 2009, x).

Hence, this first characteristic of the new emerging paradigm shift is holism, focusing not on the constituent parts, but rather on trying to encompass the whole. The new science is interdisciplinary in nature and the interest is ". . . in between the usual scientific boundaries." (Miller and Page 2007, 7). Within Complex Systems, Emergence Theory is the foundational science that seeks to bridge reductionism with holism.

The move to holism leads to the second shift from linearity to nonlinearity, the recognition that the explanation of many phenomena in the real world requires more than understanding their constituent parts. Stephen Kellert writes that, until recently, "Education in the natural sciences created the impression that linear and solvable systems were the only ones (or at least the only important ones) – and impression that came very close to being a prejudice of systems as regular and predictable as clockwork" (Kellert 1993, 134). So while scientists recognized that the real world data consisted of distribution curves, they steadfastly held on to the notion that the average was the only real solution. So even though ". . . chaos has surrounded us since human life began. . . . Scientists 'ignored' chaos in the sense that these observations were passed over and not considered worthy of further investigation." (Kellert 1993, 124)

But as computers enabled researchers to analyze more and more data, enlarging the tails of distribution curves and recording rather than throwing away "spurious data," it became increasingly clear that most linear systems models could not account for all observed phenomena as empirical data, when collected and analyzed in greater amounts, in many cases had multiple "averages." The increased understanding of "sensitivity to initial conditions" was what led to the development of the science of chaos. In time, researchers began to conclude that traditional science tools ". . . with their emphases on average behavior being representative of the whole – may be incomplete or even misleading." (Miller and Page 2007, 14) Mitchell thus writes, "Linearity is a reductionist's dream, and nonlinearity can sometimes be a reductionist's nightmare." (Mitchell 2009, 22)

The greater understanding of importance of nonlinearity and the understanding of sensitivity to initial conditions led to the third shift, that systems were in reality not static, in fact, never static, but dynamic in nature. This dynamism cannot be ignored since minute perturbations in process (the butterfly flapping its wings) are as influential as a system's initial conditions. Dynamic systems analysis is then critical in understanding the emergence of phenomena. Kellert writes that "The method of understanding their appearance is by the construction of models, not by breaking systems into their components and then constructing ahistorical deductive schemes, but rather by using experimental procedures that concentrate on holistic properties and historical development." (Kellert 1993, 114) In truth, dynamical systems include nearly every system "that you probably can think of. Even rocks change over geological time. Dynamical systems theory describes in general terms the ways in which systems can change, what types of macroscopic behavior are possible, and what kinds of predictions about that behavior can be made." (Mitchell 2009, 16) As such, "Chaos theory shows us that the need for diachronic methods of understanding is much broader than previously thought" (Kellert 1993, 96).

The removal of the reductionist, linear, and static bias and the increasing inclusion of the holistic, nonlinear, and dynamic character of real world complex phenomena results in the fourth relevant shift, from empirical to metaphor. The recognition of human limitations forces the necessity that any scientific endeavor is inherently "fuzzy." Kellert argues that this however,

> . . . does not lessen our understanding or render much of nature incomprehensible. For in the first place, it gives us new general information about the relationships between the large-scale properties and long-term behavior of systems, even allowing new predictions. And in the second place, like quantum mechanics, it gives an intelligible and enlightening account of when predictability will go out the window, and even an account of how it is that this happens. (Kellert 1993, 100)

This in fact provides a much broader range of benefit in the process of scientific inquiry. Kellert continues, writing that

> Quantitative investigations can provide very accurate information about a dynamical system by solving the equations of motion, but for nonlinear systems [i.e. most natural systems] this information is typically limited to just one solution and some small vicinity around it, and any accuracy secured rapidly disappears with time. Qualitative understanding is complementary; it predicts properties of a system that will remain valid for very long times and usually for all future time. (Kellert 1993, 101)

Miller and Page agree, writing that "if we want to investigate richer, more dynamic worlds, we need to pursue other modeling approaches. The trade-off, of course, is that we must weigh the potential to generate new insights against the cost of having less analytics." (Miller and Page 2007, 21)

What resulted in this paradigm shift was the opening of eyes. For Kellert writes that though complexity and chaos were

> . . . as common as daffodils in spring (Ford 1986, 3), yet even when looking right at it, scientists often saw nothing of interest. On some occasions, students may well have been directly instructed not to pay attention to anomalous disorderly behavior. In other cases, the training had an indirect effect through methods, concepts, and resources designated as appropriate. "You don't see something until you have the right metaphor to let you perceive it" (Robert Shaw, quoted in Gleick 1987, 262). (Kellert 1993, 136)

With the right metaphor, however, the hard sciences, everything from physics to biology to geology, have undergone a revitalization in light of the Complex Systems Science. With the right metaphor, scientists have begun to look again at what has been studied before and are now discovering new insights in the midst of old data.

One of the most important metaphors is that of looking for order over and against science's current pursuit of predictability. Keller writes

> The law-based conception of understanding seeks iron-clad rules that will dictate why things are constrained to turn out the way they do. Such an approach would typically respond to chaotic behavior dismissively, assigning it to uncontrolled outside causal influences ("noise") or writing it off as the unintelligible result of too many competing and interacting simple mechanisms (the Landau model).
>
> But chaos theory looks to the geometric mechanisms that will show how patterns arise alongside unpredictable behavior, providing an understanding of "how it happens" rather than of "why it had to happen." Such an investigation reveals order.... [Evelyn Fox] Keller recommends an emphasis on order rather than laws so as to revise our conceptions of science and the natural world for the better.... an interest in order rather than law may be expected to lead to a shift toward "more global and interactive models of complex dynamic systems."(Kellert 1993, 112-113)

Minimizing the constraints of empiricity, scientists began to see metaphors – and a whole new universe opened up before their newly adjusted eyes. Instead of reductionism, scientists now look to the whole. Instead of the focus linear connections, scientists now look to the noise. Instead of isolating the static, scientists now pursue the dynamic.

What led to this new "mazeway?" All this has come about as a result of the introduction of sufficient computational power to extend the range of humanity's epistemology, for "... it took the digital computer to make chaos accessible to scientific inquiry." (Kellert 1993, 128)

3.3 From Simple to Complex in the Soft Sciences

The same revitalization has begun in the social sciences, as the metaphors from Complex Systems Science overflow from the hard sciences; however, what is different is that these new metaphors provide a revitalized epistemology for what social scientists were already observing. Mosko and Damon write "Ironically, it may be that anthropologists have displayed seemingly little conscious interest in chaos theory because many of its tenets have struck them intuitively as all too familiar!" (Mosko and Damon 2005, xi)

What Complex Systems Science has done, however, has been to provide a means for the other social sciences and hard sciences to conceive of the vast diversity of human cultures and societies. "Chaos theory does not show us what the world is like, or what thought or even representation may be like; it only shows us *how* they are like themselves." (Mosko and Damon 2005, 43). Mosko and Damon write that Complex System Science

> ... presents social anthropology with something more valuable than merely formal descriptions of seemingly analogous cultural phenomena. Chaos theory, in other words, offers a way to integrate an otherwise heterogeneous collection of many of social anthropology's most provocative and far-reaching theories and postulates of recent decades: Evans-Pritchard's analysis of the dynamics of segmentary opposition (1940); Levi-Strauss's canonic formulation for myth (1963c; 1988; 1995; Mosko 1991a; Maranda 2001); the widely acknowledged indeterminacy of historical events; Leach's (1954) model of societies in "moving equilibrium"; homologous structural replications across cultural domains; Forte's (1970) formulation of the development cycle in domestic groups; the unpredictable influence of individual personalities on historical events; the structural pervasiveness of binary constructions in sociocultural systems; structural analyses of history (e.g. Sahlins 1981; 1985; 1991; Levi-Strauss 1995); Dumont's (1980) theory of religious and political hierarch; Wagner's "obviation" theory and particularly his grasp of representation in symbols standing for themselves (1986a; 1986c; 2001); Marilyn Stratherns' portrayal of Melanesian sociality (1988; 1992a; 1995; 1999) and her discussions of scale and proportion (1991a; 1991b; 2000; 2001); and Appadurai's (1996) perception of patterns shaping current processes of globalization. The current developments in chaos theory necessitates, therefore, not so much a new departure for social anthropology as a consolidation and appreciation of a disciplinary coherence until now only simply and incompletely perceived. (Mosko and Damon 2005: 5-6)

If the same paradigm takes hold in the social sciences, the "integrative investigations by new social anthropologists making connections between biological, social, and cultural realms in the social monism might just have the desired revolutionary effects." (Reyna 2002:183)

Similarly, in the field of sociology, Complex Systems Science provides a means to integrate the disparate theories that have resulted in the division created by postmodernism. The ingrained linear and reductionist approach of traditional science has resulted in a fractured discipline. Walby summarizes the potential for unifying the various camps of sociologists, writing

> Social theory faces a challenge in theorizing the intersection of multiple complex inequalities. To do so adequately it must address the ontological depth of systems of social relations of inequality in the institutional domains of polity, violence, and civil society rather than flatten this to a single dimension of culture or economics. But the old concept of social system did not allow for more than one major axis of inequality in each institutional

domain. This led many of those that prioritized the significance of multiple inequalities to reject the concept of social system. However, in so doing they lost the capacity to simultaneously theorize their ontological depth. To theorize simultaneously the ontological depth of each of these inequalities as well as their intersection it is necessary to revisit and revise the concept of social system, so that it can meet this challenge.

Complexity theory[5], which has developed across a range of disciplines, provides the conceptual toolkit that enables this to be done. . . . it offers a series of conceptual innovations to the concept of system that may be synthesized with selected traditions of social theory. . . . allow[ing] the transcendence of some of the old polarities of modernism and postmodernism. . . . The complexity notion of the system/environment distinction enables a more nimble conceptualization of systems and their interactions. . . It enables the rejection of the notion that parts must be nested within a whole, and thus a rejection of the reduction of one set of social relations of inequality to another. Complexity theory provides the theoretical flexibility to allow systematic analysis of social interconnections without the reductionism that so marred the old. (2007, 466-467)

Hence, Complex Systems Science is seen not as a new approach that replaces existing approaches, but as a means of providing an expanded, integrated, and interdisciplinary space, much like what Shaw described in chapter 2, where all the various approaches can find their significance and relationship with one another.

With regard to the study of religion, Purzycki *et al* write, "Current approaches to religion maintain that religion evolved as a byproduct of cognitive mechanisms that were naturally selected or functions unrelated to religion. . . . we argue that it is necessary to widen the scope of analyses to encompass religious concepts, behavior, and sharedness, and how they interact with each other and their environment." (2012)

In summary, the integration of Complex Systems Science holds great promise since multicultural environments are now in the majority of human societies which have been shaped by urbanization and globalization. Complex Systems Science-framed metaphors, models, and methods provide greater fidelity, robustness for analyzing increasingly complex data, and as well, a clearer pathway to its visualization to spark a *Gestalt* perspective that Wallace describes as the necessary catalyst for revitalization; but unlike Wallace, Complex Systems Science breaks down the boundaries of closed systems and

---

[5] Complexity Theory is a subdiscipline of Complex Systems Science that is best suited for describing living systems in contrast to Chaos Theory which is better suited to describe mechanical systems. Please see 4.1.1 for a more detailed explanation.

opens the field to not just a single mazeway, but multiple, simultaneous, yet integrated and networked, mazeways of study.

3.4 Visualizing Complexity in Social Systems, Organizations and Leadership

Of all the social sciences, the field of economics has made the greatest strides in the practical applications of modeling and visualizing complexity in social systems. Immersed in the intrinsic heavily data-oriented nature of economics, researchers have generally been cognizant of, and adept at analyzing, complexity. With the growing accessibility to ever increasing computational power, the result was the development of the subdiscipline of Agent-based Computational Economics (ACE), the computational study of processes modeled as dynamic systems of interacting agents (Testfatsion 2006, 835). Leigh Tesfatsion writes,

> As the other disciplines began to recognize the importance of integrating complexity into their fields, ACE models served as the basis for visualizing complexity. Agents that have been successfully represented in ACE models include individuals (e.g. consumers, workers), social groupings (e.g. families, firms, governments agencies), institutions (e.g. markets, regulatory systems), biological entities (e.g. crops, livestock, forests), and physical entities (e.g. infrastructure, weather, geographical regions.). Thus, agents can range from active data-gathering decision-makers with sophisticated learning capabilities to passive world features with no cognitive functioning. Moreover, agents can be composed of other agents, thus permitting hierarchical constructions. (2006, 835)

The robust nature of Complex Systems Science-framed models allows one to study processes at all levels of social systems. Using the fractal properties of Chaos Theory, which involves the replication of phenomena and processes on multiple scales, ACE models have been successfully used to represent data from the micro-scale, such as data from human subjects experiments (Duffy 2006), to the meso-scale level, such as the understanding how differences in network structure impacts a community (Wilhite 2006), and on to the macro-scale level, such as event history analysis (Uhl-Bien and Marion 2008, xx). Such flexibility allows researchers to narrow or expand their spectrum of focus depending on how complex a model they desire to develop. But as well, the ever present nature of scalability forces researchers to be constantly aware of reductionist tendencies, thereby mitigating the potential for bias.

Of particular interest to this book are the Complex Systems Leadership Theory studies of organizations, the role of leadership, and the evolution, development, and resolution of conflict. These have direct bearing on both the book's focus on Wallace's understanding of leaders and their roles in revitalization movements and the group interactions in Chinese churches in the diaspora journey.

The interdisciplinary integration of Complex Systems Leadership Theory and revitalization studies is non-existent, yet this is fertile ground for bearing significant discoveries. It is interesting to note that although not a single source in the primary literature of Complexity Leadership ever cited Wallace, nevertheless, the parallel discussions are striking. Specifically, Complexity Leadership Theory studies how leaders and organizations navigate the "Cusp of Change," this process being defined as "criticalization." Jeff Goldstein, James Hazy, and Benyamin Lichtenstein write,

> Criticalization is perhaps the most difficult time in the life of any organization, as a whole or in part, since it is all about the effect of internally or environmentally generated shocks that disrupt the inner workings of the company. This disruption can show itself in a growing recognition that current operating models are not sufficient and small fixes are not enough to deal with the scope and pace of change. Criticalization often signals a time of conflict and differences of opinion, a period of cognitive dissonance and information overload. Critical periods, however, also offer unique opportunities for transforming an organization through innovation. (2010, 48)

If one compares this definition with Wallace's understanding of the revitalization process, one finds them nearly identical.

But unlike Wallace's revitalization model, Complexity Leadership Theory is not biased toward a single leader or event, but expands the focus to look at the entire system as a dynamic process. On the one hand, Complex Leadership Theory does recognize the importance of leaders, as David Schwandt and David Szabla write, "Effective leadership required a shift of mind in which leaders perceived the whole system and reasoned and made judgments based on the interrelationships between system components both inside and outside the organization. 'Seeing systems' became a critical cognitive ability for leaders." (2007, 54) Again, their definition is eerily striking of Wallace's understanding for a leader's ability to *Gestalt* change. But on the other hand, Complexity Leadership Theory equally recognizes the possibility of change through emergent properties by organizational individuals and their network interactions. David Schwandt and David Szabla write,

> Researchers began to use the complexity sciences to explore leadership (Griffin, 2002; Stacey, *et al*, 2000). They found that conventional leadership

thought did not accommodate a new division of labor that was interdependent and dispersed. Leadership was being talked about as a phenomenon that emerged from and was embodied in the interactions of participants. The research was intense and several leadership conceptions based on this new framework emerged, including *shared leadership*, which was defined as "a dynamic interactive influence process among individuals in groups for which the objective is to lead one another to the achievement of group organizational goals" (Pearce & Conger, 2003:1), and *distributed leadership*, which was characterized by the criterion of "conjoint agency" (Gronn, 2003). (2007, 55)

Consequently, "leadership became known 'as a process, not a person (Hollander 1978, 4) that "involves an going transaction between leaders and followers" (p. 12). (Schwandt and Szabla 2007, 54)

Complex Systems Leadership Theory concludes that leadership is, in fact, defined not by an individual, but "*leadership* in Complex Systems takes place during interactions among agents when those interactions lead to changes in the way agents expect to relate to one another in the future." Furthermore, "*effective leadership* occurs when the changes observed in one or more agents (i.e. leadership) leads to increased fitness for that system in its environment. We define fitness in relation to some metric of sustainability..." (Hazy *et al* 2007, 7) Consequently, in Complex Systems Leadership Theory,

> ... the questions of interest related to the dynamics of the system and not a superior acting on a subordinate. These new questions like the following began sparking our interest: How does leadership emerge from within the dynamics of a system? To what extent and by what mechanisms does individual agency influence system dynamics? Does collective agency emerge? If so, how does this come about? Was leadership a function of one individual exercising power over another or was more [it, sic] about a dynamic that emerged across groups of people in interaction? What we were seeing therefore were explorations of leadership as a *systemic* event rather than as a personal attribute. (Hazy *et al* 2007, 13)

Additionally, unlike Wallace's model of revitalization which is descriptive in nature, Complexity Leadership Theory not only describes revitalization movements, but, as well, has the potential to model and predict how revitalization may occur. Utilizing Chaos Theory, "To understand how to navigate through these critical conditions it can be quite helpful to appreciate the dynamical systems notion of 'attractors,' an abstract representation of the underlying structures within ecologies and organizations that enable stability." (Goldstein *et al* 2010, 55)

Here, "attractor" refers to a Lorenz attractor, a concept from Chaos Theory that is defined by the equations:

$$x' = -sx + sy \qquad y' = -xz + rx - y \qquad z' = xy - bz$$

The system of equations has been used on numerous occasions to model human systems and is ideally suited for such use. First, the equations are bipolar and thus helpful in describing dyadic phenomena such as reciprocity, decision-making, and communication. Second, they are nonlinear equations that reflect sensitivity to initial conditions and variations; as such, they are well suited for modeling the variabilities of human interaction; in contrast, linear models require "exact fits." As such, instead of spending hours debating whether a particular entity was undergoing revitalization or not, missiologists may find it more fruitful to look for parallels across phenomena. Third, the equations form a system which allows one to understand how different variables influence one another. Russ Marion writes

> The strange attractor is an obvious metaphor for social phenomena. It is stable but its trajectory never repeats itself; likewise, social behavior is stable but never quite repeats itself. The strange attractor has the capacity to change. It can grow or it can shrink to encompass a broader or narrower range of behaviors; it can alter its appearance; it can convert to a dramatically different attractor; and it can even fade away. Social behavior is similarly more inclusive at times less inclusive at others. . . . Like mathematical attractors, social behavior drifts across time: Fads come and go, mores change, our relationship to institutions alters, our definition of family evolves. Social attractors occasionally experience radical change – witness what happened to the USSR in the late 1980s, for example. Systems, like attractors even fade away. (1999, 22)

He concludes that, while "Such metaphorical comparisons don't prove, of course, that social behaviors are Chaotic attractors, but, as the old saying sort of goes, if it looks like a dog and barks like a dog, why don't we see if it will tell us something about dogs." (1999, 22)

Marion was perhaps unaware of it at the time, but other sociologists did in fact find that real world data could indeed be modeled as a strange attractor. Dooley *et al* (1997) found that data from Adolescent Childbearing in Texas from 1964 – 1990 looks exactly like a strange attractor. What seemed chaotic and random, when plotted weekly, monthly, and yearly, across the period of 26 years, reveals cyclic phenomena with periodicities of 7 days, 28 days, 1 year, and 10 years. Dooley *et al* were able to provide plausible reasons for the 7-day periodicity to clinic practices of inducement and the 28 day and 1-year periodicities to the school year, but could not explain the 10-year cycle. Nevertheless, the application of Complex Systems Science-framed approaches proved their effectiveness in revealing patterns in what had been considered chaotic data.

Andrew Abbott argues that the social sciences now have in their ability to consider the study of historical scale. He writes,

> We now possess important and substantial social data sets that have experienced real historical change in the nature of the coded categories. Not simple drift in the usage of words, but actual drift in the nature of the things denoted, in both content and structure. The most familiar examples come from the census, where occupational and ethnic classifications have changed with regularity over the years. As the epoch of electronic data gathering continues, more and more data will have this quality of true historical change, constitutive change in the underlying categories. A central challenge for the future of all social research is to figure out how to handle this category change without simply sweeping it under the rug (2000, 299)

The following figures illustrate how a Lorenz attractor is visualized from data. Figure 9 are representative axial plots of the time evolution of chaotic (nonlinear) yet stable data of a Lorenz system.

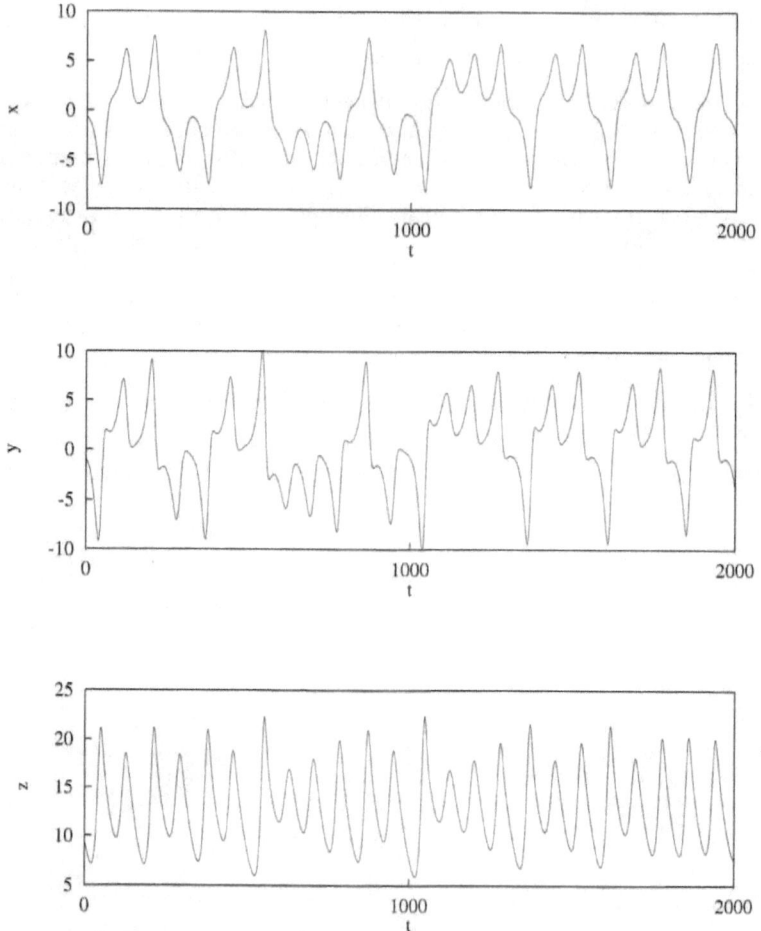

Figure 9 - Time evolution of x, y, and z from the Lorenz system
(Flake 1998, 171)

Figure 10 is an illustration of how variability is a result of minute changes that are made to the initial conditions of the variable "x." The system is still stable, but the trajectory will shift slightly, no longer overlapping one another.

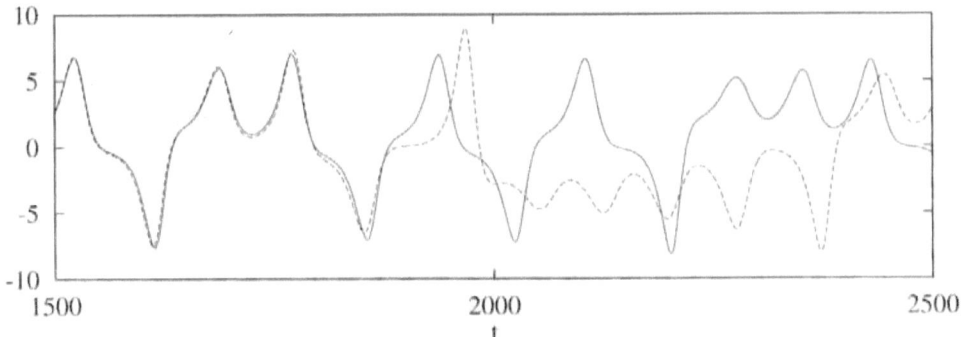

Figure 10 - Two time evolutions of x with an infinitesimal initial difference
(Flake 1998, 169)

The resulting Lorenz attractor is shown in Figure 11.

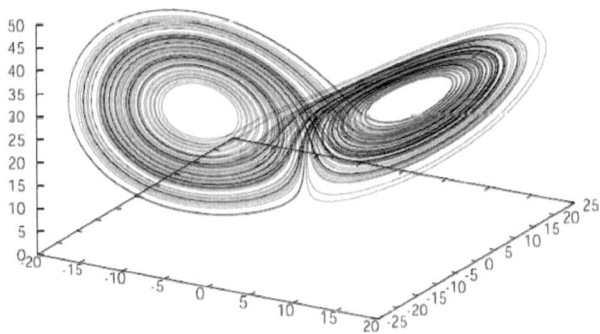

Figure 11 - An illustration of a Lorenz Attractor (Flake 1998, 172)

This plot is in actuality a family of similar systems of equations, each with small differences in the initial conditions. Each trajectory is similar to the others, implying that each system that is plotted is stable, yet, equally important, they are dissimilar (in fact, no two are alike) as a result of infinitesimal differences in initial conditions. Though not shown, the trajectory's shape may change with changes in the environmental conditions defined by the coefficients.

The Lorenz attractor is considered a complex system because, while stable, it is not linear, that is, it does not repeat itself in the exact trajectory. Specifically, it describes a system "on the Cusp of Change," a dynamic process that oscillates in liminality between a static system and turbulence, that is, total chaos.

ACE researchers recognized that such Complex Systems can be used to model human interactions. Goldstein *et al* write,

> Attractors represent the organization in its stable condition, in other words, when the operative constraints are balanced and steady. Thus the two constraints introduced earlier, namely, the levels of opportunity tension and of informational differences across the organization, plus the organization's history as embodied in the routines, norms, and functions that have developed over the years, determine the attractors that are operative in the organization. (2010, 56)

In Figure 12, they model how individuals or organizations follow specific patterns of behavior, but when faced with change, their trajectories' patterns change over time. This models the process of "criticalization," and what Wallace might consider the *Gestalt* phase of revitalization.

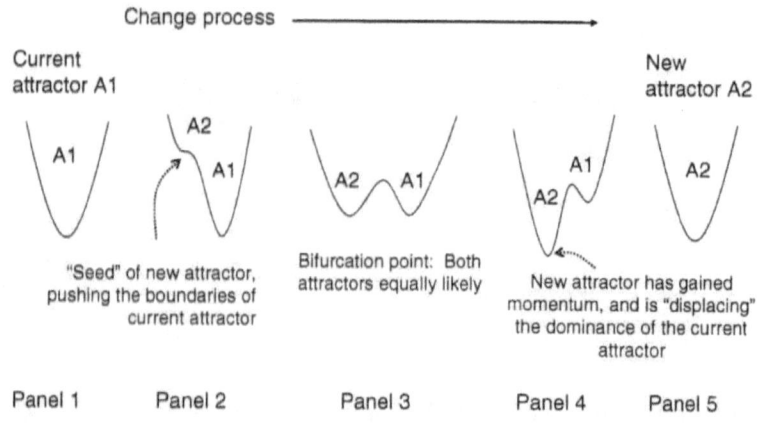

Figure 12 - Emergence of a New Attractor (Goldstein et al 2010, 62)

To illustrate the efficacy of Complex Systems Science-framed models, Goldstein *et al* looked at how two companies, Oracle and IBM, responded to changes in the markets. Figure 13 illustrates the robust nature of Complex Systems for *gestalting* a mazeway through change and charting its trajectory. Oracle's approach was a dramatic company-wide shift in approach. This resulted in "catastrophic" re-structuring, which led to massive lay-offs, and substantial resource costs. This is illustrated in Pathway 1 where the movement is discontinuous from one plane to another plane. In contrast, IBM took a more circuitous route over the course of three years. This is illustrated in Pathway 2 by gradually changing the location of attractors (i.e. corporate values and approaches) thus altering IBM's trajectory of transition. Both companies moved from A1 to A2. But the phase transition of IBM (Pathway 2) was gradual, predictable, and ultimately less damaging than Oracle's (Pathway 1) radical and catastrophic trajectory that resulted in substantial loss due unpredictable consequences. Goldstein et al thus illustrated how Complex Systems provided a more robust model of organizational response to change that could both analyze as well as predict how organizations traverse change.

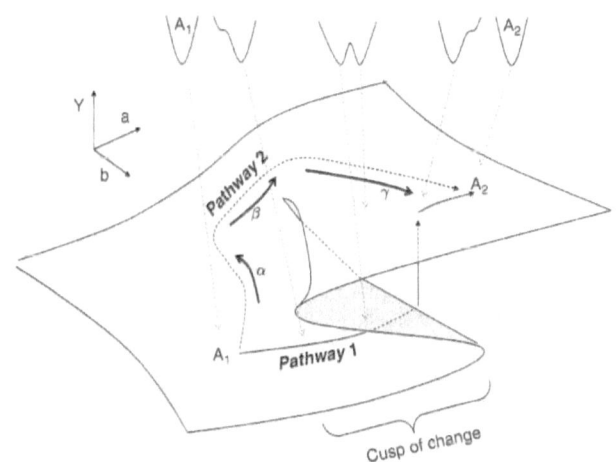

Figure 13 - Representative Pathways for Attractor Change
(Goldstein et al 2010, 70)

Figure 14 shows how the interaction of different individuals might look like in an organization. In this diagram, each of the trajectories represents the trajectories different individuals may take in an organization. Although each may seem unrelated and unique, nevertheless all the trajectories are related because they all circumnavigate a single attractor. As such, the organization is considered "chaotically stable."

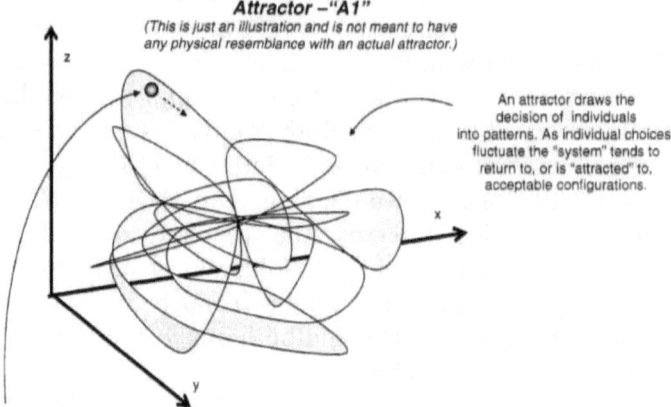

Values for variables (x, y, z, ...) describing the organizing system assume a constrained set of allowable configurations among various possibilities. (One such configuration is shown here as the grey ball, rolling around as events occur or individual choices are made.) The variables, like employee attendance, are drawn to particular configurations as biasing norms that constrain behavior, such as "report to work daily at 8:00 AM" versus "stay home," operate to "attract" the organization into acceptable configuration patterns. Some individuals resist, other conform.

Figure 14 – Stylized Model of an attractor in an organization with multiple individuals (Goldstein et al 2010, 59)

Of special relevance for our discussion is the application of Complex Systems Leadership Theory, with its focus on interactions, to understanding the relationship between about communication and conflict. Pekka Aula and Kalle Siira recognized that bidirectional character of communication and one's ability to communicate change are inter-related in a dynamic, complex process that is illustrated in Figure 15 (2007, 377).

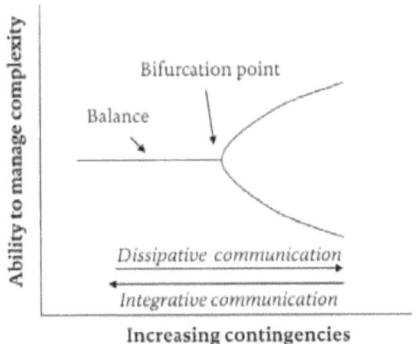

Figure 15 – The Emergence of Dissipative Systems Complemented with the Dual Function of Organizational Communication (Aula and Siira 2007)

Using real-world case studies to generate data for an ACE model, they explored the relationships through the metaphors offered by the Complex Systems Science-framed model. They concluded that

> From a social complexity perspective, conflict is considered as a natural phenomenon of complex human systems. Needs and desires of organizational agents 'are not homogeneous and, therefore, their goals and behaviors are likely to conflict" (Rouse 2000, 144). The social complexity view on conflict and communication opposes that conflict situations are about false, wrong, or errors in communication, and, instead posits that they are, by definition, communication events. . . . "thus communication is not an input, moderator, or mediator of outcomes; it becomes the conflict itself" (Putnam, 2006:18). Conflict is critical in renewing organizations, as it is an antecedent and an outcome of diversity in organizations.

Understanding that conflict is communication, leadership then is not about ". . . simply keeping peace or providing answers, but to create the conditions 'in which followers' behaviors can produce structure and innovation (Uhl-Bien and Marion, 2001:398)." (Aula and Sirra 2007, 379)

If one reflects back to my personal journey through the Lilly Renewal grant and the conclusions drawn, one will find that they are identical with those drawn by Aula and Siira. As will be discussed in Chapter 6, the methodology, models, and metaphors of Complex Systems Science provide a new mazeway in understanding the complex phenomena I encountered in ministry.

In summary, the efforts of ACE modelers reveal the potent possibilities of Complex Systems Science for missiology. The new metaphors, models, and methods offer more robust tools for missiologists to better understand the increasingly complex world of the twenty-first century.

3.5 Visualizing Complexity Missiology and Revitalization

In the introduction, I have already described the increasing challenges of using Wallace's existing model of revitalization in urbanizing and globalizing realities; in the above subsection, I have argued that the increasing inadequacy of linear models is not an isolated phenomenon, but a reflection of increased recognition of the need to incorporate complexity in analysis in all fields - *including missiology.*

Missiologists, though they may not yet have the terminology or the concepts to describe complexity in their research, nevertheless are already aware of its existence. As I began work in Intercultural Studies in 2009, words like "multiple centers," "dialectic tension," "competing centripetal and centrifugal forces" were littered through my classes. When it came to the study of "people groups," there were no longer any clear cut boundaries, but there was the recognition that they were increasingly fuzzy and interpenetrating.

My mentor, Mike Rynkiewich, perhaps because of his training as an anthropologist, was one of the first missiologists to recognize the need to incorporate complexity into analyses, writing, "We need to understand how culture is contingent on regional and global flows, how culture is constructed from materials brought into the present over historic and geographic distances, and how culture is constantly being contested in daily life. If we do not have such an understanding, we fail to grasp the missionary situation and to communicate the gospel properly." (2002, 316)

As if to recognize the emerging understanding of the new context we are in, it is no coincidence that the new 2013 cover of *Missiology* is that of a complex network. The covers no longer reflect different topics or venue each month, but now remain static, as if to imply that complexity is the ever-present condition of our human world.

Recognition is but the first step; one wonders if missiologists are willing to take the next step to develop the tools with which to analyze the complex realities of twenty-first century human cultures and societies? As the bias problems of Wallace's revitalization model were described previously, the same can be said of missiology. It is one thing to say "hold things in tension," but what does that actually mean? What is the balance between "pilgrim" and "indigenizing?"

How can one be "centripetal" and "centrifugal" at the same time? How do "multiple centers" interact with each other?

In truth, personal bias more often than not pulls a person to one side or another side, not to stay balanced between two opposing poles. Similar to Wallace's model of revitalization, not unlike the bias that Kuhn describes in science, there is a natural tendency toward simple explanations that are biased by one's perspective. This bias is also recognized by Andrew Abbott (2001, 32) as "self-similarity" and Paul Hiebert's understanding that knowledge is paradigmatic – that is, we see what we want to see (1999, 42).

Russ Marion likens it to the fold tale of three blind men describing an elephant, writing

> One blind man feels the tail and says the elephant is like a rope. The second feels the elephant's leg and concludes it must be a tree. The third feels the trunk and says it is like a snake. Each man focuses on different perspectives and creates a different explanation of elephant.
>
> A test of model goodness [that is, the metaphors people use to construct our perceptions of reality] is in its generalizability, thus the snake model, if reasonably accurate, should work for the opposite end of the mammoth, but of course it doesn't. Our blind scientists could argue that the elephant is so complex that theorists must focus on one part of the animal at a time. When models are restricted to their intended uses, they are reasonably appropriate. Still, these models are problematic because they do not impart a full sense of elephant, and the blind scientists will inevitably be bothered by the lack of connection among the theories. (1999, 11)

What is needed is a means to what Paul Hiebert calls "critical realism;" Complex Systems Science-framed approaches offer a mazeway to critical realism because it requires researchers to step back and look from a broader, systemic perspective and consider other possible factors. "Critical realism offers an alternative that is more humble but also more proactive in its response to the human dilemma. . . . It affirms the presence of objective truth but recognizes that this is subjectively apprehended (1999, 68). . . . Critical realism draws on community hermeneutics, metacultural grids, and a broad range of rational analysis to test the validity of theories (1999, 74)." This is in essence what happens when the galaxy of traditional science approaches are forced to step back and understand its place in the broader universe of Complex Systems Science. Hiebert writes,

> . . . higher levels of knowledge involve logical processes – the mental abilities of forming abstract concepts, relating these in complex theories, and testing between competing theories. Critical realism accepts the validity of the formal algorithmic logic that is the basis for positivism and postpositivism, but it broadens the concept of rationality to include the other types of

reasoning. It recognizes the role of metaphors, analogies, and other tropes in shaping human thought. (1999, 86)

This essentially describes the paradigm shift from traditional approaches to Complex Systems Science-framed approaches.

Recognizing the increasing complexity of the global contexts, the consultations of the World Christian Revitalization Movements recognized the limitations of the existing model of revitalization. Steve O'Malley *et al* write,

> To view Christian revitalization as a *mosaic* is to recognize the complexity, significance, and beauty of countless interlaced components and patterns. A complex web of numerous interdependent dimensions and components characterized each revitalization movement. The configuration of the intertwining elements varied from movement to movement, but every movement demonstrated some significant form of ecclesial renewal and reconstitution, testimony of divine encounter, and evidence of personal transformation. (2013, 163)

Hence, with such complexity, those in the consultation called for new methods to study revitalization. Eunice Irwin writes,

> The challenge will be to study but also move beyond analysis of single movements one at a time, and to discover broader and more universally recognizable ways to understand and articulate revitalization as it has been observed, while avoiding the reduction of findings to any type of uniformity. Todd Johnson's suggestion of employing an approach of examining characteristics rather than devising models or taxonomies has merit (2011, 241)

How then can such a *Gestalt* moment be realized? What will provide the "aha!" or "eureka" moment where one has a *Gestalt* experience, when one understands how individual pieces fit with the whole, for example, when Victor Turner drew a picture of the ritual process, he finally understood how all the pieces fit together as a reflection of the Ndembu culture and their cosmology (Turner, 2008:30)?

For simple systems, a simple illustration is more than sufficient to explain a cause-and-effect relationship. For example, in the graph provided by Hiebert *et al* (Figure 16) to explain Wallace's theory of revitalization movements, one can understand all the basic elements of the model.

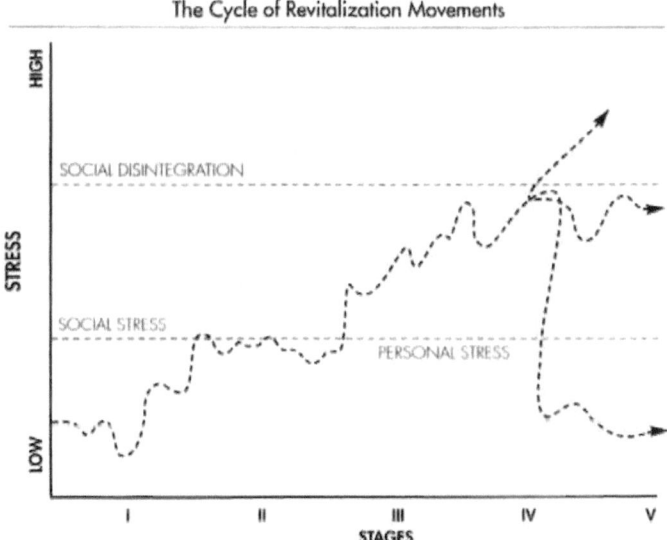

Figure 16 - from Hiebert *et al*, 1999:349

But in reality, Heibert's model does not describe a simple process; rather, one finds it eerily similar to the axial plots of the Lorenz equations (Figure 9) and the bifurcation plot (Figure 15). Its convolutions reveal that in reality it describes a complex process because the outcomes are not additive; because of the possible paradigm shifts, a multitude of outcomes are possible, even more than the three illustrated. And if one begins to look cross-culturally, the parameters grow exponentially and it becomes much more difficult to understand the relationships between variables. For example, consider the illustration below (Figure 17) which seeks to define a homeostatic system with individual and social levels.

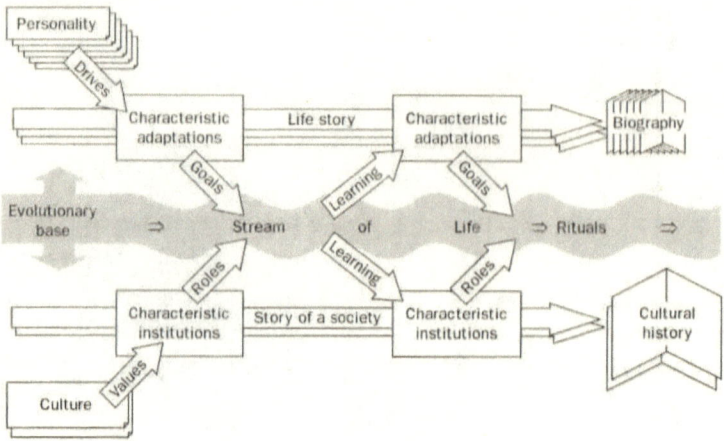

Figure 17 – Illustration of Cultural Homeostasis (Hofstede *et al* 2010, 467)

Visually, this is fairly easy to understand. But if one looks at the rest of Hofstede's book, there are a lot of charts, but very few graphs, the reason being that it is very difficult to visualize interconnected, complex data in a way the human mind can *Gestalt*. Even though Hofstede's illustration only hints at complex, nonlinear, and dynamic nature of the system through the use of cascading boxes, he nevertheless initiates a *Gestalt* moment for readers.

Another example is the map found in Rynkiewich's article describing the influence of various Christian missions to Misima in New Guinea (2002:311). The map shows multiple lines of contact in contrast to the "traditional regional flow" that shows just one line. Visualization of the complex data Rynkiewich details provides a *Gestalt* moment for his readers.

Complex Systems Science can provide the means by which to both analyze and visualize the multi-faceted context missiologists increasingly face in globalized, urbanized settings by expanding vocabulary and the metaphors which can be used to describe what is observed. In particular, three characteristics - that of bifurcation, sensitivity to initial conditions, scalability and nonlinearity provide the means of integrating the diverse theories, models and issues in missiology.

Consider, for example, how Complex Systems Science may help to unify the multitude of paradigms described by David Bosch (1991) and the "constants in context" by Stephen Bevans and Roger Schroeder (2004) with regard to world Christianity and local Christianities. A possible model metaphor can be found in the Lorenz attractor as illustrated in Figure 18.

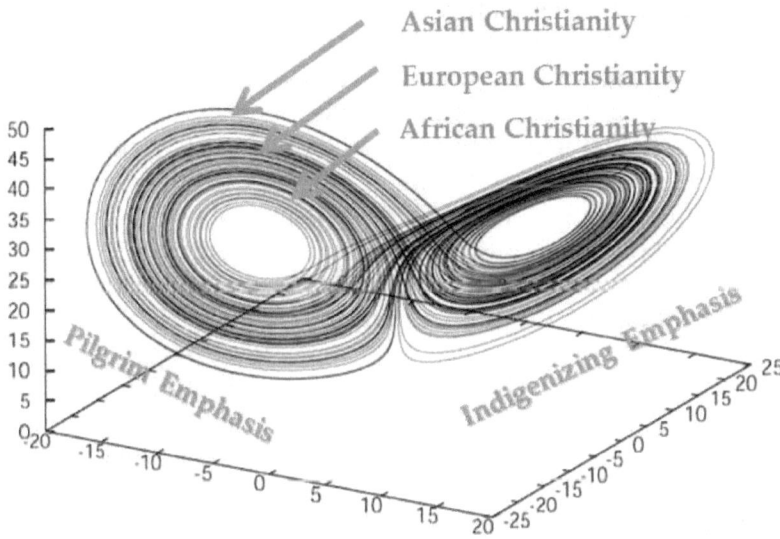

Figure 18 - Lorenz Attractor with application to missiology

The bifurcating nature of the Lorenz attractor provides a means to integrate many missiological principles which tend to be dialectic. Such pairs include "spiritual" and "material," "centripetal and centrifugal," and "pilgrim" and "indigenizing." One may understand the tensions conceptually, but modeling the dialectic relationships as a Lorenz attractor allows one to visualize both polarities as part of a single system. It is not an either/or relationship, but a both/and relationship. As the Lorenz attractor allows for multiple equilibrium centers, one does not need to choose between one position or the other. Both are equally valid positions and where a particular local Christianity is will depend on its own particular context.

As well, the Lorenz attractor places local Christianities in the larger universe of world or global Christianity. One now has a way to place a local Christianity within a larger framework. Furthermore, the diagram enables one to model interactions and a means to determine how new patterns can emerge.

And because the Lorenz attractor is a mathematical model, it is not merely a qualitative metaphor; it also provides a quantitative model that field researchers can collect, process, and analyze real world data. And perhaps what is most exciting is that once a model is developed and verified with real world data, missiologists will have in computationally adaptive models that can serve as a "test tube" to alter variables and predict how they alter the trajectories of change of other variables and the entire system. No longer would social scientists be limited to static studies, but as Andrew Abbott noted, social scientist may once again study historical change with a degree of validity (2000, 299). Since Abbott's keynote symposia, hundreds of Complex Systems Science models for social science have been developed (Epstein 2006, Castellani and Hafferty 2009).[6]

The same tools can be adapted for missiology. For example, the system of equations for the Lorenz attractor is:

$$x' = -sx + sy \qquad y' = -xz + rx - y \qquad z' = xy - bz$$

Computationally, one can, through a survey, evaluate how much a particular group is influenced by the "pilgrim" or "indigenizing" principle and quantify it with 's' of the Lorenz equations (see above). For example, the data for Figure 17 can be derived by looking at a particular religious group's theology. Their level of remaining "pilgrim" or indigenization can be quantified, then entered into the equation to generate the attractors. The resultant "attractors" can then be used to determine whether or not it is a stable system and visualize the interaction and relationships of the two influences. The shape, separation, and other relational characteristics of these attractors can provide a digestible visual representation of complex, ethnographic data for the missiologist.

The variables "r" and "b" describe the model's "air" (Kellert, 1993: 11) and provide a means to describe how a culture's trajectory may differ as a result of initial conditions; in other words, these variables can be used to describe the sensitivity to a society's characteristics and its social contexts. For example, they may be used to describe a society's traditional or progressive nature, whether it is communal or individualized, or it degree of isolation or globalization.

---

[6] for examples and actual programs, see www.personal.kent.edu/~bcastel3. accessed September 27, 2014

The characteristic of sensitivity to initial conditions allows for differences without having to discretely define a society's state. It bears similarity to the benefits of Hiebert's centered set theory (Hiebert 1991, 110) which allows for broader definition of conversion, belief, and faith by defining one's dynamic relationship to Christ rather than a static state if one uses the model of bounded sets. The example of Figure 18 allows for differences in African, Asian, and European Christianities without the need to challenge each culture's orthodoxy or requiring that each follow the exact same trajectory. In Chaos Theory, each "Christianity" would be considered "stable," in other words, "orthodox," though each travels a different trajectory as a result of differences in their initial cultural contexts.

Finally, the third characteristic of scalability and nonlinearity provides a means to integrate the global and local parameters of a society. Both subfields of Chaos Theory and Emergence Theory are based on a system's nonlinear nature and recognize the characteristic that something may be more than the sum of its parts. In other words, it counters reductionism with the inclusion of emergent, systemic processes. Complexity Theory integrates these relationships even more because of its focus on relationships – interactions between agents and the environment and internal dynamics of the networks of agents. Marion writes that attractors in a Complex system ". . . map their environment by resonating, or correlating, with them; that is, they interact with, and become a part of, their environment. Different attractors within a system resonate with one another, thus augmenting the capabilities of the broader organization." (1999, 82)

For example, the relationship between downward and upward causation provides a means to analyze and visualize the relationship between supracultural, global factors and local factors such as "spiritual" and "material," "pilgrim" and "indigenizing," etc. These could be incorporated in the variables to describe the "air" of Figure 18.

Hence, Complex Systems Science-framed metaphors, models, and methods inherently provides a qualitative and quantitative means to describe nebulous opposites and visualize how they interact with one another, something that may prove more satisfying than merely stating that they are to be "held in tension." The benefit of Complex Systems Science is that its focus is not merely on describing a state of being, but focuses on the interaction between states and how they change over the course of time. As such, two states, even polar opposites, are considered part of the same system. Consequently,

Complex Systems Science-framed approaches allow for the study of multiple poles and centers that are already being evidenced in missiology.

In summary, similar to its application in the social sciences, Complex Systems Science and its associated subsystems provide a means of integrating the diverse and oftentimes diverse aspects of missiology. It is a shift that missiologists Charles Van Engen has called for, writing,

> In all aspects and at all levels of society, we are in the midst of profound changes like nothing seen since the Industrial Revolution. Given the paradigm shift that the church and the world are undergoing, we must free ourselves to re-conceptualize the foundations, the forms, and the goals of ministry formation in the future. Ministry formation must likewise undergo a radical paradigm shift so that it can appropriately serve the church in the world of tomorrow. (1996: 241)

Responding to his challenge, this book argues that Complex Systems Science provides new terminology and new metaphors that can provide new lenses to *Gestalt* the increasingly complex changes that are occurring and define new mazeways for the contexts of twenty-first century realities.

3.6 Complex Systems Science and Social Movement Theory

At this juncture of the discussion, it is prudent to discuss how Complex Systems Science, and specifically the subfield of Complexity Theory which best describes the complex nature of living systems (see 4.1.1 for a more detailed discussion) and Social Movement Theory, considered as an enhanced or alternate model for Christian revitalization, are similar or dissimilar. To frame the relationship, the best analogy is, like traditional science, to understand Social Movement Theory within the larger universe of Complex Systems Science. One may consider Wallace's model of revitalization and Social Movement Theory as separate solar systems in a star system of social theories. This star system is then placed in the galaxy that is traditional science. Finally, the galaxy of traditional science is placed within the universe that is Complex Systems Science.

In review, Social Movement Theory has been used to describe Christian revitalization movements (Rynkiewich 2007, Foreword). Greg Leffel defines social movements as "... non-institutionally organized human collectives, that put meaningful ideas into play in public settings, that actively confront existing powers through the strength of their numbers and the influence of their ideas, and that grow in size and power by inspiring others to act, in order to create or to resist change." (2007, 48) As such,

> Social movements challenge those who control institutional and cultural power. Their members function as outsiders trying to force changes in the ways in which power is used to shape social life. They attempt to do this by provoking a crisis of decision through the display of collective dissent. Their most significant resource is social power, the amassing of large numbers of people who act together to apply the pressure that is required to create change. (197)

From the definitions, while one recognizes the shared understanding of the importance of the collective constituency, one immediately notes a stark contrast between Complexity Theory and Social Movement Theory in terms of systemic perspective. Unlike Complexity Theory, which seeks to integrate all components into a single, continuous system, Social Movement Theory intrinsically polarizes and differentiates components into "challenger" or "non-institutional," and "institutional." In other words, it pits "bottom up" with "top down." In contrast, Complexity Theory is able to objectively integrate both components as part of a larger system. Complexity Theory does not define institutional powers as the *status quo* and the challengers as the change agents. Rather, both are equally weighted as change agents.

Additionally, Social Movement Theory understands revitalization as possible only when the collective constituency reaches critical mass; in contrast, Complexity Theory allows for incremental and individual change agency. As such, although Social Movement Theory recognizes the importance of micro-level agents, it nevertheless is unable to define revitalization until such agents become a macro-level collective constituency. Such bias creates blind spots in analyzing change phenomena on the micro-level. In contrast, Complexity Theory has fewer blind spots as researchers must consider micro-level agency as part of the holistic research approach.

Further, Social Movement Theory focuses primarily on the development of crisis and the creation of change in contrast to the more long-term perspective of Complexity Theory. In this respect, Social Movement Theory shares greater similarity with Wallace's revitalization model; both are looking at a discrete period of time where conflict and change are occurring, perhaps a shared trait that emanates from an aversion to historical change theory (Abbott 2000, 299). If so, then Social Movement Theory shares the same biases as Wallace's revitalization model with regard to modeling continuity.

In contrast, Complexity Theory places no limits on change phenomena, and as such, removes the bias to isolate and reduce phenomena.

Without a doubt, Social Movement Theory enhances Wallace's revitalization model by removing its bias towards leaders through incorporating the agency of the collective constituency. However, Complexity Theory, as it is free to travel in the universe of Complex Systems Science rather than reside merely in the domain of general linear reality of traditional science, remains a more robust and comprehensive model to understanding Christian revitalization through its more objective, holistic analysis. And because Social Movement Theory shares similarities with Wallace's revitalization model, Complexity Theory can in many aspects similarly enhance Social Movement Theory.

Social Movement Theory has, in fact, already been framed within Complexity Theory. Marion used "social solitons" to describe social movements within a broader framework provided by Complexity Theory, writing

> These social solitons are everywhere. We can see them in fads, rumors, cliques, mobs, riots, lynchings, *social movements* [italics mine], clans, crowd behavior at sporting events (the phenomenon known as the "wave" is a good pun here), camaraderie within army platoons, political campaigns, and rock star concerts – any form of what sociologists call "collective behavior." . . .. Social solitons distinctly represent what we are calling Complex behavior (1999, 35)

As such, a Complexity Theory, as it is not bounded by traditional approaches, but moves about in the universe of Complex Systems Science, remains a more robust and comprehensive model and is able to incorporate both Wallace's revitalization model as well as Social Movement Theory.

3.7 Using Complexity Theory to Visualize Mazeways through Complex Change

Complexity Theory and its associated mazeways, metaphors, and analytic tools has the potential to go beyond being a research tool for missiology or to better study revitalization in complex contexts. It may also serve as the catalyst by which to initiate or sustain revitalization by providing a means for a community to *Gestalt* a new mazeway.

Wallace's revitalization model relies on a visionary leader to analyze and process the factors creating stress to see a new mazeway through to a new stable state. But as mentioned earlier, in complexity, the human senses may not be able to comprehend such wide and multivariate factors. In the global complexities of twenty-first century contexts, humanity struggles ". . . with complexity, complexity within the environment and within organizations themselves. For the most part, complexity is considered an unknowable, largely undifferentiated condition . . . ." (Marion 1999, 11). Hence, the frequency of revitalization movements of the kind that is defined by Wallace may be increasingly diminished as human society becomes increasingly complex.

But with the development of social networking, it has become increasingly evident that the network is the change agent. In the terminology of the seminal work of Evelyn Fox Keller and Lee Segel in 1968, no longer are "pacemakers" or an "executive branch" needed for change. Rather, change can also come from "bottom up" and simultaneously throughout an entire community and increasingly across communities. (Johnson, 2001: 17-18) If true, then for complex contexts, it may be very well possible that revitalizing *Gestalts* will be generated through social networks instead of a single leader.

An example of this is Randolph Roth's re-examination of the Second Evangelical Awakening in the United States in the 19th century (Roth 1992). Roth was able to challenge Wallace's simple linear model by showing how nonlinear systems analysis looking through the network could reach the same conclusions with greater correlation. He not only revealed flawed biases as a result of simple modeling, but showed how a more complex model expanded the understanding of the processes which were occurring. He writes that historians ". . . may benefit by placing greater emphasis on processes that encompass many narratives and by viewing stories as illustrations of how processes might have played out rather than as evidence that processes played themselves out in particular ways. . . . such narratives may improve inquiry across disciplines, teaching the importance of all things human and nonhuman, and encourage modesty and restraint among the powerful and hone among the powerless." (Roth 1992, 237)

Additionally, mated with computational modeling, complexity theory provides not only the means by which to visualize the interactions across complex networks, it is also able to distill and communicate complex data in a form that can be comprehended by the human senses. These are what Mitchell calls "*idea models* – models that are simple enough to study via mathematics or computers but that nonetheless capture fundamental properties of natural complex systems."

(Mitchell 2009, 38). The end result is "... the ability to see their deep relationships and how they fit into a coherent whole – what might be referred to as 'the simplicity on the other side of complexity.'" (Mitchell 2009, 303).

One example is James V. Spickard's computational model that simulates Rodney Stark's understanding of religious behavior (2005). Using Stark's parameters for individual units and their context, Spickard developed what is known as an agent-based model which visualized sectarianism over time. He concluded that these Complex Adaptive System (CAS) models "... are powerful tools for testing both models and theories in the social sciences." Roth agrees, writing that ". . . nonlinear processual metaphors can enrich our causal imagery and lead to useful models and heuristics. They may also, as Beyerchen (1989) [considered the father of nonlinear systems analysis] hopes, legitimize interest in the complexity of human affairs and encourage creative collaboration among students of humanity, society, and nature." (Roth 1992, 238)

It should be noted that researchers in Complex Systems Leadership Theory, independent of Wallace, have already drawn the very same conclusions of human organizations. Change is often through networks of interactions among a system's agents and in the "base programming" (i.e. ability to learn) of each agent. "Accordingly, leadership events are not constructed by the actions of single individuals; rather, they emerge through the interactions between agents over time." (Lichtenstein *et al* 2007, 135). This can occur at any level, among the collective constituency, between leaders and constituency, or between leaders across network nodes.

In conclusion, just like Turner's drawing of rituals or Rynkiewich's map, Complex Systems Science-framed Cusp of Change models, metaphors and methodology can be used to visualize complex data that enables one to *Gestalt* complex patterns from massive amounts of data, leading potentially to new insights and paradigm shifts or revitalizations in thinking. With the right perception and perspective complex realities, missiologists can be freed from relying solely on Wallace's linear revitalization model and see with a more robust perspective that "... goes beyond the myths of the hero or the scapegoat, and instead reflects the dynamic and emergent nature of leadership as it is enacted every day by supervisors, subordinates, and peers across all organization." (Dooley and Lichtenstein 2008, 288) As Marion concludes, "... the goal is to provide a crucial foundation for pushing back the darkness of surrounding complexity in social structures, to provide yet another way for blind scientists to understand nature, including human nature." (1999, 13)

3.8 Chapter Summary

1. Complexity Systems Science is now the normative research approach in the hard sciences and is rapidly becoming the normative research approach in the soft sciences.
2. The move from Traditional Linear Systems Science to Complex Systems Science has four main characteristic changes: 1) reductionism to holism; 2) linear to nonlinear analysis; 3) static to dynamic; and 4) empirical to metaphor.
3. The discipline of economics, with its mathematical foundations, has made the greatest progress in developing analytical tools for Complex Systems Science. Two subdisciplines, Complexity Leadership Theory and Agent-based Modeling (ABM) are of primary interest with regard to creating a more robust model of revitalization.
4. Many missiologists are already observing complexity though most lack the terminology, metaphors and methodology to describe their observations. Increasing numbers of missiologists recognize the need, and are calling for, more robust research approaches in missiology.
5. An example of how Complex Systems Science can be applied in missiology is provided.
6. Social Theory Movement, considered as an alternative to Wallace's model of revitalization movements, is framed within the subfield of Complexity Theory in Complex Systems Science.

Chapter 4

Developing a Complex Systems Model

In this chapter, our goal will be to develop and evaluate the efficacy of Complex Systems Science models, metaphors, and methodologies to a specific complex context in the field of missiology. The two axes of research are to analyze the interactions between culturally different populations, and discover, then model how each population changes over time. The analysis of the data will then be distilled into variables with which to develop a conceptual metaphorical (a theoretical representation of reality derived with qualitative data, but requires validation with additional quantitative data) model, the Lorenz attractor, that can be used to develop a Complex Adaptive System (CAS) model for revitalization in the context of missiology. While the actual implementation in a computational model is left for future research, I provide an adequate framework sufficiently detailed for the development of a computational model. This chapter sets the delimitations of the theoretical framework, describes the study population, and describes the steps taken to develop a conceptual model metaphor. Readers unfamiliar with Complex Systems Science may refer to Appendix 1 which contains definitions of essential terms.

4.1 Theoretical Framework Delimitations:

Complex Systems Science is an emerging paradigm that is broadly extant and continues to be actively developed. As such, Complex Systems Science is in flux; hence, it necessary to delimit the theoretical framework in order to sustain a cogent discussion. This section delimits the parameters of the Complexity Theory model as defined by Russ Marion (1999), to a region that is termed as "the Cusp of Change" by Goldstein *et al* (1992, 55), and though much of the discussion is derived from Weak Emergent properties, also incorporates Strong Emergence as defined by Paul Davies (2006).

4.1.1 Complex Systems Science, Chaos Theory, and Complexity Theory

As an emerging science, Complex Systems Science encompasses many overlapping theories, fields and disciplines; with a focus on social science, for our discussion, we will delimit the theoretical framework to Complexity Theory as defined by Russ Marion (1999, 5). Marion recognizes that Chaos Theory and Complexity Theory overlap in many aspects and that there is much discussion as to which one is the general theory of nonlinear dynamics and which one is the subdiscipline. But when living systems are the to be characterized, Marion argues that Complexity Theory, as opposed to Chaos Theory, is more reflective of reality. Marion writes that

> Chaos is a bit too mechanical, although there certainly is an element of the mechanical in social behavior. It seems more appropriate for describing physical systems such as weather and fluid turbulence than for describing human behavior. There is an element of life missing in Chaos Theory....
>
> Adaptation, deliberative behavior, and the such [sic] are conscious and unconscious activities that are based on past experiences and, often anticipated outcomes. Social systems, for example, carry information about themselves and their environments, and are able to act on such information. That information allows them to spawn reproductions of themselves or to replicate their ideas at remote sites; it allows them to make reasonable accurate predictions of the effects of their behaviors; it lets them interact with their environment. Chaotic systems fluctuate too unpredictability [sic] and mechanically to carry information of this sort, but Complex systems to not.
>
> Complexity Theory layers Chaos Theory on top of more traditional theories of stability, but the result is a unique theory in its own right. A Complex system is more stable and predictable than are Chaotic systems; even so, it borders on the state of Chaos – it possesses sufficient stability to carry memories and sufficient dynamism to process that information. This balance between order and Chaos enables the ability to reproduce, to change in an orderly fashion, and as we shall see, to self-organize, or emerge without outside intervention. (1999, 6-7)

Goldstein *et al* (2010, 7) concur with Marion in their understanding of the development of Complex Systems Science found in Figure 19. Hence, the theoretical framework will draw from Complexity Theory to develop the conceptual model metaphor.

Developing a Complex Systems Model 83

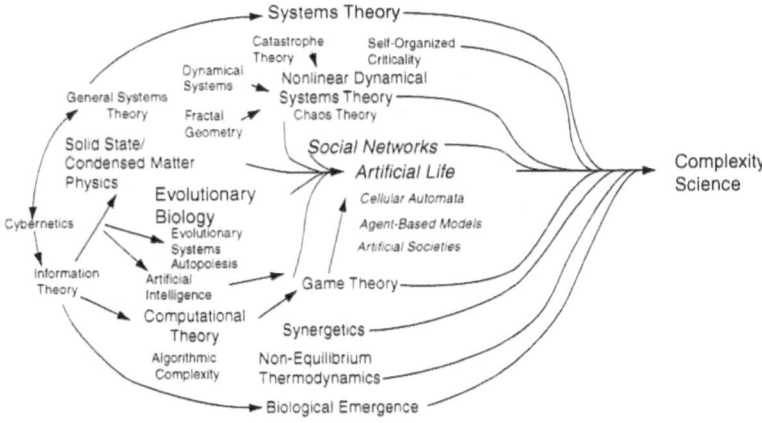

Figure 19 - Scientific and Mathematical Fields Making Up Complexity Science (Goldstein *et al* 2010, 7)

4.1.2 Stability, Chaos, and the Cusp of Change

As the focus of this book is on revitalization, where a society makes a cultural *gestalt* to a new mazeway, the theoretical framework for model development will center on what Marion (1999, 32) terms the phase transition period between stability and Chaos, what Goldstein *et al* term "the Cusp of Change" and the process, as described earlier, is known as "criticalization." (2010, 48) This phase is also what M. Mitchell Waldrop would call this "the edge of chaos" (1992, 12). The Cusp of Change framework is similar to Wallace's understanding of revitalization as "Social systems are poised at the Edge of Chaos, and unpredictable, change events can throw them over the precipice. Things that have limited impact on the system one day can cause major dislocation the next." (Marion 1999, 264)

But unlike the traditional, linear model of revitalization, Complexity Theory is able to model complex, network systems that are reflective of twenty-first century contexts. At this Cusp of Change on the edge of Chaos, Marion writes that in complex systems,

> ... small networks exist that are tentatively linked with a limited number of other networks. The networks are sufficiently ordered to carry information about themselves, but close enough to Chaos that they experience its tug and are doing dynamic things. Here, biological networks are active enough to reproduce and sufficiently stable to have information that can be passed on to another generation. They remember that certain other units will do harm to hem, and are active enough to act on that knowledge. They can explore

new opportunities without forgetting where they came from – in case the new opportunities don't pan out. They are sufficiently isolated that they can act without disturbing other networks, but if they discover something useful, they are sufficiently linked that other can learn about it. Life can – and does – exist here. (1999, 33-34)

He later adds more detail, writing

Complex Systems Theory identifies three states of behavior: stable, Edge of Chaos, and Chaotic. Neither stability nor Chaos is capable of exhibiting the characteristics associated with Complex systems; Complex behavior can exist only at the Edge of Chaos. Edge of Chaos attractors are sufficiently stable to maintain information about themselves and their environment, yet sufficiently vibrant to process that information. These attractors map their environments by resonating, or correlating, with them; that is, they interact with, and become a part of, their environment. Different attractors within a system resonate with one another, thus augmenting the capabilities of the broader organization. (1999, 82)

As these characteristics reflect Wallace's model of revitalization and twenty-first century global, modern, and networked realities, this book narrows the timeframe of analysis to develop a Complex Systems Science-framed model at the "Cusp of Change."

4.1.3 Emergence Theory in the Strong

Because the subfield of Emergence Theory has both ontological and epistemological implications, in addition to the extant acceptance of Weak Emergence, this book takes the position of acknowledging the presence of Strong Emergence as missiology has an inherently theological component and as such, must allow for the transcendent and the mysterious. Here, Strong Emergence is understood to be phenomena which is "top down," or phenomena that cannot be explained by physical means or a result of any aggregation or amalgamation of lower material constituents. Although most complexity scientists, still grounded in reductionist, positivist, traditional science, accept only Weak Emergence, that is, that no external, supranatural, entity exists, the Strong Emergence position is nevertheless allowed as "emergentism is consistent with theism but does not entail it" (Broad 1925, 94, quoted in Clayton and Davies 2002, 6). It is, in fact, the position of many scientists that include Newton, Galileo, Bacon, Maxwell and Von Braun among a host of others.

The inclusion of Strong Emergence position allows for the presence of God's work in both directions, upward and downward. Davies writes,

> The founders of physics, such as Galileo, Kepler, and Newton were all religious, and they believed that in doing science they were uncovering God's handiwork, arcanely encoded in mathematical laws. In this world view, God sits at the base of physical reality, underpinning the mathematical and rational laws of physics, constituting what Tillich calls 'the ground of being.' Religious emergentists might [also] be tempted to locate God at the *top* of the hierarchy, as the supreme emergent quality. There is thus apparently a tension between reductionism and emergence in theology as well as in science. (Clayton and Davies 2006, xiii)

It is in essence the scientific parallel to the apostle Paul's epistle to the Colossians when he writes of Jesus, "He is the image of the invisible God, the firstborn over all creation. For by him all things were created: things in heaven and on earth, visible and invisible, whether thrones or powers or rulers or authorities; all things were created by him and for him. He is before all things, and in him all things hold together." (Colossians 1:15-17, NIV)

In summary, the inclusion of a Strong Emergence position, in addition to Weak Emergence, taken in this book recognizes that beyond the physical or material realm, the existence of supernatural, transcendent entities should not be discounted. Allowing for both Weak and Strong Emergence thereby allows for a bridge between reductionist-biased scientism and theology, bridging a chasm that opened up during the Enlightenment and has grown wider ever since (Hiebert 1999, 23; Jorgenson 2011, 204); accepting both as possible is, in reality, the more objective and unbiased position (Keener 2011, 647).

4.2 Study Population

To develop a CAS (complex adaptive system) revitalization model, multi-congregational, multilingual, multicultural Chinese churches of the Chinese diaspora in North America were chose. Monocultural (single-language, single-congregation) churches were excluded for the purposes of this study.

4.2.1 The Heterogeneous Nature of the Chinese Diaspora

One might assume that all "Chinese" share a similar cultural background, but akin to accepting a simple system model as a proper reflection of reality, such an assumption would be far from realistic (X. Yin 2007, 122; Zhou 2009, 73). To use an analogy, if one desires to eat at a Chinese restaurant in the United States, more often than not, one will find a buffet restaurant or a restaurant with dishes from multiple provinces and regions – and their iterative combinations. For example, the ubiquitous "Crab Rangoon" found in most Chinese restaurants is not Chinese, but rather is of North American origin with a Burmese name. Hence, a singular definition of "Chinese food" would be an exercise in futility because their origins are myriad. As will become clear, the same can be said of "Chinese" in the multivariate churches studied.

For background, the U.S. Census Bureau recorded that the Chinese population doubled between 1860 to 1940 to 77,504, and doubled again to 198,958 in 1960 (Yang 1999, 32) But it was not until the full repeal of the various Chinese Exclusion Acts since 1882 in 1965 that the population exploded. From 1960 to 2000, the Chinese population grew fourteen-fold to 2.7 million (Barnes and Bennett 2002, 9). As of 2006, the US Census Bureau estimates that there are approximately 3.5 million individuals of Chinese descent.[7]

In terms of composition (see Figure 20), using US immigration data, approximately 1.1 million who immigrated from China after 1980 can be classified as "mainland Chinese" with a world view that was formed through the Cultural Revolution. Those who are considered "overseas Chinese," or OBC for Overseas-born Chinese, defined by Enoch Wan as "people of Chinese descent residing outside the People's Republic of China (PRC)," (Wan 2003, 35) generally have a more traditional Chinese worldview and are comprised of the 21,000 who immigrated from China between 1950 – 1970, the 485,000 who immigrated from Hong Kong after 1950 and the 444,000 who immigrated from Taiwan after 1950.[8] The remaining 1.5 million individuals of Chinese descent are American-born Chinese (ABC) and ethnic Chinese from countries such as Singapore, Vietnam, Philippines, etc., as descent is not delimited in immigration or census data.

---

[7] Asian Community Survey, US Census Bureau, 2006. http://factfinder.census.gov/servlet/IPTable? bm=y&-geo_id=01000US&-qr_name=ACS_2007_1YR_G00_S0201&-qr_name=ACS_2007_1YR_G00_S0201PR&-qr_name=ACS_2007_1YR_G00_S0201T&-qr_name=ACS_2007_1YR_G00_S0201TPR&-ds_name=ACS_2007_1YR_G00_&-reg=ACS_2007_1YR_G00_S0201:035;ACS_2007_1YR_G00_S0201PR:035;ACS_2007_1YR_G00_S0201T:035;ACS_2007_1YR_G00_S0201TPR:035&-lang=en&-redoLog=false&-format=. Accessed October 1, 2010

[8] United States. Department of Homeland Security. *Yearbook of Immigration Statistics: 2009*. Washington, D.C.: U.S. Department of Homeland Security, Office of Immigration Statistics, 2010, 8 - 10

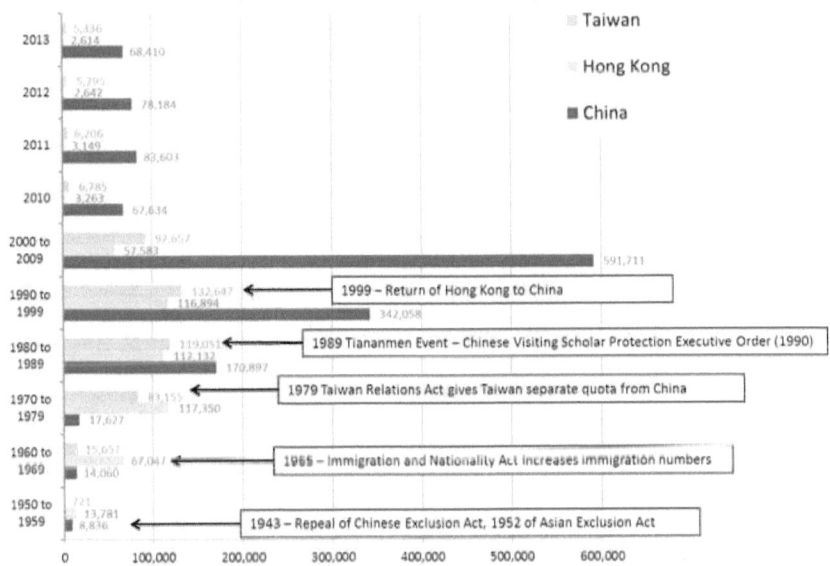

Figure 20 - Immigration Numbers with Historical Timeline of Key Events (from 2013 Immigration Statistics Yearbook; X. Yin 2007, 125)

The number of Chinese churches followed in lock step the rise in the Chinese population[9] (see Figure 21). From only 44 Protestant Chinese churches in 1931 and 66 churches in 1952, by 1979 there were 366 churches. By 1997 there were 697 Protestant Chinese churches (Yang 1999, 6). As of 2003, there were roughly around 1000 Chinese churches throughout the US (Wan 2003, 40).

---

[9] Dr. Philemon Choi, General Counsel. Chinese Coordination Council on World Evangelism Annual Conference, Keynote Address, 1986

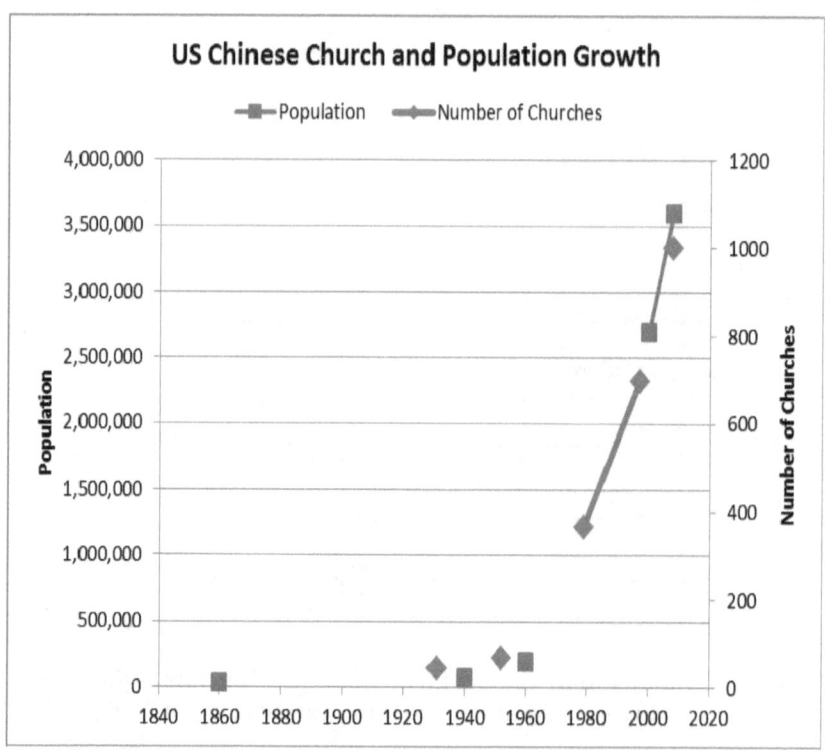

Figure 21 - Chinese Immigration plotted with number of Chinese churches

My Lilly Endowment study looked primarily at the differences and the interactions between three specific subpopulations based on the most commonly found language-based congregations in multi-ethnic multi-congregational Chinese churches. These are the Mandarin-speaking, Cantonese-speaking and English-speaking congregations and are found in all the churches studied. While there are other language congregations found in other North American Chinese churches, such as Teochew, Taiwanese (Hokkien), and Hakka, as their language groups are synonymous with cultural distinctiveness, they tend to congregate as small, monolingual churches and are not considered for the purposes of this study. Additionally, none of the six churches included in the dataset have such language groupings.

Additionally, my research differentiated the Mandarin-speaking subpopulation into Diaspora Chinese from mainland China and OBC (overseas born) Chinese. It is generally noted that although they share the same dialect, they are culturally differentiated due to distinctions in historical, political, and social contexts (Lien 2006, 73; X. Yin 2007, 122; Zhou 2009, 46).

With regard to the Cantonese-speaking subpopulation, it is generally assumed that these are Chinese who have immigrated from Hong Kong or Southeast Asia. Although they may originate from different geographical origins, they all share the same general cultural distinctiveness (Zhou 2009, 30).

The English-speaking congregations are the amalgamation of all the second generation descendants of immigrant Chinese. Whether their parents are from mainland China, Taiwan, Hong Kong, or American-born Chinese, they share the cultural distinctiveness of a strong westernized and American cultural influence.

Although not differentiated in the original dataset, for the purposes of the discussion, each language subpopulation was further divided by generation, covering the three primary generations populations of the North American Chinese Diaspora extant in the first decade of the twenty-first century. Specifically, the three generational groups to be studied are those born after 1990, those born after 1970, and those born after 1949. The reason for the delimitation of 1949 is that this generation corresponds to the most recent major Chinese immigration group following the 1965 immigration reform which exponentially increased the US Chinese population (Zhou 2009, 45). Additionally, 1949 marked the end of the Chinese civil war, leading to a "baby boom" as both mainland and overseas Chinese finally had some semblance of peace after nearly two decades of constant war. While Chinese born prior to 1949 are extant in the churches, for the purposes of this study, they are considered to be in the same group as those born between 1949 – 1965. The second generational group, born after 1970, constitutes the children of this first generation and represents a transition group. The last generational group, born after 1990, coincides with global changes and increased cultural networking that perhaps make them the most "modern" (or "postmodern" [born after 1990]) of the three groups. In aggregate, these generational groups make up the majority of the congregants in North American multiethnic multicongregational Chinese churches in 2014.

In total, twelve groups, four geographic groups across three generations were studied. These are listed in Table 1.

	Exiled overseas Chinese – Mandarin-speaking (Taiwan)	Hong Kong Both resident and exiles – more "Westernized"	Mainland Chinese (post- Tiananmen)	American-born/ American-raised
1949 – 1969	Born in exile, holding strongly to traditional roots – first group to immigrate to US after 1965 Immigration act	Born in exile, holding strongly to traditional roots – first group to immigrate to US after 1965 Immigration act	Born in current form of Chinese society, having undergone the Cultural Revolution and radical modernization	Most likely born of long-time immigrants, reflects American culture
1970 – 1989	Born in a rapidly modernizing society, loss of traditional Chinese culture and identity (due to loss of UN status), considered "Taiwanese" rather than "Chinese"	Born in a rapidly modernizing society, identity strengthened as bridge between China and "West"	Raised in Communist ideology which resulted in disillusionment as a result of Tiananmen	Considered "third cultural" generation, "betwixt and between" (Lee 2003) – conflicted with traditional and American values
1990 - present	Outwardly Confucian, inwardly more modern, strong self-identity, do not see a need to study abroad or immigrate for "better future"	Outwardly Confucian, inwardly more modern, strong self-identity, do not see a need to study abroad or immigrate for "better future"	Outwardly Confucian, inwardly more modern, strong self-identity, takes advantage to study abroad to "help nation," may or may not immigrate for "better future"	While retaining some Asian values and traditions, predominantly reflects American culture

Table 1- Matrix of Generational and subcultural diaspora Chinese study populations

For the case study, I use Fenggang Yang's Theoretical Framework of Adhesive Identities (1999, 184) illustrated in Figure 22. This is similar to the identity framework proposed by Walby (2007) and Grant (2011). Yang models the primary, binary, and tertiary cultural identities as three circles which move in relationship to one another. The size of the circle provides a measure of each culture's influence on the individual. The overlap provides a measure of the relationship between each identity. Here, the three cultural identities are Chinese (C), American (A), and Christian (X).

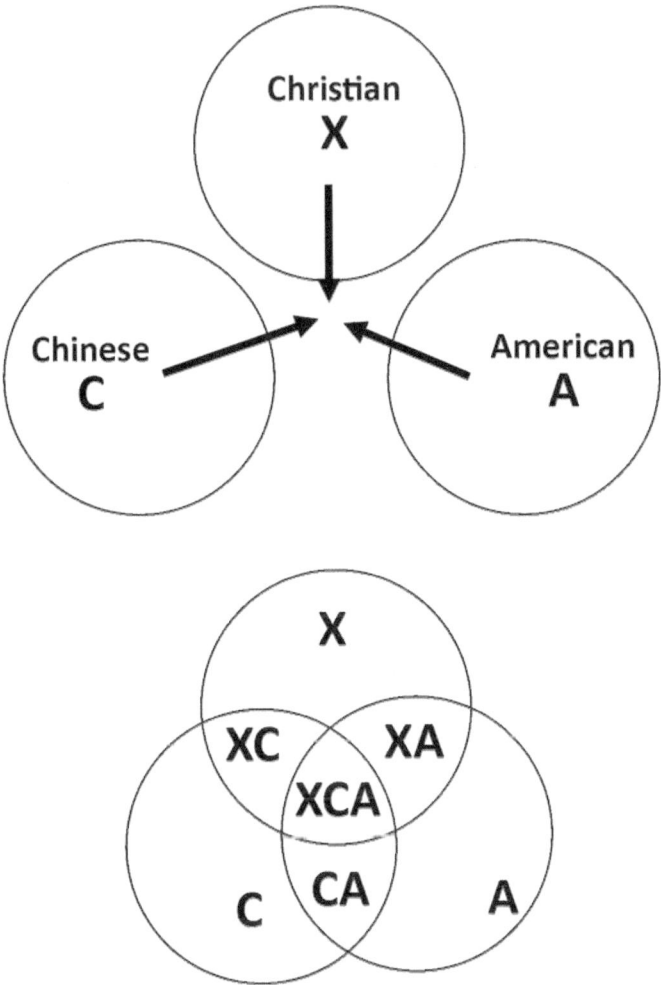

Figure 22 - Co-existence of Multiple Identities to form an Adhesive Identity - from Yang (1999, 184)

4.2.2 Study Population Delimitations

It should be noted that there are other Chinese subgroups such as Filipino Chinese and those from Southeast Asia, and they also are present in the churches studied; however, to delimit the scope of the dataset, their distinctiveness and role in the churches was not considered in my research. The reason is that their cultural backgrounds are much more diverse due to the additional intervening immigrant phases and as a consequence, problematic in disentangling cultural influences.

4.3 An Overview of the Churches Studied

These churches presented in the following chapter were originally selected because they were most similar to my home church, a multilingual, multi-cultural church with multiple congregations. These churches are among the largest in their metropolitan area, ranging from 800 to 2500 in Sunday attendance. The churches have at least three language congregations, Mandarin-speaking, English-speaking, and Cantonese-speaking. Several have two congregations in the same language subpopulation, and some even have separate campuses. Most of the churches were founded in the 1960s or early 1970s as a result of the flood of new immigrants after the repeal of the Chinese Exclusion Act in 1965, and as a consequence, have been in existence between 50 – 60 years.

Demographically, the churches are generally identical in composition. Each of the churches has a healthy, age spectrum with the median being middle-aged members with teen-age children and skewed more toward the younger population than the elderly population. However, the elderly populations in each church are not insubstantial.

Educationally and economically, the church populations are generally composed of upper, middle-income professionals. All the churches are found in metropolitan areas which have at least a handful of institutions of higher learning and/or research centers, and several major Fortune 500 companies that require a highly-educated work force. With the exception of the elderly, the majority of members hold at least a bachelor's degree and at least a quarter of church members hold a master's and/or doctoral degree, or a professional (medicine and law) degree. All the churches have budgets in excess of one million dollars.

Spiritually, these churches have a healthy core of mature believers with the majority of children and youth having been raised in Christian homes. Here, "spiritual health" is defined as having the ability to sustain vitality by adapting to a changing context, in the spiritual formation of church members, from evangelism to the equipping of the laity for social justice ministries and missions, and with ministries extant for all age groups (Thompson 2003, 186). This core of mature believers generally come from the overseas-born Chinese, both Mandarin and Cantonese-speaking, and English-speaking second generation members. The mainland Chinese members tend to be younger Christians with less than ten years since their conversion.

4.4 Methodology for Data Collection

Data collection was through the Case Study Method (R. Yin, 1993). The first set of data was drawn from unpublished case studies collected as a result of my 2005 Lilly Endowment Clergy Renewal study which have yet to be analyzed in detail. Although relevant conclusions were drawn as part of the problem statement, the records contain much more detail such as understanding the attitudes of church leaders and members, conflict issues and history, details pertaining to the relationships between the Chinese subpopulations, both social and with respect to ministry.

The data set, collected over the course of one year from July 2006 to July 2007 through visiting nine multicultural, multi-congregational and multigenerational Chinese churches in the United States and Canada. The cities were Vancouver BC, Orange County CA, and Houston TX (two churches) in Summer 2006 and Minneapolis, MN, Boston MA, Newark NJ/New York NY, Washington DC in Summer 2007, as well as my home church in Seattle WA. Another two were case studies were collected in Taipei, Taiwan in December 2006 as well.

Data collected included videotaping the various services, interviews with both church leaders and select members, the collection of church documents such as bulletins, histories, ministry plans and visioning papers. However, recording was only performed for eight primary churches, those in Boston, Newark/New York, Washington, DC, Houston (two churches), Seattle, and Taipei (two churches). In total, over forty hours of recorded interviews with pastors and elders from these eight churches were collected. Leaders from all the congregations of each church were interviewed.

For the purposes of this book, in order to maintain uniformity and reduce bias, only data from the six US churches in which the full battery of questions were collected via recording will be used to form the primary dataset. Data collected from the other churches, which contains many insights, were used primarily to enhance or support conclusions drawn from the primary dataset of six churches.

A second set of data was collected in 2013 to determine the diachronic change of each church. Church leaders and members from each church were contacted again by e-mail with follow up questions in the form of a survey to ascertain how each subpopulation had changed, how the ministries had changed and how relationships between the groups has changed over the course of time.

4.4.1 Axis 1: Subpopulation Differentiation and Interaction (2006-2007)

Pastors overseeing each of the different congregations in each church were interviewed. The interview questions were divided into three categories: general questions regarding the church, regarding spiritual formation practices in the church, and specific questions regarding each congregation, divided between Chinese-speaking (Mandarin and Cantonese) and English-speaking congregations. The questions asked are found in Appendix 2.

As time permitted, further questions were asked in order to develop a picture of each church's unique situation. Of particular interest were questions regarding differences or conflicts among church leaders, whether within a congregation or across congregations.

For the purposes of this book, the answers from these interview questions are not reported in full. Rather, as the purpose of analyzing the data is to discover parameters critical in developing an analytic model, results reported are based on repetitive and prevailing themes from the interviews and presented in summarized form.

4.4.2 Axis 2: Evaluating Change over Time (2013)

To understand change over time, a subset of seven leaders and members, at least one from each church and two from one church, were contacted again from Fall 2013 to Winter 2014 to ascertain what changes, if any, had occurred in the church. All the leaders and members from the first time point were not able to be contacted due to transitions in pastoral staff and congregational displacement. However, every attempt was made to ascertain a valid perspective of the context of the churches at the second time point. Data collection involved the use of a survey which was sent by e-mail (see Appendix 3). No visits were made to the churches.

4.5 Confidentiality of Participants

Because of the nature of the interviews, participants were promised the condition of anonymity. Although the interviews were videotaped, each participant was informed that names would not be revealed nor any of the recordings broadcast without their prior consent. It was hoped that this would promote more truthfulness as they evaluated their own church ministries.

For the purposes of this book, following Institutional Review Board guidelines, each church will be assigned a letter designation and a number for each participant, for example "AM1" for church A, Mandarin congregation, leader 1. Hence, each participant will remain distinct, but his/her identity held in confidentiality. Only the dissertation committee will have access to the list of churches, actual interviews and the identity of each participant to validate the authenticity of the data collected.

4.6 Data Analysis and Model Development

Because the focus of this book is on methodology, the analysis of data is intended primarily to be exploratory in nature. Hence, results discovered as a consequence of the application of the methodology, while beneficial, are of secondary importance and are used principally to illustrate the efficacy of the new metaphors and methodology of Complex Systems Science-framed models for missiology.

Data analysis was performed in two phases. In the first phase, the data were used primarily to identify qualitative trends and anomalies across the churches and subpopulations. As such, data analysis involved comparing answers to the questions in order to determine similarities and differences between the churches in terms of their history, cultural composition, church structure, and hierarchy, challenges each church is facing, and specifically the conflict history of each church. With respect to change, data from the two points were used to illustrate how rapidly change occurred.

In the second phase, the data observations were framed using the model of a Lorenz attractor as it is the best metaphor for the behavior for the case study organizations on the Cusp of Change (Marion 1999, 22). As mentioned, this model will only be conceptual and as such, qualitative. No quantitative data were collected and as such, the model is only intended to be used metaphorically as it may not accurately represent reality. The metaphorical model development used the theoretical framework developed by Robert Axelrod and Leigh Tesfatsion (2006) and Marguerite Schneider and Mark Sommers (2006) to identify the characteristics and system variables for the implementation of agent-based models (ABM) for complex adaptive systems.

Axelrod and Tesfatsion (2006) recommend that researchers should have four specific goals in implementing ABM models: empirical, normative, heuristic, and methodological. By utilizing the questions raised to address each goal, one can identify the parameters for the model. The empirical question is: "Why have particular large-scale regularities evolved and persisted, even when there is little top-down control?" The question seeks to identify emerging patterns and their loci. The normative perspective leads the researcher to determine what policies, institutions, or processes will lead to a socially desirable system. In other words, what characteristics of a social system lead not only to stability, which in reality is stagnation in the context of continuous, complex change, but to vitality, the ability of an organization to adapt and replicate itself in the context of continuous, complex change.

The heuristic perspective raises the question: "How can greater insight be attained about the fundamental causal mechanisms in social systems?" From this perspective, the researcher seeks to understand what basic characteristics are essential to the system agents and how the resulting interaction between agents is related to that the larger emergent pattern. Finally, the methodological perspective is interested in developing what these models can advance a particular field.

Schneider and Somers (2006) add to the four perspectives by suggesting three specific variables in the ABM that determine the system's survivability and ability to adapt. These are:

K: the inter-relatedness within a system

C: the inter-relatedness across systems

P: the common schemata shared by sub-units

The variables serve to qualify the patterns of relationships in the network and how the base characteristics of each agent influence the emerging patterns and thus determine the survivability and adaptability of the social system to change.

It is similar to ACE models of endogenously determined relationships. According to Nicholaas Vriend, "This concerns models in which agents not only (learn how to) play some (market or other) game, but also (learn to) decide with whom to do that (or not)... These models of endogenous interactions are to be distinguished from models in which the interactions between agents are exogenously determined." (2006, 1049) This model is well suited in that there is a variable to understand learning, allowing one to incorporate spiritual formation into our model.

4.7 Chapter Summary

1. The context of the multicultural, multicongregational Chinese church in the North American Diaspora is defined as a "Complex Adaptive System."
2. The delimitations for the application Complex Systems Science is that analysis will primarily rely on Complexity Theory as opposed to Chaos Theory and, in addition to the extant acceptance of Weak Emergence, acknowledges the position of Strong Emergence that includes the possibility of supranatural entities.
3. The study population draws primarily six multicultural, multicongregational Chinese churches in the United States using data collected from my 2005 Lilly Endowment Clergy Renewal grant.
4. These churches share the basic characteristics of being: 1) located in a major metropolitan area exceeding one million; 2) average attendance over 800; 3) three language congregations: Mandarin-speaking, Cantonese-speaking, and English-speaking; 4) economic and educational background of the church constituency are generally middle-upper income and highly educated professionals; 5) established in immigration wave following the 1965 repeal of the Chinese Exclusion Act.
5. Mandarin Overseas-born Chinese (OBC) are distinguished from mainland Mandarin-speaking Chinese (MMC) due to their distinctly different cultural contexts.
6. Delimitations of the Study Population: 1) Monocultural churches were not considered as they were insufficiently complex; 2) other Chinese dialect churches were not considered as their cultural background is different from the six churches studied; 3) immigrant Chinese outside of the three distinct subpopulation groups are not considered
7. Two axes of study are proposed: Subpopulation Differentiation and Interaction and Change over Time
8. The Complex Systems Science-framed model to be used for this case study is the Lorenz attractor as it best reflects the behavior of social organizations on the Cusp of Change. Parameters for model development are provided. Readers are reminded that this is only an exercise in conceptualizing a model, and thus, a qualitative. No quantitative data were collected, and as such, the conceptual model may not accurately represent reality.

Chapter 5

Data Presentation and Analysis: An Emerging Gestalt

The data presented in this chapter is a distillation of interviews with church leaders and members from the six churches visited in my Lilly Endowment Clergy Renewal grant. As such, they have been filtered through the lens of the researcher with parameters that he felt were significant to the development of a complex system model. There will inevitably be some bias present, but since this research is exploratory in nature and discovery in intent, any bias should not be overly adverse but may skew the selection of variables.

Herein lies one of the first advantages of the complex system model and the traditional pre-(complex) model. In Complex Systems Science-framed models that look at the relationships between variables, the results would still be valid. The subsequent results may not prove to be the most significant variable, but nevertheless the results would still be valid because the results are based more on the relationships between variables. In contrast, using the traditional model, because it is descriptive in nature and oftentimes seeks a "single solution," any bias introduced will intrinsically skew data interpretation and result in potentially incorrect conclusions. Furthermore, because the initial conditions have been skewed, any such model would mostly lead to even greater distortions as it tries to predict the trajectory of future pattern changes.

5.1 Overview of Church Contexts

Table 2 provides an overview of the six churches studied. While their placement on the table has been randomized, no attempt was made to hide their geographic context.

Each of these churches share similar histories and ministry contexts. Each is the largest Chinese immigrant church (CIC) in their particular metropolitan area and each church is located in geographic regions in which the percentage of Chinese is considerably higher than the national average (US Census Bureau 2006).

	A	B	C	D	E	F
Church Attendance	1000	1400	2000	800	1200	1000
Number of Congregations	3	6	3	3	6	6
Number of Campuses	1	2	1	1	2	2
Pastoral Staff	7	8	6	10	13	6
Subpopulation Origin of Primary Leader	Hong Kong immigrant	Mandarin immigrant	Mandarin immigrant	Mandarin American-raised	Cantonese American-raised	Mandarin immigrant
Subpopulation Ranking by congregational Size	1. Mandarin 2. English 3. Cantonese	1. Mandarin 2. English 3. Cantonese	1. Mandarin 2.English 3.Cantonese	1.Mandarin 2. English 3. Cantonese	1. Cantonese 2. English 3. Mandarin	1. Mandarin 2. English 3. Cantonese
Year Church Founded	1971	1967	1979	1991	1961	1976
Growth Reported in 2006/2007	10% 6 previous church plants	15 – 20% 4 previous church plants	5 – 10% 1 church plant	10 – 15% One previous church plant	<5% One church plant	10% 5 previous church plants
Growth Reported in 2013	Stagnant/slow growth (<2%)	Slow growth (<2%)	Stagnant/ declining growth	Rapid growth via new church plant (>10%)	Moderate growth (5-10%)	Moderate growth (new church plant) (5-10%)
Metropolitan Population	2.1 M	3.8M	2.1M (19M)	1.5M	6M	1M
Asian/Chinese Population	6.1% 73,000	13.6% 80,000	9.1% 65,000 (570,000)	11.5% 80,000	7.52% 198,000	14.7% 50,000

Table 2 - Overview of Churches Studied

There are however some differences to be noted:

1. In Church E, the Cantonese subpopulation represents the largest congregation because its history places it at a time where the Cantonese population was the largest group in the city. It was founded prior to the repeal of the Chinese Exclusion Acts and the oldest the six churches. However, it should be noted that the contemporary immigration trends for this church are similar to the other churches, i.e. the Mandarin-speaking mainland Chinese subpopulation is the fastest growing congregation. The pastor of Church E believes that the Mandarin congregation will become the largest congregation in the next decade.

2. Church E, because its primary focus had been the Cantonese subpopulation in the past did not experience the rapid growth reported by the other predominantly Mandarin-speaking churches. But as noted in (1), when it embraced outreach to the Mandarin-speaking subpopulations, the church began to experience similar rapid growth as the other churches

3. Church B and E have a multi-campus structure. This however is not believed to a major differentiating factor when compared to the other churches.

4. While all churches have planted churches in the past, only churched D and F are currently in the process of planting churches at the time of this writing

5. The geographic and social context of Church C is an order of magnitude larger than the other churches, and it is the largest of the six churches. While it is located in a city population similar to the other churches, it draws from a much larger metropolitan area.

Of interest to this study is the current rate of growth reported in Table 2. Of the six churches, one is experiencing rapid growth, two are experiencing moderate growth, and three are stagnant or experiencing slow growth. One goal of my research was to understand why there are differences in growth rate despite the similarities these six churches share with each other.

5.2 Summary of Church Distinctiveness and Ministry Characteristics

Table 3 summarizes the responses of church leaders from the various churches with regard to each church's distinctiveness and characteristics of ministry. It should be noted that these are their responses and may or may not reflect reality. However, their responses are useful in understanding the perceptions of the leaders as well as their inherent desires for the church.

On first perusal, one finds four common characteristics; two are distinct, one is probable, and one is inferred. From Table 3, based on the answers from the leaders, all of these churches share two common characteristics: a self-proclaimed emphasis on *biblical* preaching/teaching and a commitment to ministry through small groups. A third observed, shared trait is stated explicitly by the leaders of Church B and F, and implicitly by the leaders of Church E – an emphasis on strong children's and youth ministries. Visits to each church and interviews with members revealed that the children's and youth ministries are both an essential and primary emphasis of all the churches. This suggests a strong generational aspect in the structure and ministry of these churches.

CHURCH MINISTRY APPROACH AND EXECUTION	A	B	C	D	E	F
Church Distinctives	• Longevity of leadership relationships • Minimum bureaucracy • Biblically based preaching • Strong evangelism and mission emphasis	• Diverse congregational base • Emphasis on Bible teaching • Full service church • Strong childrens' and youth ministries	• Evangelistic • Strong biblical preaching • Fellowship and small groups	• Small groups • Strong preaching • Family ministry	• Strong preaching • Community presence • Full service ministry • Vibrant young adult ministry	• Family oriented • Strong preaching • Full service church • Strong childrens' and youth ministries
Evangelistic Approach	• Member training • Small groups • Evangelistic meetings	• Evangelistic meetings • Small groups	• Small groups • Evangelistic meetings	• Member training • Small groups • Community outreaches • Church planting	• Small groups • Community events	• Evangelistic meetings • Small groups • Church planting
Discipleship Approach	• Integrated across church ministry • Preaching • Sunday School • Discipleship class • Small groups	• Small Groups • Sunday School • Discipleship Class	• Small groups • Sunday School	• Small groups • Continuous leadership training • Strong Sunday School program	• Sunday School • Small groups • Discipleship class	• Small groups • Sunday School • Discipleship program
Perceived Implementation of Ministry Goals	Generally intentional	Generally intentional to Ad hoc	Generally intentional	Intentional	Generally intentional	Generally intentional

Table 3 - Church Distinctives and Characteristics

A fourth shared characteristic is a strong emphasis on evangelism and missions. Although this is only explicitly stated by the leaders of Church A, a review of the ministries of all the other churches reveal active efforts in evangelism and missions. This can be implicitly confirmed by noting that all the churches actively host evangelistic or community events throughout the year and all leaders responded without hesitation at least one means of outreach. The same can be said of member responses in each church.

With respect to discipleship approach and perceived implementation of ministry goals, the responses were much more varied. Only in one church were leaders certain that their ministry goals were intentionally implemented. Leaders from four churches (A, C, E, and F) could only respond as "generally intentional" and leaders from church B responded with "generally intentional to *ad hoc*." Interviews with members corroborated the leadership responses. The lack of clarity suggests that while each church has a strong evangelistic and mission emphasis, spiritual formation is a desire that has yet to be fully fleshed out.

5.3 Overview of Church Leadership and Structure

Table 4 summarizes the responses to questions regarding leaders' *perceived* characterization of church leadership and church structure. The responses reported are a composite summary of all leaders within a single church. Hence, the summary includes what may be "ideal" and what may be reality as *perceived* by various church leaders, both senior leadership and the rest of the pastoral staff.

CHURCH LEADERSHIP	A	B	C	D	E	F
Senior Church Leadership Responsibility	• Set vision • See church as a whole to work together • coach	• facilitator • ministry integration • rotate (every year new leader)	• coordinator • oversight (ensure things are done)	• Team building • Understanding staff and entire church	• Set vision and direction • Understand church as a whole • Consensus builder	• Set vision • oversight
Perceived Leadership Structure	Hierarchical with Team building in mind	Team, but in reality fragmented	Team, but in reality hierarchical	Team, open leadership culture	Team, open leadership culture	Partnership, but in reality hierarchical
Perceived Leadership Agreement on Vision	General to strong agreement	Agreement "in principle"	General to strong agreement	Strong agreement	General to strong agreement	General agreement
Ministry Oversight Distribution	By congregation and by ministry purpose	By congregation	By ministry purpose and by congregation	By congregation and by ministry purpose	By congregation	By congregation
Subpopulation Origin of Primary Leader (2007)	Cantonese (HK) immigrant	Mandarin American-born	Mandarin immigrant	Mandarin American-raised	Cantonese (HK) American-raised	Mandarin immigrant (Korean-raised)
Subpopulation Origin of Primary Leader (2013)	Open Former senior pastor retiring	Mandarin immigrant	Former leader retired, Cantonese immigrant from staff	same	same	same
How to Maintain Church Unity	• Begins with leadership, leaders must be friends • Joint services and activities • Joint meetings	• Combined curriculum once a year • Joint services and activities • Cross campus, not much across language groups	• Leadership seen as belonging to all • Leadership by ministry focus, not congregation • All pastors/elders preach in all congregations	• Strong staff relationship • Groups and congregations serve each other (e.g. EM help with child care during gospel camps) • Joint service projects	• Begins with senior pastor to understand needs of each group • Shared ministries (e.g. community service projects) • Joint services activities	• Begins with leadership to understand whole church • Joint services • English Ministry is "glue" of church via childrens' and youth ministries
Perceived Effectiveness in Unity	strong	Marginal, needs improvement	acceptable	strong	Could be better, more emphasis on cross-campus than cross language	Marginal, needs improvement
Change in Conflict/ Future Challenges	Conflicts increased, vision unclear	Conflicts increased, vision unclear	Recovering from conflict, vision clearing??	Challenged, but future perceived as positive	Challenged, but future perceived as positive	No apparent change, future perceived as positive

Table 4 – Characterization of Church Leadership and Structure

In the first category of "Senior Church Leadership Responsibility," it is interesting to note the varied responses. All the churches have a permanent senior pastor with the exception of Church B and C that have leaders rotating through the senior leadership position. Three senior leaders see their primary role as setting vision and direction for the church (Church A, E and F), two senior leaders see themselves has a coordinator or facilitator (Church B and C), and one senior leader see his role as a team builder (Church A). It does not mean that all the senior leaders do not share similar roles. For example, all senior leaders did mention their need to set vision and direction. As well, the senior leader from Church A also saw himself as a coach and the senior leader from Church E saw himself as a consensus builder, much as the senior leader from Church D who saw his primary responsibility as a team builder. However, the chart highlights what each senior leader perceived as their "primary" responsibilities.

In the second row, the perceived (composite) leadership structure is reported. All churches reported that their leadership structure was a "team" or "partnership." However, based on a composite perception, only churches D and E had complete agreement among their leadership. Leadership in the other churches expressed a more "realistic" perception of the actual structure. In three of the churches (Church A, C, F), there was a hierarchical component and many of the leaders in Church B responded with perception of "fragmentation."

It should be noted that a hierarchical structure is not incompatible with a team approach. If the leaders have a high respect for senior leadership and are willing to accept his leadership, church unity can be strong (see Perceived Effectiveness in Unity, Church A). As well, while both Church D and E have a strong open and team-based leadership culture, their senior pastors in actuality have substantial authority over church matters (e.g. veto power over the Elder Board), but in their tenure, they have rarely had to exercise "hierarchical" power.

One correlation of note is that when a senior leader sees one of his (all the leaders are male) primary roles as a "coach," or "team builder" or "consensus builder," the rest of the leaders tend to be in higher agreement with the senior leader. Church leaders in these churches (A, D, and E) have a higher agreement with respect to vision (row 3, Perceived Leadership Agreement on Vision) and overall church unity (row 8, Perceived Effectiveness in Unity). The senior leader of Church D who saw his primary responsibility as "team building" had the strongest agreement both in his leadership (row 3) and from church members (row 8).

Of note in this table are the origins of senior leaders (rows 5 (2007) and 6 (2013)). Those that had a higher level of agreement (row 3), unity (row 8), and a more positive vision of the future (row 9) tend to be bicultural. They tend to have grown up in a culture not of their origin (Church B (2007), D, E and F). And with the exception of Church B, there is an aspect of longevity in leadership in these churches. Also of note is the correlation with row 7 (How to Maintain Church Unity) where there is an active effort on by church leaders to see the church as an integrated system and that unity must be exemplified by the relationships among church leaders.

In contrast, where conflicts or a less clear or negative vision of the future exist (Change in Conflict/Future Challenges, row 9), senior leadership have origins from a single culture (Church A, B (2013), and C (2007)). In support, the shifts in Church B and C occurred when there was a leadership change from a bicultural to a monocultural leader (Church B) or a monocultural leader to a bicultural leader (Church C). As well, in the churches where conflict had occurred or is now occurring, it was primarily from one individual or group that sought to have greater power or priority in the church.

In rows Row 7 and 8, which report on unity, churches in which leaders and ministries proactively promoted "unity in diversity" were the most successful. All churches had meetings and events which sought to build unity; but the churches that succeeded took more proactive measures, such as leaders building friendships or strong relationships with one another (Church A and D). In the churches that intentionally developed unity, leadership is seen as corporate in nature (church C). As such, church leaders, led through mutual interdependency in unity with one another (Church A, E, and F). Additionally, senior leaders understood the whole church (church E and F). In contrast, the churches which merely emphasized "facilitation" (church B) and "coordination" (church C) or "oversight" (church F) reported lower levels of perceived unity (row 8).

5.4 Summary of Cultural and Generational Issues

Table 5 is a summary of comments freely submitted by interviewees about cultural and generational issues observed across the different subpopulations. The purpose of this table is to see whether or not there were similar or dissimilar comments made across the various churches. Similar comments would suggest an intrinsic trend whereas dissimilar comments would suggest that the observation was church specific and random.

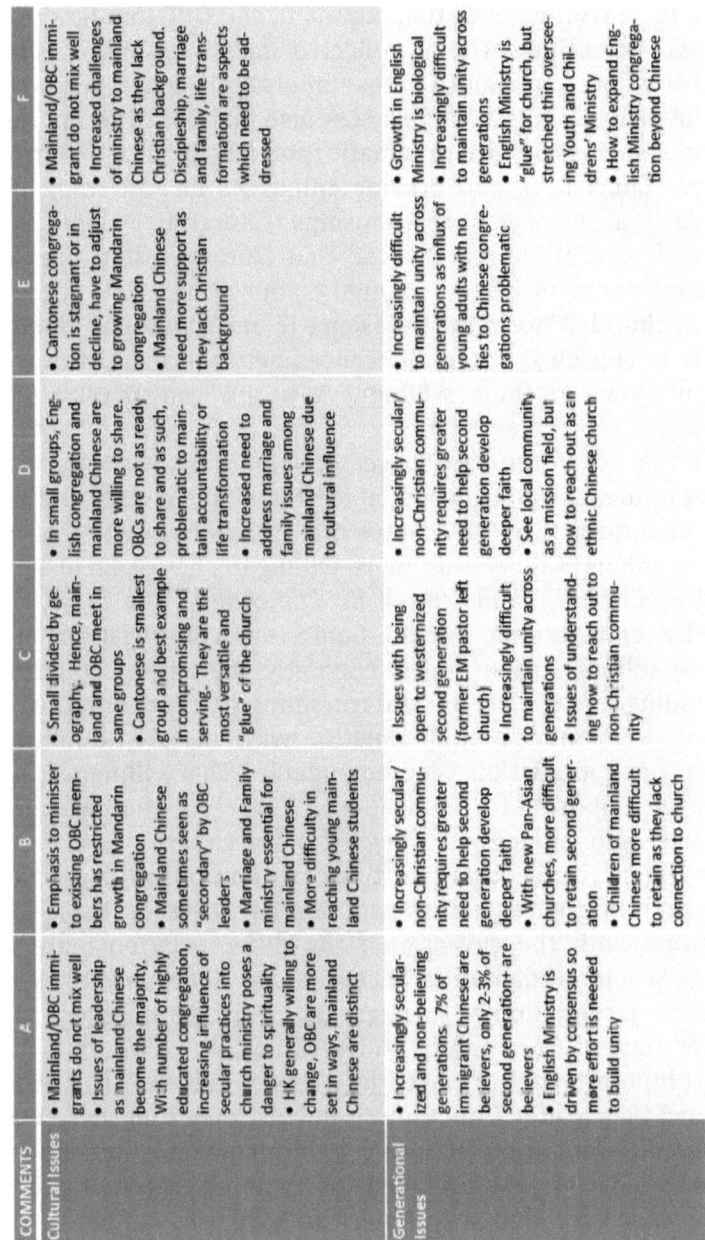

Table 5 - Cultural and Generational Issues

The table reveals similarities in the relationships across subpopulations, particularly with respect to mainland and overseas (OBC, Overseas Born Chinese or diaspora Chinese) Mandarin populations. Churches A and F explicitly indicated, as well as the other churches (though to a lesser extent), that mainland and OBC immigrants to not mix well. Oftentimes, this is reflected in ministry approach, as in Church B where mainland Chinese ministry is considered "secondary." But as well, cultural differences also indicate different ministry challenges such as a more pragmatic (and less spiritual) approach to ministry (Church A), and greater emphases on Christian lifestyle, particularly in the area of relationships (Church B, D, E, F). As well, leaders of several churches noted that cultural differences impact the effectiveness of certain ministry approaches. For example, a leader in church A notes the difference in one's ability to change, and a leader in church D notes differences between mainland and OBC subpopulations in their willingness to be transparent in small groups.

With respect to the Cantonese subpopulation, it is interesting to note the influence of one group on the rest of the church, in this case, a positive impact. Church A notes that Hong Kong (HK, that is, Cantonese-speaking) Chinese are more willing to change, an observation echoed by Church C and Church E. The observation of Church E is especially enlightening as the Cantonese congregation was the founding subpopulation and is currently the largest congregation. Their willingness to start a Mandarin ministry, even with the realization that the Mandarin subpopulation will one day outnumber the Cantonese subpopulation, is commendable. This willingness to compromise is supported by one leader of Church C who noted that the Cantonese subpopulation is "the glue" of the church.

The second row reports selective comments which highlight similarities and differences across generations; however, these must be understood with the caveat that the differences emanate not so much from generational differences, but the difference in the degree of cultural assimilation as immigrants. This can observed through attitudes toward Christianity and secular culture (Church A, B, D) among Chinese born but raised in Western culture. This is further confirmed by a leader from Church B who noted that there was generational differentiation between young mainland Chinese in comparison to older mainland Chinese as he noted that young mainland Chinese were very similar to American born/raised Chinese in their attitudinal resistance to Christianity.

The increased difficulty to maintain unity reported in almost all the churches (Church A, B, C, E, F) illustrates the importance of understanding the root issues and how they are reflected across generations. The responses reveal differing reasons, from a greater need to build consensus due to the more westernized polity of second generation OBCs (Church A) to a lack of relationships with the second generation of mainland Chinese converts with the church (Church B and E).

The observations illustrate that two change engines are operating: one in America and one in China. This adds even more complexity as Chinese immigrate at different periods in the change timeline. Thus, a 60-year old immigrant who just arrived is not the same as a 60 year old resident born in America; nor is a 20-year old newly arrived immigrant like a 20-year old born in America. In fact, none of them are alike. The differences in generation coupled with migration history coupled with the change in the society of origin and the society of destination exponentially increase the level of complexity.

Comments on the generational issues also highlight the challenges second generational Chinese Christians face with regard to the future. On the one hand, the English congregations are critical for the CIC to maintain the youth and children's ministry (Church F), a distinctive mentioned by many churches in Table 2. But on the other hand, English ministry Christians also see the need to reach out to their community and their peers (Church C, D, F) as the US religious landscape becomes increasingly secular. As such, Chinese churches must discern the path of their second generation believers, whether to embrace them or send them off, with the understanding the path may very well transform the CIC church itself.

5.5 Summary of Reported Changes between 2006-7 and 2013-14

Table 6 records the responses for a subset of church leaders and members from interviews in Fall 2013 and Winter 2014 in comparison with interviews from 2006-7. This table highlights the nature and rate of change that occurred even in a brief seven year span.

Looking at row one (Growth in 2007) and two (Growth in 2013), one should note that all the churches, with the exception of Church E were growing numerically at a rate of ten percent or higher in 2006-7. If one factors in that several of the churches were also planting new churches, the rates were probably much higher. But by 2013-

14, only one church (Church D) maintained the rate of growth. For context, one should note that this may be reflective of the geographic demographic change in population (row 7), though this would not explain Church B which had slow growth despite a rapid increase in the Chinese population.

CHANGES	A	B	C	D	E	F
Growth Reported in 2007	10% 6 previous church plants	15-20% 4 previous church plants	5-10% 1 previous church plant	10-15% Church plant in progress	<5% One previous church plant	10% 5 previous church plants
Growth Reported in 2013	Stagnant/slow growth (<2%)	Slow growth (<2%)	Stagnant/declining growth	Rapid growth via second church plant (>10%)	Moderate growth (5-10%)	Moderate growth (new church plant) (5-10%)
Subpopulation Origin of Primary Leader (2007)	Cantonese (HK) immigrant	Mandarin American-born	Mandarin immigrant	Mandarin American-raised	Cantonese (HK) American-raised	Mandarin immigrant (Korean-raised)
Subpopulation Origin of Primary Leader (2013)	Open Former senior pastor retiring	Mandarin immigrant	Former leader retired, Cantonese immigrant from staff	same	same	same
Change in Conflict/Challenges	Conflicts Increased, vision unclear	Conflicts increased, vision unclear	Recovering from conflict, vision clearing??	Challenged, but future perceived as positive	Challenged, but future perceived as positive	No apparent change, future perceived as positive
Shifts in church ministry approach	No change	No change, new building	No change	Establishing Church plant	New congregation	Establishing Church plant
Chinese population change	Stagnant to slow increase	Rapid increase in suburb, moderate increase metro core	Stagnant to slow increase	Rapid increase	Slow increase	Moderate increase
Change in Church demographics	• Increased percentage of mainland Chinese • More difficult to reach second/third generations, both immigrant and local • Fewer Chinese in ministry area	• Aging Mandarin-speaking congregation • Increased percentage of mainland Chinese • More difficult to reach and retain second/third generations both immigrant and local	• Increased percentage of mainland Chinese • Loss of English congregation after EM pastor left, in rebuilding phase	• Increased percentage of mainland Chinese • More secular and non-Christian community (need to outreach to non-Chinese)	• Increased percentage of mainland Chinese • Declining Cantonese-speaking population • Growing Mandarin-speaking congregations	• Increased percentage of mainland Chinese • More difficulty to reach and Retain second/third generations both immigrant and local

Table 6- Changes in the Churches between 2006-7 and 2013-14

Rows Three (Subpopulation Origin of the Primary Leader 2007) and Four (Subpopulation Origin of the Primary Leader 2013) report changes in church leadership (also reported in Table 4). Three senior leaders remain (Church D, E, F) and three had changes (Church A, B, C).

Row Five (Changes in Conflict/Challenges) reports changes in conflict or future challenges. Church A and B reported increased conflict with the vision unclear. Church C reported that it was recovering from conflict and that the vision was becoming clearer. Church D and E did not report conflicts, but did report continuing challenges, although the future was perceived as positive.

Row Six (Shifts in church ministry approach) reports changes in ministry. Churches A, B and C reported no changes though Church B did report a new building. Church D and F were in the process of planting churches and church E was establishing a new congregation. These changes can be used to draw inferences with respect to the vitality of each church. In other words, churches that have building projects, planting churches and establishing congregations generally suggest that they are vibrant, growing churches.

Rows Seven (Chinese population change) and Eight (Changes in church demographics) report demographic changes. Row Seven shows changes in the overall demography of Chinese in the metropolitan areas each church is located and row eight reported any changes in the demography of the church. As was noted above, the rate of growth among the churches is reflective of changes in immigration patterns that are expressed in the overall metropolitan population change with the exception of Church B. With respect for church demographics, all churches noted a continuing increase of the mainland Chinese population.

In addition, Church A, B, and F show increasing difficulty reaching and retaining successive immigrant generations. Church C suffered a decline in the English Ministry after its senior English Ministry pastor left. Church E, which is dissimilar from the other churches in that its largest congregation is Cantonese, reported a declining percentage of Cantonese-speaking members, again reflective of immigration patterns. It however reported moderate growth after years of slow growth (row one) as it has expanded its Mandarin-speaking ministries. Church D also reported an increasing secular and non-Christian environment in its community, highlighting a need to evangelize beyond the Chinese population.

5.6 Selection of Primary Variables Investigation

From the perspective of any revitalization model, it is important to understand change and how people, particularly leaders, respond to and adapt to change. In reviewing the data, looking for similarities and differences, certain variables are noted for investigation.

5.6.1 Immigration Patterns

With respect to change, the most obvious parameter of change is the immigration pattern as it heavily influences the character of CIC community. Immigration patterns generally define the demographics of each church, specifically, which congregation grows and which congregation declines.[10]

This is evidenced, for example, by Church E as one looks through time. It is one of the earliest CICs, founded in 1961 with a majority Cantonese Chinese population (Table 2). This period was prior to the repeal of the Chinese Exclusion Act of 1965, before Taiwanese began to immigrate in larger numbers and before 1989 when mainland Chinese began to immigrate in large numbers. Church E is unlike the other Mandarin-speaking churches in the study which were founded through Chinese immigrants from Taiwan.

Immigration from Hong Kong slowed dramatically after it was repatriated to mainland China in 1999. Prior to 1999, many Hong Kong residents left out of fear for the potential loss of freedom. But after 1999, when mainland China established a 50-year limited change policy, many Hong Kong residents returned and the US actually experience a net efflux of Cantonese-speaking immigrants. As a consequence, the growth in Church E was stagnant during this time as a reflection of minimal immigration of Cantonese-speakers. In contrast, the other Chinese churches grew rapidly during the same period as immigration increased from both Taiwan and mainland China (Table 6). It was only when Church E began to expand its Mandarin ministries that it began to grow rapidly.

As well, the subsequent immigration surge of mainland Chinese after 1989 has impacted all churches requiring shifts in ministry approach and direction (Table 5 and 6). For example, as the percentage of mainland Chinese grew, because their cultural background lacked the Christian background of Hong Kong and Taiwanese Chris-

---

[10] Philemon Choi, Chinese Coordination Council on World Evangelism Annual Conference, Keynote Address, 1986. see also Figure 19

tians, it presented both opportunities as well as challenges. On the one hand, the atheistic background left a great spiritual vacuum resulting in large numbers of mainland Chinese to convert to Christianity. On the other hand, because they lacked an understanding of the "Christian lifestyle," it created a great need for transformational discipleship, much like the first century church as large numbers of Gentiles were converted. Thus, changing immigration patterns is perhaps the primary variable to influence CIC systems. The growth or stagnation of churches can in large part be correlated to how well a church as responded to the demographic changes arising from shifting immigration patterns.

5.6.2 Leadership Flexibility in Adapting to Change

A second variable that appears significant is the flexibility of church leadership - how quickly leaders prepare for and adapt to change. Flexibility may be characterized as an amalgamation of visioning and intentionality. In churches which are growing, senior leadership places visioning as a priority (Table 5, Church A, E and F). Visioning suggests that church leaders acknowledge that their context is changing and desire to set a future direction for the church to respond to the changes. As well, intentionality is a measure of commitment to change.

Visioning is often in contrast to leaders who are seeking to maintain the *status quo*. For example, one leader of the Church B Mandarin congregation, an OBC, responded, "Our church was founded as a Mandarin-speaking [OBC] church and the majority of the church's resources should continue to be channeled to maintaining this heritage" (see Table 4, row 1, column 2). Of all the congregations among the six churches, this was the only congregation that numerically *declined* despite a rising Mandarin-speaking population in the city. I also noted that the congregation is disproportionately skewed toward the OBC elderly. As well, the growing mainland Chinese congregation members are considered as a secondary ministry.

Church growth appears to have a stronger relationship with visioning and intentionality than evangelistic intents and efforts. As Table 3 demonstrates, even stagnant churches place priority on evangelism with regular outreach activities. In fact, interviews all indicate that outreach events are generally well attended across all six churches. However, whether or not newcomers choose to join a church appears to correlate more with church vision and intentionality than whether or not there is an evangelistic desire.

5.6.3 Level of Systemic Comprehension or Unity

A third variable that appears significant is church leadership's level of systemic understanding of their church – the level their congregations and ministries are integrated. Conversely, from a corporate perspective, this variable can be a measure of unity, how much effort was made with regard to church unity.

It should be noted that this variable is not a measure of central or distributed leadership, that is, the level of hierarchy in the church. Both organizational structures were observed among the churches. Rather, the variable would be a measure of how leadership and members mutually understand and accept their roles or function within the church body.

Churches where leadership and members understood their respective roles were those that tended to maintain growth through changing contexts without much conflict. Where church leaders understood their role as helping the church to work together (Church A) or understand the church as a whole (Church D and E), unity was strong (see Table 5). The answer from the senior leader of Church D is notable as he sees his responsibility as one of understanding *both* his staff and his church. Indeed, in the interviews, one noted the reciprocal nature of esteem share between the senior leader and his staff. This is in contrast to the more muted responses from other churches, particularly those where senior leaders viewed their role as "facilitator" (Church B) or "coordinator" (Church C) or "oversight" (Church F). I noted that the perceived level of unity in these churches were only marginal, bordering on conflict.

The differences in understanding specific roles of each congregation in the church can also be observed with the manner in which the church maintains unity. Where a lack of systemic comprehension was apparent, ministries to maintain unity were superficial (e.g. Church B). In contrast, where there was strong unity and an understanding of respective roles, unity was an intrinsic part of church life (e.g. churches D and E).

5.6.4 Level of Transcultural Identity

A fourth variable that appears significant is that of transculturality. This is manifested in two ways.

First, I noted that whether the background of senior leadership is monocultural or multicultural appears to influence the flexibility and systemic understanding of the church in church leadership (Table 5).

In 2007, churches with greater unity and less conflict had senior leadership who were transcultural (Church A, B, D, E, and F). It should be noted that these were generally the fastest growing churches, and consequently, the largest Chinese churches, in their geographic area. But at the second time point in 2014, when the senior leader was replaced by a senior leader who was monocultural, unity diminished and conflicts increased (Church A and B). Conversely, when a senior leader with a monocultural background was replaced by a senior leader with a transcultural background, conflict diminished (Church C).

Second, transcultural groups were often seen as the most willing to adapt to change and were seen as being the "glue" of the church. This was noted of those who immigrated from Hong Kong (Table 4, Church A and Church C) and the second generation (Church F, Table 4 and 5). Through the examples of these groups, the other groups in the church learned how to mutually respect one another and work together.

It should be noted that several church leaders have noted this important variable in the spiritual formation of new converts (Liu 2003, 9). It was noted that numerical and spiritual growth was slower in Chinese churches that lacked transcultural groups.

5.6.5 Intentional Spiritual Formation

A fifth variable that appears significant is the level of intentional discipleship. Although this is not well represented in the tables, it was nevertheless an important aspect of the interviews collected in 2006-7. The "passion" for spiritual formation was apparent in the way that church leaders responded to the interview questions. Churches that emphasized a comprehensive intentional discipleship developed members who understood their role in the church and how various ministries and groups of the church formed the corporate body (Table 3). This was noted especially in church D which grew the fastest between 2007 and 2014 by planting two churches. Members were equipped, sent out, and were able to establish new fully functional churches. In contrast, while other churches also had spiritual formation ministries, they tended be disjointed or *ad hoc*. Interviews with members in these churches revealed vagueness in understanding their role in the church and in ministry.

One may understand this variable of spiritual formation to be that of intentionally developing the transcultural or supracultural nature of the Christian identity. When believers understand that they are all in Christ, "there is neither Jew nor Greek, slave nor free, male nor female." (Galatians 3:28, NIV)

5.7 The Gestalt Process: Capturing the Variables into an Integrated Model

Following Axelrod and Tesfatsion (2006) and Marguerite and Somers (2006), model development is a three step process that integrates empirical, normative, and heuristic characteristics of the data. The empirical aspect of the model seeks to address the question, "What are the large-scale regularities that have evolved and persisted, even when there is little top-down control?" The normative aspect of the model seeks to address the question "What processes result in socially desirable system performance over time?" And the heuristic aspect seeks to ask the question "How can greater insight be attained about the fundamental causal mechanisms in social systems?"

These aspects are then quantified into three distinct variables "N," "K" and "P" defined by Vriend (2006, 1076). Utilizing the Lorenz attractor as the metaphor model, "N" is the overarching equation that defines the composite trajectories of the Lorenz attractor. The dependent variables "K" and "P" must have a bifurcating nature; in other words, they must have two poles and a relationship between them.

If one considers the five variables that categorize the data, it is evident that the immigration pattern is the large-scale regularity. This pattern is observed in all the churches. As well, church leadership essentially has little control over the immigration pattern because it is defined by the external context. Further, the various stages of the immigrant cultural assimilation process are similar across the various groups. This correlates to the "N" variable which describes the inter-relatedness across systems.

Yet, it should be noted that though the immigration pattern is the large-scale regularity, the groups are also differentiated by the point of history that each group enters the US social context. At the point of emigration from their homeland, characteristics of origin such as vocabulary, cultural memories, and social mannerisms, are fixed and tend not to change throughout their journey in the US. It is this stasis of culture of origin that serves as the differentiating initial condition that defines the specific trajectory of each group.

The variables that would describe the processes within CIC churches are those which characterize Leadership Flexibility in Adapting to Change and Systemic Comprehension or Unity; these would address the normative understanding of the model. The levels of these two variables were different and appeared to show interdependency across the churches. As such, it is reasonable to suggest that these variables describe ongoing processes in each CIC church system. This correlates to the "K" variable which describes the inter-relatedness within a system.

Lastly, the level of Transcultural Identity and Intentional Spiritual Formation would serve to characterize the heuristic understanding of the model. Intentional Spiritual Formation transforms one's transcultural identity, and transcultural identity influences one's systemic comprehension as well as one's flexibility in adapting to change. If church members are considered the agents in the model, discipleship, an integral aspect of church ministry that impacts every member, can be considered the fundamental causal mechanism that can alter the entire social system. This would be the "P" variable that describes the common schemata shared by all sub-units.

5.7.1 Meso-level Model

Taking each variable into account, one may then develop a meso-level model that takes into account all the variables using the metaphor of the Lorenz attractor (Marion 1999, 22. Please see Section 3.4 for discussion of its relevance) as illustrated stylistically in Figure 23. The resulting integrated model may then be used to understand the state and relationships between all the subgroups. Readers are reminded that this figure is merely a metaphorical representation, and requires actual, quantitative physical data for validation. Actual representation would require much more detailed data collection over time and/or data generated from a computational model. Additionally, the trajectories are probably more convoluted, similar to those of Figure 14; however, the simple Lorenz attractor used allows for more clarity as its properties are described. What the reader should understand is that the system is stable and that all the trajectories, each describing a particular subpopulation, maintain their orbit around the same attractors, here representing a shared community.

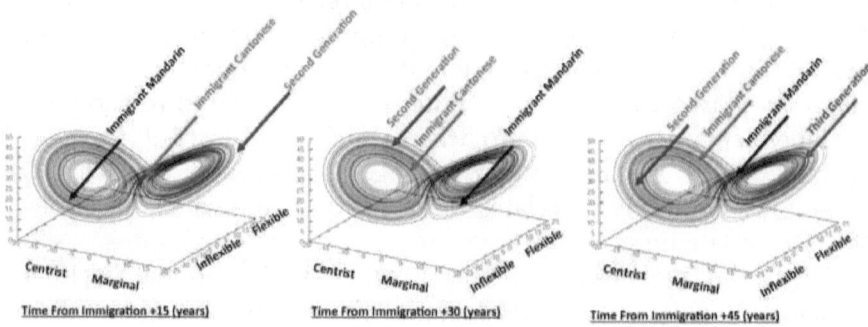

Figure 23 - Complex Description of a CIC Church

In this representation of a complex system, each trajectory describes each immigrant subgroup. Their place in immigration history (stylized by the trajectory) serve is the initial condition which differentiates each trajectory. However, as the process of cultural assimilation is similar, each subgroup's trajectory is similar to one another.

The two axes represent the two normative variables of Systemic Comprehension or Unity and Flexibility in Adapting to Change. The figure can be used to describe the state of each subgroup or each leader.

The model provides normative understanding in four ways.

1. The figure suggests that there are an infinite number of states, that is, positions along each trajectory. In other words, there are no "right" and "wrong" positions.

2. Second, because the states form trajectories, the figure suggests that each group or leader is in flux and changes over time. Again, the figure affirms that there is no "right" and "wrong" position; in fact, all groups are travelling on similar trajectories.

3. With changing contexts, certain states may provide for a healthier church environment at different times. With the flow of time, each congregation may move along the trajectory to be more flexible, less flexible, more centrist, or more marginal. As such, the figure affirms that there is no "right" and "wrong" position, merely which positions may be best suited for different contexts in relation with the other congregations.

4. The figure provides a means to understand the relationships between different groups. Although three, and later four, groups are represented, it is possible to incorporate all sixteen groups into the

figure. The figure allows for a more comprehensible *gestalt* of the church's relationship system.

With such a model, one may then establish a means to heuristically alter the transcultural identity of individual agents, leaders or church members, through intentional spiritual formation and run simulations to determine the effect on individual trajectories and inter-relationships. With this understanding, the model would provide a means to help churches navigate anticipated changes in context.

5.7.2 Micro-level Agent-based Model

A micro-level Agent-based Model (ABM) can also be developed using the same variables. These micro-level agents then can be represented in computational models to simulate and visualize, analyze, and predict the interactions and trajectory of the meso-level model above.

Using Yang's theoretical framework of Adhesive identities, Figure 24 illustrates how the variables can form a micro-level agent. Row 1 is a review of Yang's three cultural identities. Row 2 illustrates the spiritual formation journey of an individual agent before a conversion (no Christian identity) to conversion to spiritual formation. Note that the diameters of the circle represent the growing or decreasing influence of a cultural identity. Row 3 illustrates what a congregation of micro-agents might look like and how the congregation changes over time. In row 3, C' and C" are used to differentiate new immigrants from different time points in the immigration journey. Each new immigrant's original cultural identity will be different because their culture of origin will have changed from that of earlier and future immigrants. As such, the originating cultural identity will be different and needs to be accounted in the representation of each micro-agent.

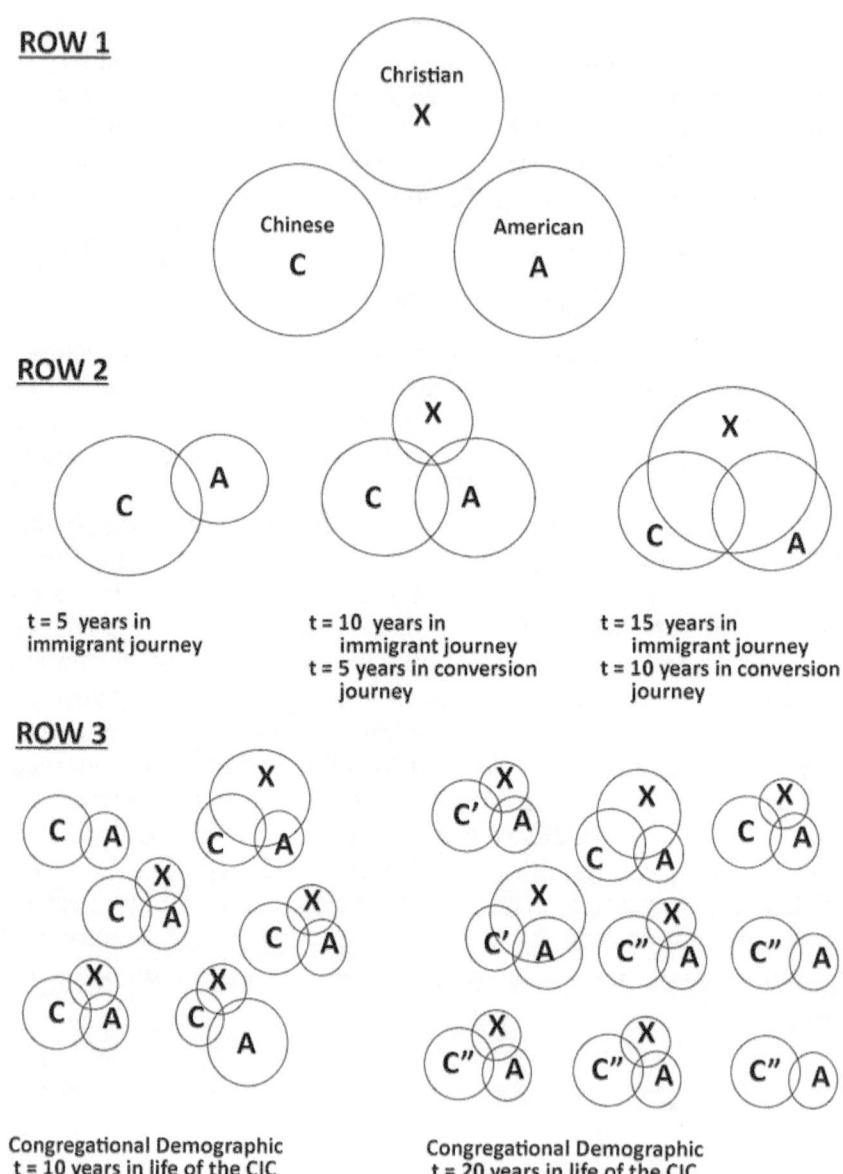

Figure 24 - Micro-agent Model depicting changes in Adhesive Identity over time

Note that the model exponentially increases in complexity as the number and variability of micro-level agents increases. Additionally, the congregants number only six and nine members in Row 3 for illustrative purposes. But in an actual congregation, congregants may number in the hundreds or thousands. Furthermore, the Chinese churches in the case studies range from three to six congregations, increasing the level of complexity of the models social network.

But as much as the complexity has increased exponentially, computational tools are more than able to account for the increased number of data points and increased variability. As will be discussed in Chapter 8, missiologists need only add one additional step, that of collective quantitative data, in existing research methods to develop computational models and methods to integrate Complex Systems analysis.

5.8 Chapter Summary

This chapter has illustrated one method in which missiologists can frame data into a Complex Systems Science-framed model. It has shown how data can be used to ascertain model variables, how such variables may be integrated into a metaphorical complex system model, and how the model can integrate complex multivariate data that adds to the ability of researchers to *gestalt* and draw significant inferences. As well, the process lays the groundwork with which to develop an agent-based complex adaptive system model that may help churches understand future change and provide a means to respond accordingly.

5.8.1 Observations

1. Church growth, stagnation, or decline is strongly tied to immigration growth, stagnation or decline, respectively, in Chinese-American churches. The growth in the number and size of Chinese churches in North America mirror the rising influx of immigrants, and thus does not seem to be related to the variable of how they changed their ministry. The same can be said of church stagnation and decline.

2. However, if the growth of a Chinese immigrant church deviates from the changes in the population of immigrants to its metropolitan area, it is suggestive of internal issues in the church that prevent a church from adapting to its changing contexts.

3. The character of flexibility appears to be the variable that describes how quickly a church can adapt to changes in the immigration pattern.

4. Visioning and intentionality appear to be highly influential factors in determining the character of flexibility of a church's leadership. As well, visioning and intentionality are better predictors of church growth than priorities placed on evangelism and regular outreach activities.

5. The ability of church leadership to systematically understand their church and integrate ministries across the congregations appears to be a valid measure of church unity. The number of activities which promote church unity is not an accurate measure of church unity.

6. Churches in which their leadership understand their organizations systematically are better able to maintain growth without much conflict.

7. The mutual esteem between a senior church leader and his/her staff appear to be a measure of the level of systemic understanding.

8. The breadth of a church leader's cultural background appears to influence the characteristics of flexibility and systemic understanding. As such, church leaders with bicultural backgrounds appear to have more flexibility and systemic understanding than those with monocultural backgrounds.

9. Anecdotally, numerical and spiritual growth appeared slower in Chinese churches that lacked multicultural groups.

10. The intentionality of spiritual formation is a measure of church unity.

5.8.2 Model Development

1. The macro-level variable "N," describing inter-relatedness across systems was modeled as the immigrant assimilation journey, the common denominator across all congregations.

2. The meso-level variable "K," describing the inter-relatedness within a system was modeled as Flexibility and Systemic Understanding.

3. The micro-level variable "P," describing the common schemata shared by all sub-units was measure of Intentional Spiritual Formation that formed the Transcultural (Christian) identity.

5.8.3 Normative Insights from the Complex Systems Science-framed Cusp of Change model

1. Because congregations are modeled as sharing the same journey, in understanding conflicts, there are no "right" or "wrong" parties.

2. Focus is shifted from relative differences across groups or leaders to an emphasis of understanding changes in trajectory and contexts

3. The model provides insights as to how a healthier church environment can be fostered at different locations along the trajectory of the church's journey.

4. An integrated model, understanding how all groups in the church are inter-related, fosters a systemic, transcultural identity.

5. The model provides a mazeway that helps church leaders and membership a way to mazeway to navigate through future change.

Chapter 6

Discussion – A Tale of Two Paradigms

It is this chapter's goal, by way of example, to illustrate the greater fidelity, more robust, efficacious, and comprehensive nature of the Complex Systems Science-framed approaches compared to traditional approaches. In this line, this chapter compares the Complex Systems Science-framed Cusp of Change model of Christian revitalization with Wallace's model of revitalization using observations and questions raised by the contemporary consultations on Christian revitalization as a template for dialogue.

The framing of this chapter uses the following observations drawn from three consultations on Christian revitalization from 2011 – 2013 that were sponsored by the Center for the Study of World Christian Revitalization Movements. In total, although not inclusive, thirty-one questions and observations were summarized from the data and cases studies spanning the globe (Irwin 2011). They are as follows:

Divergent Christianity exists in new groups and churches. How should we judge them?

Is revitalization always good? All want it, but what sort? Individual or communal?

Are individual or communal forms problematic to revitalization?

How do we know what is revitalized? Dynamics complex

What cannot or should not be revitalized because it is just a refreshment of old religious ideas?

What ecclesiology dominates the revitalization moments?

What is the ecclesiology of a revitalized congregation?

Revitalization creates change in the dynamics of the status quo – some people win and some lose. How do we assess these dynamics?

If revitalization depends on social and spiritual relationships, what is the substance of these relationships?

Revitalization that is noted operates most frequently and powerfully at the level of the laity. What is implied by this realization?

Revitalization touches all dimensions and areas of human existence, even the earthly environment that sustains it. Is environmental theology an important supplement, and is revitalization as Christian environmentalism needed?

Revitalization is related to an individual or local fellowships of people, based on developing relationships and discipling, in terms of collectivity (a whole tribe) and among people at the margins

Revitalization also occurs in studied, devotional isolation of retreats.

Revitalization movements are very specific, with unique features

Revitalization is related to human markers of "time" and "place", seasons and centers. It has a temporal and a geographical rationale, including crossing boundaries of eternity and time, as preeminently embodied in the life of Jesus Christ

Do renewals show similar marks across time and traditions? Yes, these similarities can be traced, but their patterns are unpredictable.

Can standards be set, or may standards, models, and examples be used as guidelines

It is not feasible to evaluate Christian movements early on, but only much later. Issues of change are not to be factored, and the tendency of movements to morph into new forms.

Revitalization is cyclical. The vitality is recurring yet impossible to last

Revitalization is not a new burst of strength. It is a "new birth"!

The world is the locus for the relationship of God's revitalizing activity in human life

Sacrament is a visible sign of an invisible grace – and interactive dynamic, socially constructed

The church is the Christocentric presence of God in the world

The church is also an imperfect, growing body

Do movements have to move outside the church in order to take root? Can we accept new movements within existing structures, or are they created by moving outside structures?

For whom, what, and what purpose is revitalization? Revitalization of the church for the church, or the church for the kingdom of God?

Asymmetries of gender, economics, and ethnic groups should be considered seriously in evangelism, but these have been largely unmentioned so far in revitalization discussion.

> Christians are "renewalists", according to Todd Johnson.
>
> There is a rise in renewal movements at the beginning of the 21st century, according to Todd Johnson
>
> A new term, "vitalization movement" refers to a movement of person first hearing of encounter with God and Christianity
>
> It may be better to use a model, and a typology is difficult. Try to think of a Christian revitalized church by characteristics. (Irwin 2011, 239-240)

This chapter compares how Wallace's revitalization model and the Complex Systems Science-framed Cusp of Change model address these questions and observations. Biblical texts and normative texts from core curricula in missiology will be used as dialogue partners and are not intended to be definitive.

6.1 Analysis 1.0 – The Linear Approach

A traditional approach using Wallace's linear model of revitalization as a theoretical framework seeks to place a case study onto a five-phase template and compare how well the characteristics match the model. In review, the five phases of the model are the initial steady state, increased individual stress, cultural distortion, revitalization, and a new steady state. Wallace stipulates that each of these phases must be present to be considered a revitalization (Wallace, 1956; Hiebert *et al* 1999, 350-351).

The focus of most revitalization studies is the period between pre- and post- steady states to ascertain whether cultural distortion is present, whether or not cultural reformulation takes place, and how the new mazeway is routinized (see Grumet 2003). "The movements rise quickly, totally absorbing adherents and giving them a whole new lifestyle." (Hiebert *et al* 1999, 348)

Using the Wallacian model of revitalization, one would look for the direct, causal factors of stress and its impact on the culture; however, studies assume that the change agent is a charismatic leader, for "With a few exceptions, every religious revitalization movement with which I am acquainted has been originally conceived in one or several hallucinatory visions by a single individual" (Wallace 1956, 270) In fact, countering Weber, Wallace does not consider any group *gestalt* to be part of the revitalization (1956, 274)

In summary, using the traditional approach, one would have looked for, and demarcate, two static contexts and an intermediary period of change in which an observed cultural distortion stressor results in a new lifestyle mazeway and a newly defined identity. The center of this focus would be a specific leader who is the vessel in whom a new mazeway is reformulated. Much discussion about whether a case study is or is not a Christian revitalization gravitates around whether or not a sufficient number of these elements are observed (Johnson-Miller 2011, 18).

In certain contexts when such elements could be categorized and explained by general linear reality, the traditional approach and the Complex Systems Science-framed approaches would have most likely resulted in similar findings; but with the traditional approach, only certain phenomena could be classified as a case of revitalization. Others would be dismissed as what Wallace defines as evolution, cultural drift, diffusion, or acculturation (1956, 265).

But in limiting the definition of revitalization, Wallace's model does not support many of the case studies the consultations considered a Christian revitalization. At best, the traditional approach would have yielded results that were only a sliver of the observed realities. Hence, relying on the Wallacian model of revitalization, grounded in general linear reality, would have resulted in missing "non-traditional" revitalizations altogether. Consequently, without an overarching framework, the consultations could only draw nebulous conclusions and issue a call for new models and methods to better understand Christian revitalization.

Indeed, over the years, Wallace's model of revitalization has had to be repeatedly modified to account for these "non-traditional" forms of revitalization. For example, in the study of South American Pentecostalism, the model had to be modified to account for reformulation even when cultural distortion was minimal (Shaw 2008). Wallace himself also corrected this oversight in his study of the paradigm shift in the arts in the 18th and 19th centuries. He concluded that "the paradigmatic model of 'normal' incremental progress works well in many periods of artistic and technological development and that it also accounts for gradual change paradigms, contrary to the Kuhnian model of scientific change." (2003, 139)

One must then ask, is such an approach reasonable? In other words, if a model is normative, what is the point of continually adjusting the model every time there are phenomena that do cannot be aligned to its template? Perhaps such a practice suggests the model may no longer be "normative." Perhaps a more robust model would be a better alternative as the context of contemporary realities rapidly change.

Again, it is not the intention of this chapter to argue that Complex Systems analysis obviates linear analyses. Traditional, linear approaches remain valid in its bounded domain, and in some isolated contexts that can appropriately be modeled as a general linear reality, traditional, linear analyses may be sufficient and yield valid results.

But at issue is whether such methods have made us myopic in a universe of expanding scale and its associated exponential growth in diverse realities and their associated collected data. As Andrew Abbott writes, "all too often general linear models have led to general linear reality, to a limited way of imagining the social process." The consequence is that "Alternatives seem applicable only to special cases, as Kuhn says, because our current methods prevent our seeing the myriads of situation to which they apply." (1988, 183)

As such, this chapter argues that Complex Systems Science-framed approaches expand the bounded domain of Wallace's revitalization model such that exceptions and modifications no longer need to be the preferred method to account for the growing number of "anomalies." The next section discusses how Complex Systems Science-framed approaches, without making exceptions, can inclusively consider a variety of cultural change trajectories as a Christian revitalization and a greater number of possible agencies that are observed in the realities of globalized and urbanized complex societies.

As well, the next section argues that Complex Systems analyses has a predictive quality. Because full change trajectories, and not merely states, are described, such findings would remain useful for a much longer period of time - even as cultural and social contexts change. More importantly, Complex Systems analysis has the potential to mediate change itself.

Hence, as global factors become more prominent locally, and as local contexts become more interconnected with global contexts, traditional linear analyses will reach their effective limits of validity. It is in this expanded spectrum of contexts that the addition of Complex Systems analyses should strongly be considered. As Ramalingam argues:

> Complexity thinking can help describe and explain our world, our relationship to it, and to each other far better— with far greater realism and fidelity— than the tools we have had handed down to us from nineteenth-century physics. It seems clear that complex systems research will prove of growing interest and value for those dealing with problems of the twenty-first century ... (2013, 362)

As Complex Systems analysis is much more robust because its holistic approach allows researchers to account for historical change through a larger network of relationships, and empowers an interdisciplinary approach that integrates diverse theories and models into a single system. Complex Systems analyses results in a broader series of findings that include a deeper understanding of the interactions across congregations, and more importantly, not merely to place blame on a particular cultural group as the source of conflict and obstacle to revitalization, but understands the respective roles each group plays in the larger system over time. As such, through Complex Systems analysis, conflict is not seen as an abnormal, negative situation, but rather, as a critical and intrinsic phase transition, a criticalization, in the transformational trajectory on the Cusp of Change at the edge of Chaos.

Through the case study, this chapter concludes that the Complex Systems Science model of the Cusp of Change is more compatible with the observations of Christian revitalization by the consultations. With the lens of Complex Systems Science, Christian revitalization is defined as an ongoing, continuous process of Christian praxis sustaining Christian communities in the Cusp of Change at the edge of Chaos in the globalized, networked twenty-first century context of rapid, complex change.

6.2 Analysis 2.0 – The Complex Systems Approach

A Complex Systems approach forces researchers to step back and look at the forest and its context. While a single tree may be at issue, such an approach reduces bias toward linear conclusions by requiring researchers to evaluate other factors. Hence, if the issue involves more than one tree, Complex Systems analyses would be able to capture the interactions involved in the processes.

Specifically, the Complex Systems approach expands analysis in three aspects: historicity, networks, and dimensional and subsequently, interdisciplinary, integration. This is in contrast to the traditional linear approach which is static, singular, and reductionist.

6.2.1 Historicity: The Dynamic Nature of Complex Systems

Because Complex Systems analysis is by nature heavily dependent on understanding initial conditions, the trajectory of a particular context is a crucial element in the process of understanding the entire system. Conclusions are drawn not from a specific point in time, but on how the system changes over the entire history of a given context. Complex Systems Science recognizes revitalization as a continuous, ongoing process.

As it happens, the twenty-first century context is one of rapid, complex change. The normative state *is* change. A state of continuous stress from change is no longer the exception.

In such a continuous state of change, with even a period for revitalization, the only logical result would be collapse. Rebecca D. Costa writes,

> *A society advances quickly when both human needs – belief and knowledge are met.* In other words, we thrive when facts and beliefs coexist side by side, and *neither* dominate our existence.
>
> But as social processes, institutions, technologies, and discoveries mount in complexity, obtaining knowledge becomes more difficult.
>
> Suddenly, water we once fetched directly from our well comes from a faucet, and we no longer can discern where it originated, how it was processed, distributed, priced, or allocated. The same goes for our monetary system, laws, taxes, satellite television, and terrorism. Every aspect of life accelerates in complexity. Not only does the number of things we must comprehend grow, the intricacy of these things also exponentially increases. So the amount of knowledge our brains must acquire to achieve real understanding quickly becomes overwhelming.
>
> When complexity makes knowledge impossible to obtain, we have no alternative but to defer to beliefs; we accept assumptions and unproven ideas about our existence, our world. This is the second symptom: the substitution of beliefs for fact and the gradual abandonment of empirical evidence.
>
> *Once a society begins exhibiting the first two signs – gridlock and the substitution of beliefs for facts – the stage is set for collapse.* (Costa, 2010: 12)

How then is revitalization possible in such a context? It is only possible if the normative state of revitalization is in fact, continuous change.

In Complex Systems Science, revitalization is understood to be a stable phase transition, a chaotic equilibrium, between stagnation and collapse or chaos. In Complexity Theory, revitalization is defined as maintaining an organization "on the Cusp of Change," such that it is able to continuously respond to change.

> The Cusp of Change is an abstract model based upon complexity ideas that describes a very tangible experience: when opportunity tension and informational differences both increase, there is a point where there emerges a split between the stability associated with the current "old way" of operating, and the emerging stability of a "new way" of conceiving an organization. In complexity science this is explained as a shift in the

organization's attractor, which is the dominant logic that guides all of an organization's action. In the Cusp of Change the organizational attractor literally splits: on the one "side" of the cusp is the old way of doing things, and on the other side is a new way. Between, within the cusp, both attractors compete for the hearts and minds of the people in the organization.... This is when generative leadership is particularly important. As the two attractors pull in different directions more and more people question the previous model, and as informational differences are exploited to a greater and greater degree, members are increasingly challenged with greater indeterminancy and ambiguity. There are literally two answers for a while.

Generative leadership can help resolve this tension and encourage the movement from one attractor to the next. (Goldstein *et al* 2010, 183)

Complexity Leadership Theory seeks to sustain the organization in the Cusp of Change so that it can continually adapt in the context of rapid, complex change. With the concept of revitalization as continuous change process being the normative condition, one must then understand the *continuous* trajectories of agents within the organization.

Unfortunately, recognizing this broader historical process of revitalization is a critical strategic perspective that has been found lacking in missiology. For example, consider the conversion of a society or culture to Christianity in terms of the traditional model of revitalization. Many short-term missionaries are satisfied with "decisions for Christ," and many long-term missionaries depart once a church has been established using the worship format they passed on to them. If converts look and act like the missionaries themselves, for some missionaries, the conversion process is considered complete. After all, by Wallace's revitalization model, their change in life-style could be defined as having moved from their indigenous steady-state to the steady state of the missionaries. (Gow 2006).

Yet from his own experiences, Vincent Donovan recounts,

> History, of course, has also offered us the opportunity to understand better the mission of the church, but for some reason we have rarely availed ourselves of this opportunity.... there have been factors at work which have deflected missionary work from true center and which leave us today, in any discussion on the matter, floundering on the periphery. (3) ... The gospel is, after all, not a philosophy or set of doctrines or laws. That is what a culture is. The gospel is essentially a history, at whose center is the God-man born in Bethlehem, risen near Golgotha.
>
> At the moment facing me was that vast, sprawling, all pervasive complex of customs and traditions and values and dictates of human behavior which was the Masai culture, a nation in the biblical sense, to whom I had to bring the gospel. At this point I had to make the humiliating admission that I did

not know what the gospel was. During those days I spent long hours thinking long, difficult thoughts, and sometimes frightening ones, about the momentous task that faced me – the bringing together of a culture and the gospel [i.e. history]. (31) (1982)

From his reflections on the historicity of the gospel, Donovan thus concludes, "The goal of evangelization and the basis for its urgency, it to put all things under the dominion of Christ. The fulfillment of the human race, the destiny of the human race, all of creation, is what is at stake. Personal salvation is a secondary question." (1982, 192)

Donovan's argument is that any understanding of conversion must be systemic and must be framed within the divine metanarrative, that is, *missio Dei*. Hence, conversion, and as such, revitalization, should not be seen as a discontinuous, isolated event, but part of the process of alternation. (Gaventa 1986; Hiebert 1991, 110)

There are many biblical examples of this conception of conversion. For example, in Acts 3:19 – 21, the apostle Peter states,

> Repent therefore, and turn to God so that your sins may be wiped out, so that times of refreshing may come from the presence of the Lord, and that he may send the Messiah appointed for you, that is, Jesus, who must remain in heaven until the time of universal restoration that God announced long ago through his holy prophets. (NRS)

Similarly, the apostle Paul writes in Romans 8:19 - 22

> "For the creation waits with eager longing for the revealing of the children of God; for the creation was subjected to futility, not of its own will but by the will of the one who subjected it, in hope that the creation itself will be set free from its bondage to decay and will obtain the freedom of the glory of the children of God. We know that the whole creation has been groaning in labor pains until now; and not only the creation, but we ourselves, who have the first fruits of the Spirit, groan inwardly while we wait for adoption, the redemption of our bodies. (NRS)

In both passages, there is an act to turn, but as well, a transformation of worldview along with the transformation of the world itself.

In the same vein, Andrew Walls argues that ". . . discipling is a long process – it takes generations. Christian proclamation is for the children and grandchildren of the people who hear it. Just as personal discipleship involves the lifelong working of 'holy word' through the personality, so national discipleship involves a generational penetration..." (2007, 31)

Walls also understands that the propagation of the gospel is not a discrete, isolated event, but from a global perspective, similar to the conclusions of Complex Systems Science, revitalization is a continuous, cycling, process.

> ... Christianity we may almost say that it exists today only *because* it has crossed [the cultural divide]. For Christian expansion has not been progressive, ... spreading out from a central point and retaining, by and large, the allegiance of those it reaches. Christian expansion has been serial. Christian faith has fixed itself at different periods in different heartlands, waning in one as it has come to birth in another. (1996, 256)

Essentially, Walls argues that Christianity is in continuous motion, always on the Cusp of Change as it exists by continually crossing cultural divides. To resituate the famous quote from Emil Brunner: "The church exists by mission, just as fire exists by burning."

As such, Christian revitalization should be understood as a continuous, ongoing process. Walls description of the Christian life is almost identical to Goldstein *et al*'s description above of the Cusp of Change.

> Complete discipleship thus implies *both* the plastered cistern *and* the ever-flowing spring. ... The holy word – the word of the Master, the word of Scripture – passes into memory. The plastered cistern does not lose a drop. But that word is not a static once-for-all possession, secured by memory and repeated enunciation. It is a dynamic, developing, growing, creative factor in the mind; ever fresh, ever bringing out new things, never getting stuck in the past, never getting state or out of date. The disciple is an ever-flowing spring. (Walls 1996, 50)

If so, one may argue that the dynamic, historically broad definition of the Cusp of Change model for Christian revitalization avoids the mistakes of the past and removes the limitations and biases of existing methodologies by shifting research paradigms from looking at case studies merely as singular events to consider that larger historical processes.

6.2.2 Networks: The Relational Nature of Complex Systems

One of the greatest strengths of Complex Systems analysis is its ability to recognize, describe, and predict a network of relationships and interactions in a specific context. Complex Systems researchers recognize that "There is a growing sense that effective organization change has its own dynamic process that cannot simply follow strategic shifts and that is longer and subtler than can be managed by any single leader. It is generated by the insights of many people trying to improve the whole, and it accumulates, as it were, over long periods." (Hecksher 1994, 24, quoted from Lichstenstien *et al* 2007, 134) As such, in addition to a single leader solution, Complex Systems analysis also provides the terminology, methodology, and metaphors to consider the possibility that revitalization can occur through a group of individuals and describe their contributions in shaping the trajectory that sustains an organization in the Cusp of Change.

For example, working from general linear reality, mission historians tended to assume that the Pentecostal revival movements in the early 20th century could be understood by showing the diffusion from one leader to another as the revitalization movement moved from Azusa Street in California to places such as East Africa and Korea (Shaw 2008, 768). But as local histories became more available, it is now generally accepted that the revitalization events occurred simultaneously and independently (Larbi 2003). Unfortunately, missiological research on revitalization movements remains overly fixated on single leaders (Larbi 2003, Ward 2013). The use of Complex Systems analysis would have avoided the bias toward linearity (i.e., cause-and-effect) as it considers the possibility of emergence from multiple concurrent sources as an equally valid explanation to a single visionary leader.

More importantly, for practical reasons, as the world becomes increasingly interconnected through the technological highways of communication, the application of Complex Systems Science and its tools for network analysis becomes the most promising option for researchers. Ben Ramalingam writes, "increasing globalization and the growing interest in complex adaptive systems go hand-in-hand." (2014, xi) For example, many sociologists have concluded that the rapid spread of pivotal social movements across diverse geographic areas from Wall Street to North Africa and the Middle East in 2012 was a result of emergent phenomena from social networks rather than a single visionary leader. Howard and Hussain write, "For the most part, however, the political uprising was leaderless in the classical sense – there was no long-standing revolutionary figurehead, traditional opposition leader, or charismatic speechmaker who radicalized the public." (2013, 19). In fact, it was the dearth of identifiable leaders that prevented governments from actively supporting – or quelling – these political shifts. Some of the most insightful observations were made by applying network analysis on the Twitter feeds (Schroeder *et al* 2012). From the analysis, Reda Benkirane concluded that "The transition from the one-to-many communication (press, radio, television) to the many-to-many communication (web 1.0 and 2.0) is a considerable change of scale. 'More' is irreversibly 'different.'" Benkirane's analysis does not discount the role of individual catalysts, what Complexity Leadership Theory describes as the "nodes of networks," an observation supported by Howard and Hussain (2013, 21), but argues against being singularly focused on individuals, calling for the need to understand the broader, systemic context. In the case of the 2012 Arab Spring, "The Arab media landscape is constituted of multiple 'levels of complexity' that correspond to a variety of media in constant interaction with equally complex social dynamics." (Benkirane 2012, 3)

As such, in the twenty-first century context, without the augmentation of Complex Systems analysis, Wallace's linear model of revitalization would prove incapable of describing and analyzing the complex nature of the movement. To fully understand the entire process, one must not fixate on visionary leaders, but rather, step back to look at the entire networked context.

If one looks through the lens of network theory, Complex Leadership also offers new insights in understanding conflict. Conflict is no longer seen as differences between two opposing parties, but because the parties in the conflict are integral elements of the network, conflict is seen as a means of communication (see Table 7).

	Complexity view	**Conventional view**
Purpose	Creation of suitable conditions	Reduction of conflicts
Control	Total control not possible, [but influence and persuasion are]	Conflicts can be controlled by a neutral authority
Styles	Fluctuating	Stable
Outcomes	Unpredictable; Disproportionate	Predictable; Proportionate
Nature of communication	Meaning construction [in between many network nodes]	[Two actors] Sending and Receiving messages
Direction of communication	[Cycles between] order and disorder	Towards order
Leadership	Leadership as dialogue	Leadership as monologue

Table 7 - Comparison of complexity and conventional views on conflict management, communication and leadership (Aula & Siira 2007, 380)

"From the interpretive perspective, conflict and communication are co-developed, 'thus communication is not an input, moderator, or mediator of outcomes; it becomes the conflict itself" (Putnam 2006, 18)." In fact, "Conflict is critical in renewing organizations, as it is an antecedent and an outcome of diversity in organization." (Aula and Siira 2007, 379) As such

> ... the aim of leadership is not simply keeping peace or providing answers, but to create the conditions 'in which followers' behaviors can produce structure and innovation (379) ... All in all, our take on conflict management is in accordance with the dialogic view on leadership that emphasizes holism and interdependence as opposed to the monologic view that accentuates the role of leaders in affection organizational outcomes. ... we would like to regard this approach more as 'conflict leadership' rather than 'conflict management.'" (384) (Aula and Siira 2007)

Beverly Johnson-Miller finds similar patterns in case studies in Christian revitalization, recognizing that conflict plays a necessary and significant role in the process of revitalization. She notes that conflict contributes to the birth of revitalization, fuels it by exposing limitations of existing organizations and provides new mazeways. (2013, 167) Hence, Complex Leadership Theory provides a new mazeway for understanding conflicts in the "complex web of realities encountered in global revitalization efforts." (Johnson-Miller 2013, 168)

In summary, the application of Complex Systems analysis has proved extremely useful in modernizing organizational theory by understanding events as *interactions*. Lichenstein *et al* write that

> ... the basic unit of organization is the 'double interact' of interdependent behaviors between individuals. ... An event is thus a bracketing of ongoing interactions to create meaning. Following this reasoning, we propose a new definition for an event, namely a perceived segment of action for which meaning relates to *interactions* among actors. All of the actors need not play equivalent roles in the action, but all of the roles are interrelated. Another way to say this is that meaning emerges in the "spaces between" people rather than in the acts of individuals ... Accordingly, leadership events are not constructed by the actions of single individual; rather, they emerge through the interactions between agents over time. (2007, 135)

It is hoped that that following application of Complex Systems analysis will prove to be equally useful.

6.2.3 Dimensional Integration: The Nature of Scale in Complex Systems

In the increasingly complex context of the twenty-first century, discovering a mazeway to integrate diverse elements in a system across global and local dimensions into a model with a single metanarrative has by far been one of the greatest challenges in many fields, including missiology. With respect to the latter, Beverly Johnson-Miller describes the complexities facing missiology with regard to understanding revitalization, writing

> ...the elements at work in revitalization are usually so deeply meshed or interlaced that they are inseparable and at times indistinguishable from the whole.
>
> No given revitalization movement could be understood apart from the web of revitalization movements throughout history, and each movement of revitalization occurs or has occurred as part of a larger picture. There was no such thing as a "solo" form or force of revitalization. No individual element, dimension, or dynamic stood alone, and the entire network of pieces and patterns are incapable of being described with completeness. Any particular aspect of revitalization that may be identified could not be contained within any single category. The pieces of the picture and pictures within the meta-picture of God's redemptive work defy or defied autonomous and linear categorization. (2013, 164)

It is in this context that missiologist Wilbert Shenk writes "The traditional interpretive framework is completely inadequate to describe and interpret the pluriform Christian reality that makes up the twenty-first century church. The task of historical interpretation must be brought into line with this new reality." (2002, xii) Consequently, "We need new tools and structures and altogether a new attitude toward the dynamic and plural nature of world Christianity. It is the only way to save and serve the cause." (2002, 114)

Perhaps the greatest contribution Complex Systems Science can offer to missiology is its ability to integrate diverse elements into a unified whole. It is in the proliferation of sub-disciplines (Shenk 2002, 28), of multiplying polarities (Schreiter 1997, 5), and of calls for interdisciplinary approaches (Van Engen 1996, 241; Escobar 2003, 21) that Complex Systems Science can provide mazeways toward integration and unity (Axelrod 2006, 1566) across all dimensions, from the local narrative to the grand metanarrative.

Of particular usefulness to missiology is the nature of fractal scales in Complexity Theory. Complex Systems Science postulates that there is unity across scales. As such, it can provide a framework for what missiologists have observed yet been unable to integrate. For example, Shenk noted that "global shifts are sometimes mirrored in shifts within local societies . . ." yet at the same time, he also despaired that "Global history becomes a kaleidoscope or collage, at best the presentation of a grand multi-cultural and multi-racial picture, at worst another attempt by the first and second worlds to initiate and determine the painting of the grand canvass." (2002, 80-81) With the already acknowledged bias toward Western Christianity, at issue now is how to integrate the pluriform Christianities in a way that equally acknowledges contributions from all actors regardless of how significant or lengthy a role one plays.

Several concepts across the spectrum of Complex Systems Science can be used to frame a model that includes all elements without prejudice. For example, consider the concept of fractal dimensionality of Chaos Theory (Lichtenstein 2007, 297). The concept recognizes that every dimension is critical to the integrity of a system without assigning priority to any level.

Another example is the Lorenz attractor, illustrated in Chapter 3, is another such function that integrates two apparent polarities into one function. As part of a single function, both are integral to the overall system and neither need be classified as "right" or "wrong." The integration of two seemingly polar entities is once again possible when the scale is expanded or contracted (Harter 2007, 347).

A final example is the use of Power Laws in Emergence Theory that allows both macroscopic and microscopic agencies to be considered as one process in one unified model (Lichtenstein 2007, 297). Both Shenk's and Johnson-Miller's observations could be well-described in the framework of Complex Systems Science.

As such, Complex Systems analysis may provide missiology with the terminology, conceptual models, metaphors, and methodology with which to build bridges across globally diverse communities, across the spiritual and physical domains, and if so, across the Enlightenment-created divide in the academy. In this section, we illustrate convergence through discussing how Complex Systems Science helps elucidate the parallel roles of individual agency on the micro-level, the roles of leaders in the meso-level, and the role of the Holy Spirit on the macro-level of a single unified system model, and subsequently, how Complex Systems Science may help to bridge the divide between the secular and sacred realms that exist in the academy.

6.2.3.1 Micro-level Agency: The Emergent Roles of Individuals

One of the greatest bias' church historians and missiologists face has been to focus on key leaders to describe the narrative of Christianity. This is due impart to the "Great Man" theory, for "... the most cherished belief about change in Western society is that it emanates from charismatic leaders.... "They are about people who dominated, and humans like to dominate." (Marion 1999, 216).

But while leaders are important, the New Testament has generally emphasized the place of the "priesthood of believers" (1 Peter 2:9). Jesus himself preached that that the church was an assembly (*ekklesia*) that should be driven by the weakest link (Mark 9:36-42, Matthew 18:1-17), a principle echoed by the apostle Paul (1 Corinthians 8).

How then can the two apparent polar extremes of the individual and the collective be reconciled?

Complex Systems analysis recognizes the critical role of both the "leader" and the "constituent" without the need to dominate or be dominated. Both have equal roles in the definition of a system and consequently, the relegation of one over the other results in the collapse of the system into chaos.

For example, concepts in Complexity Leadership are able to balance the traditional, Western-influenced revitalization model focused on visionary leaders with an understanding of the critical role of constituents, the individual agents. In the globalized, twenty-first century context, Lichtenstein *et al* write, "Traditional, hierarchical views of leadership are less and less useful given the complexities of our modern world. Leadership theory must transition to new perspectives that account for the complex adaptive needs of organizations.... leadership (as opposed to leaders) can be seen as a complex dynamic process that emerges in the interactive 'spaces between' people and ideas." (2007, 129)

As such, for identity stability and well-being of any organization in the midst of change, Schneider *et al* conclude that, "Increasingly, an organization must reside in the heads and hearts of its members." (2006, 357) As well, in the context of rapid change,

> Tapping the collective intelligence of the organization's citizenry allows for a quicker response to change. This moves the paradigm away from the single 'heroic' leader who has all the strategic answers to one where the responsibility for learning and reasons about strategic change falls onto the collective organization. (Schreiber and Carly 2007, 231)

In other words, Complexity Leaderships theorists have come to understand that as much as leaders have a role in an organization, in the organizational complexities of the twenty-first century, the determining factor of an organization's vitality and ability to adapt to change rests in the perceptions, actions, and interactions of its constituents collectively.

The corollary is equally true; if change agency is grounded in the collective constituency, then the ability to adapt rests in the process of shaping the perceptions of individual agents. Lichtenstein *et al* write that such an approach

> ... encourages all members to *be* leaders – to "own" their leadership within each interaction, potentially evoking a much broader array of responses from everyone in an organization. Complexity leadership theory provides a clear and unambiguous pathway for driving responsibility downward, sparking self-organization and innovation, and making the firm much more responsive and adaptive at the boundaries. (2007, 141)

If so, "By focusing on the structuring that is inherent in human actions and treating these acts and interactions as comprising a complex adaptive system we may not have to rely on, or default to, a person in position model of leadership." (Schwandt 2007, 120) Hence, Wallace was correct in understanding that the ability to adapt to change rested in "visions;" but he was incorrect in that it had to rest with a visionary leader; the ability of the collective constituency to adapt is equally critical, if not more in Complex Systems.

The discoveries of Complexity Leadership theorists sound eerily similar to many principles found in the Bible regarding the church and the process of disciple-making. It is also interesting that, while much of the Old Testament focuses on individual leaders such as patriarchs, kings, and prophets, many of the New Testament teachings focus on the corporate nature of God's people, the "priesthood of all believers" (1 Peter 2:9). But across both Old and New Testaments is a shared emphasis on the right identity in the hearts and minds of God's people (Deuteronomy 10:12, 2 Samuel 16:7, Psalm 51:7, Mark 12:30, Romans 15:6), on their transformation (Ezekiel 36, Romans 12:2, Ephesians 4, Colossians 3:10), and on corporate identity and unity (Philippians 2:1-11, 1 Corinthians 12, Ephesians 4). Whether leader or individual constituent, in the terminology of Complex Systems Science, an individual's "base programming" is the seedbed from which the vitality and stability of the entire system emerges.

One also finds agreement between concepts in Complex Systems Science and recent studies in revitalization. These studies increasingly point not to leaders, but to the church community as the nexus of renewal. "The point of departure for exploring revitalization is the local fellowship of followers of Christ. Revitalization operates via 'the collectivity of people,' the 'body of Christ.'" (Irwin 2011, 232) Bryan Froehle agrees, writing "Given that Christianity is inevitably an ecclesial-institutional expression, world Christian revitalization has always been rooted, in part, in struggle with this dynamic.... The institutional church is inevitably implicated: there is no other way." (2013, 149)

Complexity Theory also explains why adaptability to change comes out of the collective constituency; it is the relational network that *gestalts* the mazeway through change. As the network is the basis for perception formation, it is in the interactions across the collective constituency that enables an organization to maintain stability in the midst of change as well as promoting the organization's ability to adapt to its changing environment. Three characteristics define a collective constituency's response to change: its internal memory, which enables the organization to remain stable; the degree of resonance in the network, which mediates the organization's process of adaptation; and the diversity of the network, which determines the degree of flexibility of an organization to adapt to change.

6.2.3.1.1 Internal Memory

First, the internal memory of individual members stabilizes an organization in the midst of complex change. Much like a shock absorber creates inertia to smooth out bumps in the road, the internal memory of each member serves to dampens the effect of complex change on the network. Marion writes that this internal memory, what he terms an individual member's "map," akin to an internal mazeway,

> . . . is related to the complex system's ability to order interaction patterns and, by extension, to categorize its environment. Consider, for example, an informal social group (a group that evolves naturally) within a formal social organization. Individuals create persistent relationships because the behaviors of certain other individuals are compatible with their own internal mappings (in plain English, those involved have something in common). The individuals of this resulting group remember their relationships and the patters of their past behaviors. Such memories enable the group to maintain relationships over extended periods. . . . I argue that Complex (as opposed to Chaotic) attractors are the medium of mapping. They are sufficiently stable to retain memory; further, because of controlled interactions among attractors, sets of interacting attractors can likewise be sufficiently stable to permit memory. (1999, 72)

What Marion is saying is that as an organization revolves a particular attractor, a common identity or set of values, individual members are able to develop memories of how to relate to one another. As such, even when a system is perturbed and the trajectory is affected, the attractor serves as an inertial damper to minimize the effects of the perturbation. Hence, despite the fact that the trajectory no longer follows its original course, its orbit remains stable around the attractor.

6.2.3.1.2 Network Resonance

Second, Marion postulates that resonance between individuals or groups of members also enables an organization to adapt to change without an abrupt, discontinuous paradigm shift that Wallace's original revitalization model would require. A period of instability is created, but the system maintains stability. Stability is possible because change patterns are incrementally transmitted through resonance, that is, mutual programming through the interaction between micro-level agents. Hence, revitalization need not be discontinuous.

Resonance is possible because the internal memories of base units share a common root program, in other words, a common identity. They share a common worldview, a common vocabulary, a common form of interaction, etc. Subsequently, harmonic resonance is possible across individuals as they interact with one another.

When a system has resonance, it is able to adapt to change through what is called "positive deviance." Goldstein *et al* define "positive deviance" as

> ... a complexity science – based, nonlinear model for leading constituencies through uncertain and changing environments by leveraging internal innovations into system-wide change. This approach to leading innovation is decidedly different than traditional views. It does *not* place the leading in the role of a visionary who looks out on the situation confronting the organization, envisions a different future, then effectively designs a new kind of business model that positions the firm for that future. ... the generation of novelty is first initiated by *deviances* from the mainstream functioning of an organization (128) ... for in every community there are certain individuals ("positive deviants") whose special practices, strategies or behaviors enable them to find better solutions to prevalent community problems than their peers who have access to the same resources. (130) (2010)

Marion illustrates it similarly, writing

> Mapping means memory: The stability observed in Complex attractors allows the retention of information, hence memory. But what mechanism accounts for the implanting, or mapping, of information into the attractor? I propose an answer that is actually quite simple: An attractor maps a part of the environment by resonating, or correlating, with it. As sales division resonates with that particular part of the market for which it is responsible, the physical chemistry division of a university's chemistry department resonates with the ideas in its field, and tax lawyers resonate with fiscal laws. By *resonation* or *correlation* I mean that attractors interact with a part

of the environment, they become familiar with it; in a sense, they become a part of the environment both as observers and as actors. That is, a bit of the environment is made part of the organization. (1999, 74)

Thus, as specific individuals or groups interact with the environment, it is re-transmitted through their interactions with other members in the network. The result is a resonant wave that eventually travels across the entire network, "reprogramming" the memories of all the collective constituents. It is this relational process that allows an organization to respond to changes in the environment. "Positive Deviance not only has been successful for dealing with longstanding and what had previously been thought to be intractable problems; PD appears to change the very culture of the organizations or communities in which it has been applied" (Goldstein *et al* 2010) - in other words, a paradigm shift.

6.2.3.1.3 Organizational Diversity

Third, the greater the diversity an organization has, the better it is able to adapt. Because different attractors respond differently to the environment, the more diverse an organization is, the more avenues an organization has as options in order to adapt to environmental changes (Hazy *et al* 2007, 322). Marion writes,

Each of the constituent attractors emerge within the broader system. Each of the constituent attractors is responsible for a particular part of the environment, but their foci are interrelated. Hence the different divisions of a chemistry department are responsible for different specialties, but all are interrelated by the broader them (chemistry). Each attractor is somewhat familiar with the focus of other attractors within its network (these attractors correlate with one another and with parts of each other's environment), but is primarily responsible for its own focus. These broader networks are what lend the system its holistic strength: Through interaction across networks, the system develops a knowledge and capability that far exceeds that of individual attractors. (1999, 74)

In other words, diversity enables an organization to respond to environmental changes. The greater the diversity, the greater the possibility that at least one constituent has the means to respond appropriate to the environmental change. Such a constituent becomes a contextual "leader" whose interactions with other constituents will create resonance to be transmitted to the rest of the system.

Once again, one finds clear similarities between the above concepts of Complexity Theory and Scripture. Consider, for example, Hebrews 11:23-25, which states, "Let us hold tightly without wavering to the hope we affirm, for God can be trusted to keep his promise. Let us think of ways to motivate one another to acts of love and good works. And let us not neglect our meeting together, as some people do, but encourage one another, especially now that the day of his return is drawing near." (NLT) This was written to first century Christians in Asia who were undergoing dramatic change and beginning to face persecution to encourage them to persevere (Guthrie 1998, 20). If we interpret this passage in light of Complexity Theory, the author is calling the collective constituency to remain "stable." How is this done? First, they are to recall their internal memory, the gospel narrative of God's unfolding promise. This memory serves as an inertial damper that minimizes impulsive reactions to rapid change. The internal memory preserves the relationships with the rest of the collective in the church network and enables the church to remain stable in its orbit around the attractor in the midst of change.

As well, the apostle Paul's description of the benefits of church diversity as the Body of Christ in First Corinthians 12 reflects Complexity Theory's understanding of the role of diversity in a system. The gifts given to the church are what enable the organization to respond to change. One notes that Paul focuses on the relationships, the intrinsic character of Complexity Theory, across the gifts (1 Corinthians 13), not the gift itself. What matters most to the life and stability of the church is "love," that is, a resonant (as opposed to a dissonant or chaotic) quality of the relationship in the system.

Complex Systems Science also finds correlation with recent studies in revitalization which have drawn the similar conclusions in the two-fold calling of renewal to churches. First, churches must recognize *missio Dei*, the "internal memory and programming" of the Church. "Christian 'revitalization' is defined by an understanding of the Church and its place in this salvation history – between the saving work of Christ, and His promised return. As such, the participants of revitalization, either implicitly or explicitly, understand themselves to be a *part* of this grand biblical narrative of the *Missio Dei*." (Chung 2013, 135) It is *missio Dei* which serves as the inertial damper for the Church in the midst of complex change. As believers retain this "memory" of who they are, it will mediate their response to the impact of rapid, complex change (Walls 2002, 211).

And second, churches have been called to remember the importance of praxis. The Christian identity is

> ... irreducible to external techniques or procedures but requires a non-technical, personal and participatory way of knowing which cannot be framed in terms of detachment, universality, and utility. ... communal activity may be extended to our understanding of Christian practices, or means of grace, such as prayer and worship, the use of Scripture in preaching and teaching, evangelization, catechesis, training in discipleship, pastoral care, and works of mercy and justice. Activities of this nature are carried out in such a way to realize and demonstrate as their end those virtues, dispositions, and excellences that are valued by the church as a historical community and constitutive of its life through faith that works through the Spirit's empowerments of love. In this alternative picture, practical knowledge is seen as a fruit which grows only in the sole of a person's experience and character. One is at the same time a feeling, expressing, and acting person; and knowing is inseparable from one's life as such. (Pasquarello 2013, 173)

It is in the resonant praxis of believers that enables the collective whole to respond to change. Thus, we see that revitalization, a response to change, can be described through the lens of Complex Systems Science as occurring around two attractors, the place of the metanarrative gospel story, and the core programming of praxis that governs the loving resonant interactions between believers.

Third, the Complexity Leadership Theory principle of diversity complements the emerging nature of the Church in the twenty-first century in its pluriform fullness. Andrew Walls writes that, rather than being a source of division, diversity is the Church's strength, for

> ... the very diversity was part of the church's unity. The church must be diverse because humanity is diverse; it must be one because Christ is one. ... Believers from the different communities are different bricks being used for the construction of a single building – a temple where One God would live (Eph 2:19-22). ... This in turn brings the church's maturity, "the very height of Christ's full stature" (Eph. 4:13). The very height of Christ's full stature is reached only by the coming together of the different cultural entities into the body of Christ. Only "together," not on our own, can we reach his full stature. (2002, 77)

Hence, in many aspects, Complexity Theory complements the New Testament perspective of "one another." In the face of complex change, God's people should not look merely for visionary or charismatic leaders as the primary means of developing new mazeways forward, but rather, to the diverse body of believers God has called to be His Church.

6.2.3.2 Meso-Level: The Role of Leaders and a new 21ˢᵗ Century Definition for Revitalization

With the emphasis on collective constituents, one might think that Complex Systems Science would diminish the role of leaders, but that is not the case; rather, Complexity Leadership Theory still recognizes the critical role of leaders, and in the context of rapid, complex change redefines the role from a systemic perspective. Hazy *et al* write that

> The changing environment requires a team to engage in a sensemaking process, a dynamical search across interaction patterns among agents that tend towards two basins of attraction: formal leadership, in its function as an interface with the larger organization and thus as a source of "official" interpretations of events, and shared leadership in its function as facilitator of collective meaning and consensus understanding and action derived from individual experiences (2007, 322)

In the new twenty-first century context of rapid, complex change, leaders are not charged to *gestalt* a new mazeway for the organization. Rather, leaders are charged to *gestalt* the network and facilitate the network to find a mazeway for the organization.

Complex Leadership Theory defines this role as "generative leadership." Surie and Hazy write

> ... since group interactions must culminate in action based on a match between the model or representation of the problem and the environment, generative leaders focus on gaining rapid feedback through action. In contrast to traditional perspectives that conceive of leaders as the gatherers, interpreters, and synthesizers of feedback and those who heroically convert the information into a strategy or vision, generative leadership channels feedback through the organization's members who are in the best position to interpret and synthesize the new information into ever more useable models of the environment. (2007, 359)

In essence, leaders are called to shape and build the organizational network in a configuration that best enables the organization to understand, respond and adapt to change. Consequently, ". . . rather than focusing on individual interactions between leaders and followers, our perspective on generative leadership emphasizes the *organizational* capacity to enhance connectivity, and thereby promote innovation by synthesis and recombination of ideas from different parts of the system and adaptation to a dynamic context." (Surie and Hazy 2007, 365) In contrast to Wallace's theory of revitalization, instead of leaders primary task of *gestalting* change, generative leaders are tasked to *gestalt* the organization and its network first; *ge-*

stalting the environment is a secondary task and in practice, the task of constituent agents, the positive deviants.

Esa Saarinen and Raimo P. Hamalainen term this critical quality of generative leaders as "Systems Intelligence." It is the

> . . . intelligent behavior in the context of complex systems involving interaction and feedback. A subject acting with Systems Intelligence engages successfully and productively with the holistic feedback mechanisms of her environment. She perceives herself as part of a whole, the influence of the whole upon herself as well as her own influence upon the whole. By observing her own interdependence in the feedback intensive environment, she is able to act intelligently. (Saarinen and Hamalainen 2007, 39)

In other words, a generative leader is able to grasp the nature of the entire system and the place of the organization, of the collective constituency, including him/herself, and effect an efficacious response to a changing environment.

Even more importantly, Systems Intelligence is the quality of knowing how to improve the organization by understanding where it should be headed. A leader's objective is not merely the goal of keeping a system stable. Systems Intelligence is the quality of shaping the system such that the organization can overcome inertial ruts and ford complex change with new mazeways. "Systems intelligence is essentially applicative and essentially tied to circumstances. Its secure base is the particular and the present moment – and from that base it operates with the interest to nurture the desired outcome and cultivate its realization. The imperative of a Systems Intelligent leader is essentially one of constantly staying in tune with the possibilities and requirements of whatever is emerging." (Hamalainen and Saarinen 2007, 22)

To achieve this goal, the Systems Intelligent leader understands what is necessary to reshape the internal memories of constituents to allow them to accept and think in the new mazeway. It is not enough to have a vision of a new mazeway in the traditional linear model of revitalization; the leader must understand his/her constituents and help them make the necessary changes to adapt.

> The leader identifies the natural stress on the system that comes about when an opportunity is recognized in the environment by the members of the organization, but they also realize that, as currently configured, the system is unable to realize its potential... [then determines] the individual and groups of individuals who are already exhibiting the desired outcome within the common behaviors in the community. . . . [then implements] social interventions whereby the majority have access to and learn the new practices inherent in the novel successes of the positive deviants. (Goldstein *et al* 2010, 145).

The intended goal is to create a context in which resonance can occur.

> "Because of the fact that 'chains of consequence extend over time and many areas", the Systems Intelligent leader will place emphasis even on microinterventions. By changing something small, the Systems Intelligent leader is looking something big, through the effects and resonance brought about by the initial intervention. (24) . . . Symbols and symbol systems are the key here. The chance is to change the perspective, the frame of reference, the rules of the game via the symbolic order, and open up the road to systemic change as a result. Of all the systems available to humans, the symbolic dimension is the most accessible when reading out to the emergence of life-enhancing systems, and the way out of systems of holding back." (31) (Hamalainen and Saarinen 2007)

In summary, Complexity Leadership Theory shifts the focus from a leader needing to *gestalt* a new mazeway to a leader's System Intelligence and his/her ability to *gestalt* the organization by understanding where the system should be headed, reshaping the network configuration for maximum ability to adapt, and altering the internal memories of individual constituents such that resonance is achieved so that the entire organization can collectively respond and adapt to change.

The principles of Systems Intelligence complement what is observed in Scripture, for example, in Hamalainen and Saarinen's application of Complexity Leadership Theory to the narrative of Jesus and the Pharisees with the woman caught in adultery.

> "The teacher of the law and the Pharisee' brought in to Jesus a woman caught in adultery. 'Teacher, this woman was caught in the act of adultery. In the Law Moses commands us to stone such women. Now what do you say?'"
>
> The evangelist notes: "They were using this question as a trap, in order to have a basis of accusing him"

> But as we recall, Jesus bent down, creating a change in the rhythm of the situation. He prepared the ground for reframing of the set-up, for the emergence of a more generous and life-appreciating system. As the accusers kept on questioning him, the masterful systems intelligent countermove of Jesus was to say, "If any one of you is without sin, let him be the first to throw a stone at her." (John 8:1-7). As will be recalled, this decided the case. The accusers were stripped from their accusing advocate mode and found themselves in inquiry mode that opened the door to a bond with the accused woman. A more appreciative and forgiving system emerged, backed up by a shared experience of human connectivity and non-arrogance coming to life in the living presence. Having gotten released from the hostage system of accuse [sic] and disgust the people that came to Jesus touched upon their more generous selves, felt their own guilt and left.

This is systems intelligent interventionism; this is Systems Intelligence at the service of hope. (2007, 32-33)

Thus, in this example, we see how Jesus was able to change the entire system through Systems Intelligence. Revitalization occurred not because Jesus was visionary; revitalization occurred because Jesus possessed Systems Intelligence and was thus able to understand the relational networks, reshape it, and transform attitudes of constituents such that they could resonate in unison to become the community of the Kingdom of God.

It is interesting to note that the principles found in Complexity Leadership are very similar to Roland Allen's understanding for missionary leadership. Allen recognized that leadership is not about "gathering all authority in his own hands," (1962, 18), but in the development and equipping of leaders and lay believers. Allen understood that "leaders catalyzing others for ministry, mobilizing and sharing leadership with lay people, and emphasizing the full authority of the independent local church, infused with the power of the Holy Spirit would lead to 'spontaneous expansion.' ... This *spontaneous expansion* briefly sums up all of Roland Allen's missiology." (Mehn 2013, 161)

With this new perspective, Complexity Leadership Theory provides possible solutions for several deficiencies in current revitalization theories that missiologists have observed as necessary for the twenty-first century context. The first deficiency is a definition for revitalization and the second deficiency is a mazeway to navigate the process of revitalization.

First, in a recent consultation on revitalization, missiologists lament that there is no clear understanding of what "revitalization" means; in other words, in a period of rapid, complex change, is a paradigm shift to be expected at every "shift?" Paul Chung writes,

> There is in this sense, no clear *object* of "re-vitalization." This absence is apparent... [they] lacked for the most part the kind of language that would be consistent with the metaphor of revitalization – that of brining a dying organism back to life. Rather, they spoke of "making disciples," "new mission field," the "harvest," "heart of God," and the "sovereign plan and provision of God.'" What then is *re*vitalized in these movements? ... are we to include every such ministry under the umbrella of the term, "revitalization"? Could we do so without risking the loss of all useful meaning of the term? (2013, 131)

Looking at the various studies in the course of the consultation, Chung suggests a new understanding of revitalization, that of a journey to reach a particular goal, a *telos*. He defines revitalization as the practice of achieving a *telos* in a historical narrative,

> ... including its sometimes revolutionary changes, describes how the difficulties, problems, and obstacles in its progress to the ultimate *telos* have been overcome so far, bringing its journey closer to its *telos*.... What I am suggesting is that there is a certain kind of action ... [revitalization is] any kind of practice that has a particular purpose, which is to journey toward a definitive, through yet-unreached and distant, historical end-point. Christian revitalization is just such a practice. (134)

If one compares Chung's definition of revitalization, it is almost identical to Complexity Theory's definition of emergence, the ability to adapt to change in order to maintain a vibrant organization that is able to reach its ultimate expression.

Thus, Complexity Systems Science reshapes the understanding of Christian revitalization for the twenty-first century context of rapid, complex change. If change is continuous, Christian revitalization is not necessarily a paradigm shift, but a continuous, incremental journey of practice in which the Church achieves its ultimate *telos*.

Second, Complexity Leadership Theory provides a mazeway for missiologists and church leaders to accomplish the charge from the most recent consultation on revitalization to provide navigation, that is, leadership, in the midst of the twenty-first century context.

> Christian revitalization movements are necessarily pieces of a puzzle, the whole of which is the Divine narrative. These movements therefore are necessarily incomplete, not merely in the sense that the Church will need to be revitalized again and again, but in the sense that each movement in itself only completes one particular piece of the narrative toward the eschatological completion of the Kingdom of God. Each movement, furthermore, requires a time to orient itself to ask *where* it is in the unfolding Divine narrative, and *then* what is to be done. This act of re-orientation is constantly required throughout the history of the Church because if what I have said is correct, the Church is essentially on a *journey*, and it needs *navigation*.... theologians and scholars ... serve as navigators, mapping the past journey of the Church, and ever-looking forward to its final promised destination. Thus, they may hopefully better illumine for the rest of us the direction in which God seems to be leading His Church. (Chung 2013, 138)

Far from displacing leaders with the network, Complexity Theory re-visions the role of leaders as part of the collective constituency that is God's people, the Church, and tasked to serve the Church as guides, facilitators, and mentors to enable the collective organization to fulfill its *telos* in the twenty-first century context of rapid, complex change.

6.2.3.3 Macro-Level: The Role of the Holy Spirit

This section is somewhat sparse, more prophetic than pragmatic, because, while Complex Systems Science acknowledges the possibility of Strong Emergence, top-down causation, because hard scientists are still heavily biased toward reductionism (Keener 2011, 647), it is not an area which has been actively pursued (Jorgensen 2011) . It is why one of the 2012 Templeton funding competitions called for more active research into understanding the impact of strong emergence;[11] the goal was to provide a more balanced understanding of emergence. In the same vein, this section primarily argues for the need to include the possibility of Strong Emergence if one is to be objective across disciplines and how strong emergence properties may be included in a systems model.

Complex Systems Science inherently opens the door to explore the possibilities of macro-level variables with its demand to avoid reductionism and empiricism and the need to accept the presence of uncertainty. Even if phenomena can be explained purely through observing and analyzing local, constituent units, one must nevertheless consider the possibility of materially intangible phenomena that is systemic in nature.

Increasingly, there are a minority of Complex Systems scientists who are calling for a more objective analysis of data. Eric Dent writes,

> ... many researchers did not see God's hand in the interpretation of the data. Looking at the same evidence, however, I will suggest that many complexity theory philosophies and evidence strengthen, rather than weaken, the case for the existence of a supreme being and the religious traditions associated with such belief. ... [consequently] new organization theories based on complexity theory should be consistent, rather than at odds, with religious traditions." (2003, 124)

Indeed, Marion acknowledges it is really a question of how one interprets the data. "Again, faith and science have similar premises: Order is considered the product of sifting, and sifting represents external force, or work. The one attributes sifting to the efforts of God, the other to the efforts of natural selection: But both see order as the fruit of work. . . . Sifting, whether by God or by selection . . . represents work done to produce order." (Marion 1999, xii)

---

[11] http://www.templeton.org/what-we-fund/funding-competitions/the-physics-of-emergence. Accessed June 18, 2014

Hence, Complex Systems Science serves as a bridge between reductionist-biased scientism and theology. As Joseph Spradley concludes, Complex Systems Science introduces ". . . a new scientific world view more congenial to Christian faith." (1985, 73)

Complex Systems Science can serve as a bridge in the academy as it inherently moves toward macro-level conclusions as the goal of Complex Systems Science seeks to find simplicity on the other side of chaos. In the social sciences, Complex Systems Science seeks a metanarrative current that frames the local eddies of human interactions.

If so, then with regard to the study of revitalization, one is then obligated to consider the possibility of *missio Dei.* As Complex Systems Science, via Emergence Theory, allows for the presence of God's work on both global and local dimensions, Complexity-grounded missiological models could provide enlightenment to the rest of the academy to consider the integration of the universal hermeneutic of *missio Dei* in complex system models. In the science and theology dialogue, Arthur Peacocke challenges that academy to consider that ". . . the world is somehow located *within the divine. . .* the patterns of emergence are grounded in the divine wonder and that God continually responds to the evolutionary process, but also that the world is located within the divine being." (Clayton and Davies, 2006: 319) As such, Complex Systems Science allows missiologists to prophetically call for the recognition that beyond the physical, material realm, the existence of supernatural, transcendent entities should not be discounted.

In the case of Christian revitalization, the primary macro-level entity that must be considered is the presence and work of the Holy Spirit. "Revitalization starts with something more than just ecclesiology and personal salvation, but with the revitalization of creation. . . and we are God's created beings. So, again, it's God reaching down to us and how we respond." (O'Malley, unpublished minutes from first consultation, quoted from Johnson-Miller 2011, 14) Irwin agrees writing, "Revitalization originates from and is rooted in the Triune God; it takes place where people in specific (historical, cultural, social and spiritual) contexts experience God's enlivening and reawakening Spirit leading to a fresh encounter with the living Christ." (2011, 233)

Amos Yong, a Pentecostal theologian, believes in the primacy of the Spirit as an overarching actor in the twenty-first century global context. He writes that ". . . it is precisely because the Spirit is both universal and particular, both the Spirit of God and the Spirit of Jesus the Christ, that pneumatology provides the kind of relational framework wherein the radical alterity – otherness . . . can be taken seriously. . . . The result, perhaps, is the emergence of a new set of categories that may chart the way forward" (2003, 21) In his understanding, it will be the Holy Spirit who was, is, and will be, the bridge-maker and unifier across human divides. As such, any objective and unbiased Complex Systems analysis must include a macro-level parameter that accounts for the work of the Holy Spirit as a supranatural entity..

In summary, Complex Systems Science provides an integrative mazeway that bridges the spiritual and physical dimensions of the twenty-first century context. The inclusion of macro-level parameters will allow researchers to ask, "Will a computational model which factors in the Holy Spirit's work more aptly model real world data than a model which ignores it?" In so doing, the metanarrative of *missio Dei* may be fully visualized.

6.3 Defining Christian Revitalization: A Psychological Sickness or the Cusp of Change?

With the traditional Wallacian and Complex Systems Science-framed Cusp of Change models presented, this section now compares both through the framework of the questions and observations from the consultations on Christian revitalization. This section discusses three particular incompatibilities that have been noted throughout the chapter: 1) source of revitalization – psychological sickness or macro-level phenomena; 2) historical definition – discontinuous, isolated event or an ongoing, continuous, process of chaotic equilibrium; and 3) the locus of revitalization – visionary leader or a combination of multi-level agents with an emphasis on micro-level agency.

6.3.1 Source of Christian Revitalization

With respect to the source of Christian revitalization, Wallace's model of revitalization is decidedly humanistic, discounting the possibility of any supernatural origins, and considered an abnormal phenomenon. For Wallace, the source of revitalization is a consequence of stress, a "psychological sickness." In contrast, in Complexity Theory, revitalization is a normal, necessary emergent response to change. The locus of Wallace's model of revitalization relies on human agency. In contrast, with the provision for Strong Emergence,

Complexity Theory is sufficiently robust and allows for macro-level variables that can incorporate the systemic manifestation of the Spirit's agency.[12] Additionally, the Theory of Weak Emergence allows simultaneous analysis of micro-level variables that can incorporate the Spirit's agency in the internal memory and root programming of individual human agents. The traditional Wallacian model understands Christian revitalization as a consequence of a "psychological sickness" and the *gestalt* as a cognitive, therapeutic response. In contrast, the Complex Systems Science-framed Cusp of Change model views revitalization as a vital, ongoing, normative process that is systemic, incorporating macro-level, meso-level and micro-level variables that represent the host agents in the system and their mutual interactions.

From a biblical perspective, the source of revitalization is the Holy Spirit. Christians are called to "walk in the Spirit" (Galatians 5:16, Ephesians 3:16). In fact, revitalization is a function of an external source on the Christian. A Christian cannot transform him/herself, but must "*be* transformed" (Romans 12:2). Human effort is insufficient for transformation (Romans 7); only the Holy Spirit is able to revitalize the Christian (Romans 8). Christians are called to forget what is behind and to press ahead (Philippians 3:13), and to continue to stimulate one another to love and good works toward an otherworldly *telos* (Hebrews 10:24). As such, revitalization is a continuous process mandated by God, initiated by Jesus, and continually empowered by the Holy Spirit toward a specific *telos*. As such, biblical revitalization is not an abnormal, psychologically sick, human-initiated response to stress; in fact, Christians are not to become anxious (Matthew 6:25 – 33, Philippians 4:6).

In light of these comparisons, one must then ask which proffered source of Christian revitalization is most compatible with the observations of the consultations? Is Christian revitalization a human-initiated, aberrant, psychological response to stress? Or is Christian revitalization an intrinsic character of the nature of disciples and the Church that are journeying in an ongoing process that is mandated by the heavenly Father, initiated by Jesus, and daily empowered by the Holy Spirit?

---

[12] It should be noted that most secular scientists do not consider divine origin as a source for Strong Emergence; nevertheless, Complex Systems Science opens the door for dialogue (see Clayton and Davies 2009) and certain complex systems scientists are advocating for its inclusion (Dent 2003).

6.3.2 Historicity of Christian Revitalization

With respect to the historicity of Christian revitalization, Wallace's model definition of revitalization as an isolated, discontinuous event that is terminated when a new normative state is reached; in contrast, the Cusp of Change model defines revitalization as an organization's normative condition in the context of change and, as such, must be a continuous, ongoing process. The traditional Wallacian model of Christian revitalization understands change as aperiodic and its manifestation leads to stress in an initial steady state; hence, change is the initiator of a discrete and isolated revitalization event. Additionally, the traditional model also requires a termination of the revitalization event once a new steady state is achieved. In contrast, the Cusp of Change model understands that change is continuous; hence, revitalization must also be continuous and the normative state. As such, the inability to revitalize is the aberrant condition and, in fact, is the initiator of stagnation.

From a biblical perspective, Christians must be continually in the state of motion – of "going" (Matthew 28:18), to continually cross boundaries and cultures (Acts 1:8), and to continually abound the Lord's labor (1 Corinthians 15:58). When the Church becomes too comfortable, disciples are reprimanded (Revelation 2:1-7) and the Holy Spirit initiates trials to continue the forward motion of mission (Acts 8, James 12-4, 1 Peter 1:6-9)

Proponents of the traditional Wallacian revitalization model may argue that such a continuous, incremental shift is not a true revitalization, but a "steady-state" (fixed) or even an "adaptation" phase. But one should be reminded that Wallace himself later realized, and grudgingly acknowledged, that revitalization can be incremental (Wallace 2003, 139).

And while a Complex Systems Science-framed Cusp of Change model of Christian revitalization defines transformation as a continuous ongoing process, it does not mean that discontinuities cannot be observed. However, from a systemic perspective, such discontinuities, what Goldstein *et al* would define as "criticalizations," are more perceived than reality; such discontinuities remain a part of an overall trajectory when observed long-term, a part of the entire process, not as a single, isolated event. Described in Complex Systems analysis, such perceived discontinuities could result from a period where a trajectory curves in on itself, or when the attractor itself is shifted. Either phenomenon could mimic a discontinuity without moving the entire system into a chaotic state. And has been shown earlier (see Figure 12), an abrupt continuity can also be described within Complex Systems analysis. Hence, a Complex Systems Science-framed Cusp of Change model of Christian revitalization is more robust in nature and can explain a variety of phenomena within a single historical reality, both continuous and discontinuous.

More importantly, as mentioned earlier in the chapter, because revitalization is not an aberrant, isolated historical event, a Complex Systems Science-framed Cusp of Change model of Christian revitalization has a *telos,* a metanarrative with which a trajectory is defined. Chung writes, "These movements therefore are necessarily incomplete, not merely in the sense that the Church will need to be revitalized again and again, but in the sense that each movement in itself only completes one particular piece of the narrative toward the eschatological completion of the Kingdom of God. . . . the Church is essentially on a *journey."* (2013, 138) Revitalization then, is a continuous process that enables the Church to fulfill its eschatological journey. As such, this definition finds more compatibility with the Complex Systems Science-framed Cusp of Change model of Christian revitalization than with the Wallacian model.

In light of these comparisons, one must then ask, which historical model of revitalization is more robust in addressing the questions and observations of the consultations? Is Christian revitalization an aberrant, discontinuous, isolated event as the Wallacian model stipulates? Or is Christian revitalization an ever-moving, forward process that is fulfilling the divine *telos* of *missio Dei*?

6.3.3 Locus of Revitalization

With regard to the locus of revitalization, Christian revitalization occurs with the visionary leader in Wallace's model; in contrast, the locus of revitalization in the Cusp of Change model involves the leader, but is also grounded in the collective constituency, the micro-level agents. In the Wallacian model, it is the visionary leader who interacts with the environment to *gestalt* a new mazeway and communicates the new mazeway his followers; the locus of revitalization resides in an individual agent. In contrast, the leader in the Cusp of Change model *gestalts* the network to identify, enable and equip positive deviants, micro-level agents who have beneficial developed new behaviors in response to a changing environment; the locus of revitalization resides in the emerging interactions across agents. In the Cusp of Change model, revitalization occurs when the organization is in a condition where harmonic resonance is possible, allowing for the transmission of new behaviors across the entire organizational network through individual interactions between and across micro-level agents. Harmonic resonance occurs when all agents share the same internal memories and core programming.

Biblically, the locus of revitalization should be the Church and discipleship the basis of revitalization. In "the priesthood of all believers," (1 Peter 2:9), every Christ follower has a specific role in God's Kingdom mandate (Romans 12, 1 Corinthians 12, Ephesians 4) As well, the means of fulfilling one's role is understood to be discipleship (Matthew 28:18-19). In this model, the role of leaders is "... to prepare God's people for works of service, so that the body of Christ may be built up." (Ephesians 4:11, NIV)

As such, Complex Systems Science finds greater compatibility with the Christian conception of Christian revitalization in "the priesthood of all believers" when compared with the Wallacian model of Christian revitalization. In the context of a church, an understanding of micro-level agency provides two key insights as to the organization's revitalization efforts, the agency and the mazeway for revitalization.

The first insight is that, in the twenty-first century context, missiologists must now seriously consider that the agency for revitalization rests not with a charismatic leader, but in the spiritual formation of the "priesthood of all believers." For example, if one looks at the data from the multicongregational, multilingual, multiethnic Chinese churches of the case study, despite changes in leadership, one notes that churches that have a well-integrated path of discipleship across their ministries are able to thrive even in the context of rapid change. Hence, despite shifts in the immigration patterns, such churches continue to attract and incorporate newcomers, not merely as attenders, but as participants (Table 3). Additionally, as integrated members and their families continue to generationally participate in the church (Table 6), such churches appear better able to adapt to change by maintaining a clear vision of the church (Table 5). Such churches recognize, and are able to adapt to, cultural and social shifts that are occurring in emerging generations and in their metropolitan context (Table 4) while maintaining a sense of collective unity - even in the face of conflict (Table 5).

From a Complex Systems Science perspective, one would conclude that churches that are able to maintain their vitality, that is, their revitalization process, do so because the collective actions of their micro-level agents stabilize the entire organization. For example, an integrated network-wide discipleship ministry sustains and refreshes the long-term memories of micro-level agents. As well, such a discipleship ministry serves to "program" new micro-level agents such that they are incorporated into the organizational network. With such a shared consciousness, churches are more readily able to create resonance, allowing for the process of adaptation to change in a continuous, incremental "revitalization" rather than a discontinuous "paradigm shift."

More importantly, as mentioned earlier, one must question whether Wallace's revitalization model of a "paradigm shift" in thinking is in reality consistent with the understanding of Christian revitalization. Andrew Walls' observations on Christian revitalization movements are in fact more consistent with the micro-level concepts of Complexity Theory where the strengthening the long-term memories and root programming of the collective agency of "the priesthood of all believers" are the means of revitalization. Walls observes both that Christian revitalization occurs not from a new paradigm, but the renewal of the "long-term memory" of micro-level agents. Walls argues that

> Christian faith, therefore, is necessarily ancestor-conscious, aware of the previous generations of faith. It cannot divinize the ancestors, however, for their continuing significance comes only from God's activity in and towards them. The work of salvation is cross-generational . . . And the generations – two millennia of them since the incarnation – are parts of a single body, and that body needs them all.

Drawing from the Pietist and Evangelical movements, Walls illustrates that

> Such developments . . . had the effect of moving religion from the sphere of the public and communal to the sphere of the private and personal, and thus the sphere of group and family, and ultimately to the individual responsibility and choice. . . . These emphasized the responsibility and even the autonomy of the individual, and developed the principles of contract and association as the modes by which this responsibility could be collectively expressed. . . . such thoroughly Christian developments such as Pietism and Evangelicalism, by radically adopting the principle of personal responsibility in religion, and developing with marked success the principles of contract and association to give the religion communal form, helped Protestantism to adapt to the Enlightenment, perhaps even enabled it to survive.

> We have seen how a sense of common purpose could link groups in different countries who stood for "real" Christianity (212). . . All the springs for the Protestant missionary movement lay in the movement for "real Christianity". . .(213) (2002)

Walls, in essence, argues that it is micro-level agencies, programmed with the original memory of "real Christianity" that enabled Christianity to adapt and survive the Enlightenment. Far from a "new paradigm" and a visionary leader, it is a return to Christianity's "root programming" in micro-level agents that leads to Christian revitalization.

Howard Snyder makes similar observations regarding renewal movements through history. "Francis, Waldo and Wesley and the renewal movements springing from them (the Franciscans, Waldenses and Methodists) could be compared as differing models of renewal within the larger context of the church. Other possible parallels might include modern Pentecostalism and particularly the Catholic charismatic renewal . . . [all are] seeking to be a self-conscious subcommunity or *ecclesiola* working to revitalize . . . All these renewing forces were in one way or another radical departures from the status quo [i.e. cultural and social context they were in] . . ." (112) In all these movements, similar to Walls, Snyder concludes that the common denominator is Christian discipleship, ". . . the *way* of following Jesus Christ – based on the sure conviction that life is the only measure of real faith." (113) (1980)

In the article on revivalism and revivals in *Global Dictionary of Theology*, Mark Shaw defines revitalization as "indigenous movements of cultural change that creatively use the resources of early Christianity" (2008, 770). He elaborates as follows

> This definition suggests three interacting dynamics. The first is *contextualization* (the justice factor concerned with cultural change), which gives rise to the revival initially and is the revival's goal and outcome. The soil of revival is a collective sense of need and a discontent with the status quo. The fruit of revival is a change in the social system (when the movement is successful). The transformation that a movement of contextualization seeks may be one of statue (e.g. a change of identity from colonized victims to liberated sons and daughters of God) or a more systemic chance whereby actual political, economic or sociocultural power shifts from the status quo to the renewed people of God.
>
> The second dynamic is *indigenization*. This is the leadership factor, defining the key actors in the revival drama. . . . In global revivals leadership tends to arise "from below," from the ranks of the oppressed. The revival leadership is often plural rather than singular and inspires movements drawn from the young and the marginalized.
>
> The third dynamic is *inculturation*. This is the faith factor concerned with a return to a classic truth from which the church has drifted. . . . this "new light" of a freshly conceived Christianity penetrates deeply into the consciousness of leaders and followers during times of revival, producing a

paradigm shift in the worldview which in turn inspires a host of changes in the social and cultural systems. (2008, 770-771)

Shaw's definition is not one derived from a visionary leader, but of a process of adaptation that is channeled through micro-level agents, guided by generative leaders, and draws from internal memories and root programming. Hence, if one compares the template of Wallace's original model of revitalization and the Cusp of Change model enhanced model of revitalization, Shaw's description of revitalization finds a better fit with the latter than the former.

6.3.4 Christian Revitalization as a Spirit-imbued, Continuous, Systemic Process

In summary, following a biblical definition, Christian revitalization should in fact be Spirit-imbued as opposed to a psychological sickness, the normative state as opposed to the aberrant state, and grounded in discipleship as opposed to leadership charisma. As "strangers in a strange land" (Hebrews 11:1, 1 Peter 1:1, 17; 2:11), Christ-followers are on a pilgrimage toward the Kingdom *telos*. But far from being a geographic journey, no longer defined by a Temple, but by Christ's presence, the entire Church is in motion; ". . . normalcy would be pilgrimage. From now on their discipleship would be a liminal duet." (Zahniser 1997, 152). If so, Christian revitalization is a constant "steady-state" of Spirit-lead change in the life of the believer, not an isolated event of psychosis as a consequence of stress. Table 8 thus summarizes the comparisons between Wallace's model and the Complex Systems Cusp of Change model of Christian revitalization from this section.

Questions and Observations from the Consultations	Traditional, Wallacian model	Complex Systems Science-framed Cusp of Change model
Divergent Christianity exists in new groups and churches. How should we judge them?	It will depend on whether or not their reformulated mazeways define a new identity. New groups are to be seen as distinct groups.	Relationships between divergent Christianities are determined by the spatial relationships and shape of their trajectories
Is revitalization always good? All want it, but what sort? Individual or communal?	Revitalization is therapeutic, but is a discontinuous break with the old cultural mazeway. It is cultural, formed by a single leader	Revitalization is always good because it is part of the trajectory toward a defined *telos*. It can/should be both individual and communal
Are individual or communal forms problematic to revitalization?	Only the communal form is valid	Both forms are valid as they can be described within a single system
How do we know what is revitalized? Dynamics complex	Must follow the 5-phase definition of revitalization movements via visionary leader	Even though dynamics are complex, the model is robust enough to integrate complexity
What cannot or should not be revitalized because it is just a refreshment of old religious ideas?	Revitalization occurs only if it leads to a new mazeway	The trajectory location and the change context determines the elements to be revitalized
What ecclesiology dominates the revitalization moments?	Cultural Distortion Reformulation in visionary leader	Revitalization can occur through any agent. Diversity is strength of the church
What is the ecclesiology of a revitalized congregation?	Revitalization is leader driven	Revitalization occurs through harmony and network resonance, and in the releasing of positive deviants
Revitalization creates change in the dynamics of the status quo – some people win and some lose. How do we	Evaluation by two static states. Winners gain a new identity and are distinct from the losers	Through network analysis and the interactions among agents, winners and losers remain part of the

assess these dynamics?		same system and roles can alternate over time
If revitalization depends on social and spiritual relationships, what is the substance of these relationships?	Revitalization is a therapeutic response to social sickness	Revitalization is a transformative process through network resonance so that the entire system can achieve its *telos*

Revitalization that is noted operates most frequently and powerfully at the level of the laity. What is implied by this realization?	Problematic. Revitalization is through a visionary leader	Revitalization's core is a strengthening of internal and root programming of the laity. Positive deviants are key to informing the entire organization
Revitalization touches all dimensions and areas of human existence, even the earthly environment that sustains it. Is environmental theology an important supplement, and is revitalization as Christian environmentalism needed?	Revitalization is only organizational. The environment is only seen as the change agent	The interactions of agents, the organization, and the system are all integrated. Any change to one component changes every other component
Revitalization is related to an individual or local fellowships of people, based on developing relationships and discipling, in terms of collectivity (a whole tribe) and among people at the margins	Problematic Revitalization occurs through the visionary leader and s/he communicates it to everyone else	The revitalization response involves the entire organization, through generative leadership, positive deviants, and the resonant transmission of change through the entire network
Revitalization also occurs in studied, devotional isolation of retreats.	Valid only if this leads to a vision by the prophet or leader	Revitalization can occur through strengthening root programming and internal memory
Revitalization movements are very specific, with unique features	Revitalization is an intentional five-step process	No. Revitalization movements can occur through an infinite number of trajectories

Revitalization is related to human markers of "time" and "place", seasons and centers. It has a temporal and a geographical rationale, including crossing boundaries of eternity and time, as preeminently embodied in the life of Jesus Christ	Problematic Revitalization is a response to stress. It is coincidental and short-termed. A new mazeway may or may not include Christ in its original form.	Revitalization is a continuous process that enables an organization to fulfill its *telos*. The life of Christ defines both the root program and internal memory. It rests on the edge of chaos, in the Cusp of Change
Do renewals show similar marks across time and traditions? Yes, these similarities can be traced, but their patterns are unpredictable.	A renewal is not revitalization	Renewal can be considered an incremental step toward the larger process of revitalization
Can standards be set, or may standards, models, and examples be used as guidelines	Yes.	The model is heuristic to absorb examples, and sufficiently complex and fuzzy to integrate diversity.
It is not feasible to evaluate Christian movements early on, but only much later. Issues of change are not to be factored, and the tendency of movements to morph into new forms.	Correct. Revitalization can only be defined after evaluation of the second steady state	Incorrect. In the midst of revitalization, trajectories can determined and predict the course of the revitalization
Revitalization is cyclical. The vitality is recurring yet impossible to last	No. Revitalization is discrete and coincidental	Yes, revitalization is a continuous process and must be recurrent to achieve an organization's *telos*
Revitalization is not a new burst of strength. It is a "new birth"!	Yes	Yes. But birth is but a part of a larger process of maturity
The world is the locus for the relationship of God's revitalizing activity in human life	Revitalization is a therapeutic, psychological response to stress. There is no place for a	Strong Emergence allows for supernatural forces to exist and interact in the material

	supernatural power in the model.	environment and with micro-level agents
Sacrament is a visible sign of an invisible grace – and interactive dynamic, socially constructed	As long as it leads to the development of a new mazeway. Old sacramental rituals must have new meanings.	Sacraments are seen as the strengthening of internal memories and root programming to aid in responding to new contexts
The church is the Christocentric presence of God in the world	No. There is no place for a surpernatural power in the model	Strong Emergence establishes relationships between macro-level and micro-level agents in the revitalization process
The church is also an imperfect, growing body	The church is a homeostatic body and revitalizes only in response to stress	The church is a continuously revitalizing body that is fulfilling its *telos*
Do movements have to move outside the church in order to take root? Can we accept new movements within existing structures, or are they created by moving outside structures?	Yes. The old and new mazeways are incompatible, requiring a new identity	Revitalization can occur in a variety of trajectories, remaining within or bifurcating outward. They remain part of the same system
For whom, what, and what purpose is revitalization? Revitalization of the church for the church, or the church for the kingdom of God?	Revitalization is a response to stress and an intentional and conscious effort on behalf of humans	The purpose of revitalization is for an organization to fulfill its *telos*. An organization's vitality is when it is fulfilling its *telos*.
Asymmetries of gender, economics, and ethnic groups should be considered seriously in evangelism, but these have been largely unmentioned so far in revitalization discussion.	Not necessary as revitalization occurs in the visionary leader. The community is monolithic	The diversity of an organization is its strength. As change is diverse, so the diversity of agents enables an organization to respond to a diverse change via positive deviants
Christians are "renewa-	No. Renewal is not	Yes. Renewal is part of

lists", according to Todd Johnson.	revitalization and revitalization is only coincidental to stress	the process of revitalization
There is a rise in renewal movements at the beginning of the 21st century, according to Todd Johnson	As change is changing, organizations may not be able to maintain homeostasis and as such revitalization can be seen to be rising.	As change is changing, it is assumed that renewal movements should increase in frequency.
A new term, "vitalization movement" refers to a movement of person first hearing of encounter with God and Christianity	Only if it results in a change in mazeways, and only if the person becomes the visionary leader	It can be considered as part of the revitalization process in a positive deviant
It may be better to use a model, and a typology is difficult. Try to think of a Christian revitalized church by characteristics.	Model and its characteristics are strictly defined, though exceptions can be made	Model is comprehensive and inclusive, looks at characteristics, and is inherently fuzzy

(Irwin 2011, 239-240)

SUMMARY COMPARISON OF REVITALIZATION PROPERTIES	Christian Revitalization as defined by the consultations	Wallace's Traditional Model of Revitalization	Complex Systems Model of the Cusp of Change
Origin	Intentional *missio Dei* grounded in Scriptural mandate and the work of the Holy Spirit	Intentional, psychological, though therapeutic response, to sickness[13]	Intentional Systemic response to change in order to sustain a thriving ecology
Time Frame	Continuous Steady State	Discontinuous, discrete, and isolated between Steady-States	Continuous, Ongoing Steady State
Goal	Transformation to achieve the biblical *telos*	Construct a more satisfying culture	Achieve a systemic set of processes that sustains a thriving ecology (no end target, assuming continuous change)
Locus of Revitalization	The Church, "priesthood of all believers"	Visionary Leader	Positive Deviants in Collective of Micro-level Agents
Process	Discipleship to remember ancient identity	New Steady-State by *gestalt* by Visionary Leader with ambivalence to traditional or foreign material	Resonance through Unifying Identity through reinforcement of internal memory and "root" programming
Agency	Holy Spirit, Equipping Leaders, and the Diverse Body of Christ, the	Synthesizing and oftentimes a therapeutic process performed under extreme stress	Strong Emergence, Generative Leadership and Systems Intelligence and Posi-

---

[13] note Christian Revitalization more consistent than Wallace's understanding of classic process of cultural change leading one to question why it was used in the first place

	Church	by individuals already sick	tive Deviants
Directionality	Vertical and Horizontal Communion	Leader to Constituency	Bidirectional, Self-feeding Resonant Interaction across network

Table 8 - Comparison of Properties of Christian Revitalization reflecting the questions and observations of the consultations on Christian Revitalization

6.4 The Critical Importance of a More Complex Model

In closing, we are reminded that the choice of model is of critical importance to missiology. J.D. Payne writes,

> If our biblical and theological foundation is wrong, our missiology and methods are on tenuous grounds when it comes to the advancement of the kingdom among a population segment or people (xvi). . . . During the latter twentieth century, an evangelical pragmatism developed that resulted in many leaders seeking the latest and greatest methods to increase the numbers of people who were part of their churches. This divorce of our field-based methods from healthy missiology rooted deeply in a biblical and theological foundation resulted in numerous problems in the kingdom – the number of live bodies increased in our churches but not always with an equivalent increase in conversions and sanctification. (2013, xvii)

Consequently, Payne argues that

> The biblical and theological foundation and missionary methods are like two magnets. When turned in the proper directions, they adhere to one another. However, if their poles are changed by an improper orientation, then they repel one another. (xviii) . . . While the kingdom ethic we proclaim never changes, out contexts to change. And with changing context comes the reality of changing methods. (xix) . . . [consequently, our challenge is] for right thinking about missionary methods and the encouragement found in the spirit of mission – especially when we do not have all of the methodological answers to the challenges of our day. (xxi) (2013)

Without a doubt, Wallace's model of revitalization has served missiology well; but the twenty-first century context has changed significantly in the half century since Wallace introduced his model. Globalization has made the context more networked, more multi-leveled, and more complex. Linear system approaches and general linear realities may no longer be as useful and can be potentially harmful as they create blind spots and biases (Abbott 1988).

In response to increasing complexity, the advent of sufficiently capable computational tools has enabled hard and soft science researches to better visualize, and consequently, develop more representative models of reality. These advances have given breath and birthed from its conceptual womb the emerging paradigm of Complex Systems Science that is now matured in the hard sciences, and at least walking in the soft sciences.

As has been shown through the journal reviews, missiology hasn't even passed the mitotic stage of conception. As such, in the ever expanding and changing domain of complexity, missiology also needs to adapt Complex Systems Science-framed approaches to see the new realities of the twenty-first century. This new paradigm provides the lens necessary to missiologically contextualize the sacred and the profane in the increasingly diverse and complex contexts of twenty-first century. Hence, missiology should not be afraid to adopt new models, for such change is beneficial to God's mission.

This was made clear by Kenneth Nehrbass in his journal review of missiological journals. He used the methods of scientometrics to measure the rate at which new missiological information is being published and the rate at which this research is going out of date. He writes that the "discussion of out-dating may concern or embarrass scholars, as if it puts our credibility on the line. . . . [but] if our strategies are going out of date, this is a good indication that the world is changing and that we are continually updating our discipline in order to maximize our impact for the Kingdom of God." (2014, 291) Hence, as our hard and soft science siblings have already forged ahead with new mazeways for the twenty-first century context of continuous, complex change, it is time for missiology to adopt new mazeways as well.

6.5 Chapter Summary

1. This chapter critiques the traditional model of revitalization and argues that the Complex Systems-enhanced model of revitalization is more compatible with the characteristics and observed data of Christian revitalization.
2. Three primary characteristics of Complex Systems Science are highlighted, a call to historicity, network analysis and dimensional, and subsequently, interdisciplinary integration.
3. Historicity enlarges perspectives to see revitalization as part of an ongoing process in response to ongoing change as opposed to a response to increasing stress as a result of rapid, discontinuous change. Particularly in the twenty-first century context, change is no longer simple and linear, but complex and networked.

4. Historicity revisions revitalization as a continuous, ongoing steady-state (first differential) in the Cusp of Change. As such, Christian revitalization is the normative condition, not the exception, in the trajectory of Christianity. It is argued that by nature, Christianity itself must be continuously in change, always, in the Cusp of Change, as Christianity is defined only by crossing boundaries and transforming.

5. Network analysis enlarges the perspective to see revitalization as a resonant process that transmits change across organizational networks, not merely through the *gestalt* of a visionary leader. As such network analysis revisions conflicts as a means of communication, not a problem of communication. And it understands revitalization as a transmission process or resonance through the organization network, not a single act of *gestalt*.

6. Complex Systems Science allows for systemic integration across history, all fields, dimensions. The holistic nature of Complex Systems Science opens the doors, not just for all the subdisciplines of missiology to be integrated together, but opens the door for theology and science, including missiology, to be re-integrated into the rest of the academy after its marginalization during the Enlightenment.

7. Micro-level concepts point the locus of revitalization away from a visionary leader to understand the role of discipleship to mold the internal memories and programming of micro-level agents, the "priesthood of all believers" of the organizational network that is the global Church.

8. When shared core memories and programming are achieved through discipleship, resonance is possible throughout the organizational network of the Church, allowing for the transmission of new behaviors and patterns of thinking.

9. Through positive deviants gained through the local diversity of its collective constituents, incremental adaptations can be transmitted through the network and incorporated into the general character of churches. In the midst of rapid, complex change, Complexity Theory argues that diversity is the strength of organizations. This concept finds strong compatibility with the biblical understanding of the Church.

10. On the meso-level, Complex Systems analysis redefines the role of leaders as generative, enhanced by the degree of Systems Intelligence. As such, in contrast to the traditional model of revitalization, the role of a leader is not to *gestalt* the environment to produce a

new mazeway; rather, the role of the leader is to *gestalt* the network, equipping and enabling the network to *gestalt* a new mazeway.

11. On the macro-level, Complex Systems Science, from the position of strong emergence, opens the door to visualize the work of the Holy Spirit, and offers the universal hermeneutic of *missio Dei* as the metanarrative to interpret history.

12. Finally, this chapter argues that Christian revitalization is more consistent with a revitalization model that is a continuous, incremental steady-state process in the Cusp of Change compared to a discontinuous, isolated event.

Chapter 7

Developing Complex Systems Mazeways for 21st Century Multicultural Contexts

This chapter applies the Complex Systems Science-framed Cusp of Change model of Christian revitalization to the case study of multicultural, multicongregational, and multilingual church communities of the Chinese Diaspora in North America to demonstrate the robust and efficacious nature of this new approach, and concludes with suggesting characteristics for new mazeways for said churches for an ongoing process of revitalization in the Cusp of Change at the edge of the chaotic contexts of the twenty-first century realities. This chapter follows the three characteristics of the Complexity Theory of Christian revitalization outlined in the previous chapter: historicity, networks analyses, and dimensional integration.

7.1 *Gestalting* Historicity

Applying the Complex Systems Science-framed Cusp of Change model of Christian revitalization to the case of the multicultural multicongregational churches of the Chinese Diaspora in North America, Complex Systems analysis requires researchers to understand not just the differences between congregations at a specific point in time, but asks, "Where is each congregation's identity in their immigration assimilation, and/or revitalization, narrative?" Unlike the traditional revitalization model, Complex Systems analysis does not begin with, "Is this congregation in revitalization?" This question becomes secondary and will be answered in the course of answering the primary question.

While a Complex Systems Science-framed approach may also conclude that conflict arises from the more rigid and inflexible nature of the Confucianist cultural identity, Complex Systems analysis recognizes that conflict is not necessarily a negative factor, but merely part of the trajectory of the particular historical context of an organization shaped by its trajectory in the Cusp of Change. In contrast to the traditional, linear approach which may merely place blame on the Confucianist cultural identity as the group "in stress," the dynamic nature of Complex Systems analysis would enlarge the scale of study and take a longer historical perspective to recognize that at other points in time, the Confucianist cultural identity can also be seen as a critical necessity in stabilizing the church and not an impediment. Hence, from a Complex Systems Science perspective, every agent has a role in sustaining continuity of the revitalization condition.

For example, if one considers Figure 22, one sees that when the Mandarin-speaking congregation was in the majority, the more structured (inflexible) nature of the Confucian cultural identity would have been considered a positive influence in securing new immigrants in a strange land. More will be discussed in the section on Dimensional Integration and Micro-level Agency, but for the moment, it is noted that this observation is consistent with the observation made by John V. Taylor when he wrote about changes in attitude across generations

> In the life and growth of every young church, it seems, there is one perennial disappointment which more than any other grieves and bewilders both the missionary and the student of church history. Before the first generation of converts has passed away gospel is turned into law. The first fine careless rapture of a new discovery deteriorates into a sorry story of rules of conduct, backsliding, and church discipline. (2004, 153)

Taylor also does not place blame, but provides the context of such changes as he continues

> The converts to a new faith are under the overwhelming impact of a very few great simplicities. They have discovered, for example, that God is personal and accessible, or the name of Christ means simply that they are accepted into fellowship in a way they have never known elsewhere, or the person of Jesus himself has won their devoted though largely uncomprehending allegiance. They would rather die than deny or throw away these new-found realities. (2004, 153)

Taylor thus concludes, citing Professor Greenslade who

> ... analysed the inevitable build-up of the structures of legalism in the early centuries of church history and compared their problems with those of the so-called younger churches of the present day. Discrimination and an element of legalism, he argues, appear of necessity at the point of entry into the Christian church even before they become necessary in the fellowship of believers. (2004, 154-155)

If so, then during the initial period of the immigrant Chinese church's history, the Confucian identity was a positive critical factor, not a negative factor, that enabled Chinese Christians to hold on to their faith and survive as strangers in a strange land. It was the factor which formed *communitas* during the liminal period of Chinese immigrants (Lee 2003, Adeney 2011, 6)

But as the social and cultural contexts change and the second generation emerges, the Confucian cultural identity is no longer representative of the entire church. Had the Confucian-derived Mandarin congregation majority been less structured and more flexible, it could have been more able to readily adapt to the changing context.

For example, this was indeed the case of the Cantonese-speaking congregation who came primarily from Hong Kong, as noted from the interviews of several church leaders from different churches (see Table 4 and 5). Because their cultural identity is a centuries-long amalgamation of both Confucianist and Western cultural influences, coupled with a longer history of Christianity in their subpopulation, the Cantonese-speaking congregation tended to be more flexible, and more readily able to adapt. They would have perceived the changing contexts not as a discontinuity that needed to be challenged, but with a longer, historical perspective, merely in curve in the larger trajectory in the Cusp of Change.

As such, several church leaders interviewed commented that the Cantonese congregation was the "glue" for the church during the times of conflict (Table 4). Indeed, church leaders from Hong Kong more often than not were the mediators in the conflicts reported by different churches. They understood the curves in the trajectories and helped the entire church make appropriate adjustments to stay within the Cusp of Change.

For the older generation of overseas Chinese in the Mandarin-speaking congregations who had a more entrenched Confucianist mindset which emphasized structure and maintaining the *status quo*, they tended to be more resistant to change. In fact, as noted from the data, despite a growing Mandarin-speaking population in the city, because of their unwillingness to change, several of the Mandarin-speaking congregations stagnated and even declined in number (e.g. churches A, B, and C, Table 6). Consequently, even as the social context changed, their inability to adapt resulted in an increasing marginalization from the mainland Mandarin-speaking population, and the Cantonese-speaking and English-speaking congregations. In the terminology of Complexity Theory, these churches, though stable and remaining in the Cusp of Change because they did not split, gravitated toward the stability attractor rather than remaining balanced between the "old ways" and "new ways." What was adaptive, in changing times, became mal-adaptive.

Hence, the dynamic aspect of Complex Systems analysis not only draws the same conclusion as traditional, linear analysis, it is also able to enhance understanding with respect to the historical context. The added benefit is that Complex Systems analysis does not tie blame to the agent of conflict, but understands that conflict is a consequence of the change process. In other words, how well a church revitalizes or does not revitalize is not a question of right or wrong, but who is best able to understand, represent, and lead the church through change at each particular period of the church's history.

Such a finding retains unity in the church because it retains the critical importance of each agent within the organization. Rather than assigning blame, the Complex Systems Science-framed approach helps the entire church understand the critical and necessary role of Mandarin-speaking overseas Chinese in the larger historical framework. As well, the Cusp of Change models provides the church organization with a means of cultivating church harmony and discerning who should be leading the church to navigate change as the environmental context changes over time.

A Complex Systems Science-framed approach, because it focuses on an organization's history, understands the root causes of conflict and that conflict is merely part of the trajectory, perhaps as the trajectory bifurcates or bends as its gravitates back toward the attractor. With this frame of reference, rather than resulting in a power struggle or a church split, churches can proactively sustain a healthy and vibrant organization by shifting the attractor so that equilibrium is maintain and the organization kept within the Cusp of Change.

And in such a Cusp of Change model perspective, who is to say that in a future history context, the Confucianist cultural context might once again be needed to bring the entire church to unity? The Cusp of Change model helps marginal groups in an organization understand that they should remain in the congregation as they will most likely play a critical role as the context changes at some point in time in the historical trajectory. In Complex Systems analysis, it is not a "process of elimination," but all the agencies in the organization would realize their own critical role – as well as the critical roles of "the other" – in the unfolding story of community. For in the Cusp of Change model, as trajectories are defined by its attractors, the loss of any attractor could very well result in an organization falling out of the Cusp of Change into stagnation or chaos.

It is interesting to note that Taylor contends that critical role each group plays in the overall historical trajectory of a church. Quoting William Freytag, Taylor argued that such legalism was a necessary prelude to revival:

> There is an important truth to this. For legalism of a certain kind is a symptom of a more mature conscience. It expresses a new awareness of moral demands and a more penetrating recognition of sin. It may even be necessary for a Christian community to experience the bankruptcy of ethical self-effort and striving before it can re-discover the springs of unmerited grace, just as John Wesley had to come to the end of the moralism of the Holy Club before his heart could be 'strangely warmed' with the assurance of forgiveness. To this extent the missionary who is disenchanted by the rigidity and censoriousness of the church in which he is serving may take hope from a sense of history. (2004, 158)

In Taylor's understanding, the poles of legalism and freedom, in the case of Figure 22, Inflexibility and Flexibility, are the two poles which define the trajectory of a church. They are not in conflict, but each has its particular role in sustaining the trajectory of the whole system within the Cusp of Change, that is, within the ongoing, continuous process of revitalization.

Indeed, others have made similar observations with regard to the systemic trajectory of churches. In his seminal work, *The Life Cycle of a Congregation,* Saarinen (2001) also recognized this process in the life of the church. He writes that

> ... it seems to be a natural law that growth and decline progress from stage to stage. Experience has indicated that once in the growth phase, a congregation will progress from Infancy to Prime through the Adolescent stage and, similarly; once a congregation is in the decline phase, it will pass from Maturity to Bureaucracy through the Aristocratic stage.
>
> Second, development and decline do not progress uninterruptedly from stage to stage. Movement from one stage to another is marked by a cyclical process of dying and rising again ... (6)

Similarly, Hiebert *et al* (1999) concluded that "The life of the church, like any religious institution, depends on one generation passing on the faith to the next. The weakness is the threat of nominalism. The spiritual vision of the founders is dimmed as it is routinized in institutional life. What began as a movement becomes a bureaucratic organization." (335)

In summary, the dynamic nature of Complex Systems analysis guards researchers from focusing narrowly on a particular discontinuous point in time, but pulls them back to consider the larger historical context in order to understand the initial conditions and the trajectory the subject or group has taken. Such a perspective allows one to understand how the role of all parties flexes over the course of the historical narrative in sustaining the church in the revitalization steady-state. In so doing, it prevents researchers and church leaders from assigning blame to conflicts and problems, but instead, recognizes every party's necessary role in shaping the trajectories that sustain the church within the Cusp of Change that is revitalization. Such a perspective prevents the choosing sides and see every role not as *either/or*, but *both/and*, with each working to a larger design. In fact, the broader perspective has the potential to help churches understand who should be the leaders in each change context, allowing churches remain in a revitalization steady-state to both navigate and even mediate change.

7.2 *Gestalting* the Networks

The efficacy of a revitalization model seen through the lens of Complex Systems analysis is revealed in the case study of Chinese churches in the North American Diaspora, showing greater consistency between observed phenomena with network theory rather than the Wallacian model of revitalization. Viewed through the traditional model, the observations would lean strongly toward individual leaders in each church. From the observations of church change (Table 6), one might have concluded that it was a consequence of the loss or replacement of a new visionary leader. Nevertheless, the peripheral data reveal that some churches do not seem to fit the traditional pattern of revitalization, similar to that which was observed in the case studies in the consultations on Christian revitalization (Johnson-Miller 2013, 168-169). In these churches, the interviews reveal that development of new *gestalts* was occurring not through a visionary leader, but through a group of leaders across congregations working as a team. Leaders at the "nodes of networks" (Wilhite 2006, 1013) were generating the new *gestalt* in aggregate.)

Network analysis in Complexity Leadership is particularly helpful in understanding the leadership changes in the life trajectories of multiethnic, multicongregational Chinese church communities. Using Complex Leadership Theory to describe the leadership network of immigrant churches, one might describe the leadership structure during the initial period after their founding as that of a "star network" (Figure 25). In this initial phase, it is the senior leader who *gestalts* the changing cultural context and derives a new mazeway. But, unlike monocultural churches that do not transform in structure, as a multiethnic multicongregational church matures and the structures of churches became more complex with new leaders emerging from each congregation, the functional leadership network can be described as gradually transforming into a "ring network." In this latter, mature phase, while there may still be a senior leader, *gestalts* are progressively formulated by a leadership team rather than through a single leader.

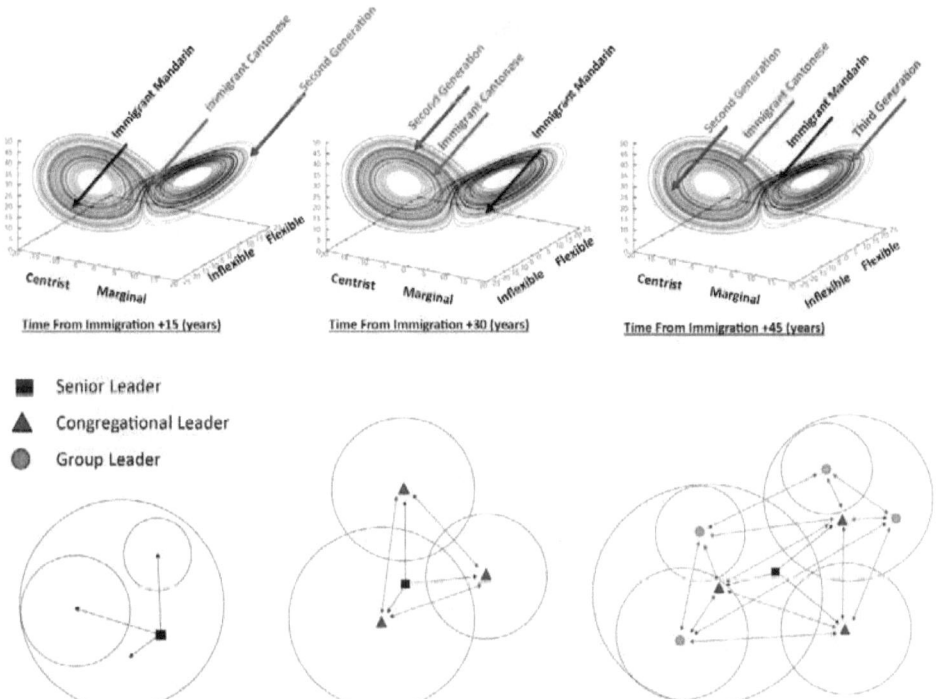

Figure 25 - Expansion of Church Networks over Time

Complex Systems analysis provides the means to understanding the shift from a star network to ring network as such transformations in leadership networks have been shown to alter the context of the entire system (Wilhite 2006, 1038). As a network structure moves from a "star" to a "ring" network, the system becomes increasing complex. The flow of communication increases by several factors with the increased number of connections, their directionality, whether unidirectional or bidirectional, and their weighting based on whether they are meso- or micro- level agents, the level of influence of each directional pathway (as seen in uneven flow of messages). It is in such complexity that the power of Complex Systems analysis is seen, being able to describe and model the leadership discourse migrating

... from an exchange between leaders and followers to leadership as dynamic interactions of lateral influence among peer members of a group.... leadership was characteristic of the entire organization, in which "leaders roles overlapped, complemented each other, and shifted from time to time and from person to person" (Barnes and Kriger 1986, 16). A more inclusive concept of leadership became fully apparent.... They found that conventional leadership thought did not accommodate a new division of labor that was interdependent and dispersed. Leadership was being talked about as a phenomenon that emerged from and was embodied in the interactions of participants. The research was intense and several leadership conceptualizations based on this new framework emerged, including *shared leadership,* which was defined as "a dynamic interactive influence process among individuals in groups for which the objective is to lead one another to the achievement of group or organizational goals" (Pearce and Conger 2003, 1), and *distributed leadership,* which was characterized by the criterion of "conjoint agency." (Schwandt and Szabla 2007, 55)

In the context of a network shift, relationships across the congregational trajectories become critical (please refer to Figure 25). During the initial phase of an immigrant Chinese church, a more rigid structure is needed to help immigrants in their liminal phase to develop new identities in their new North American cultural context. In a star network, with the relationships centered, Wallace's linear model of revitalization can be applied. As such, it is the visionary leader who identifies with the majority who *gestalts* the mazeway and leads the church through change. Such a leader is essential as the church leadership network structure is in a star configuration.

But as a multiethnic multicongregational church matures and moves to an increasingly complex structure, as immigrants move from a singular identity to a diversity of congregational identities, a single leader no longer necessarily reflects the majority identity, and most likely lacks the ability to integrate the increased complexities. Instead, separate leaders arise from the different congregations, and it is an amalgamation of these leaders' *gestalts* that provide the mazeway for the entire church. As Drath proposed "people construct reality through their interactions within worldviews ... [They do it] when they explain things to one another, tell each other stories, create models and theories ... and in general when they interact through thought, word, and action." (2001, 136 quoted in Lichtenstein *et al* 2007, 135) Hence, in this latter, complex phase of a multiethnic, multicongregational church, leaders who represent diverse views and have the flexibility to adapt are the essential ingredients to *gestalt* the new mazeway forward in order to maintain unity of the entire church.

The relationships across congregational trajectories provide insight into the rise of Conflicts. Using Figure 25 (also Figure 23), one can postulate that conflict arises when leaders from the different congregations are no longer aligned in their immigrant trajectories and begin to deviate due to differences in their velocity of travel. Here, their location along the immigrant trajectory is determined by their cultural initial conditions, their starting point, and the velocity of travel, defined by their flexibility to cultural adaptation. Greater flexibility results in greater velocity and less flexibility results in a slower velocity along the trajectory.

For bicultural leaders who have been raised in a multitude of cultural influences, such as the immigrants from Hong Kong with a long history of cultural amalgamation and second generation Chinese Americans who were raised in two cultures. These populations have a greater tendency to be more flexible and as such, have a faster velocity of adaptation along the immigration history of the cultural assimilation trajectory.

However, for monocultural overseas Chinese leaders, raised in the more rigid Confucian culture, there is far less flexibility to adapt. As such, their travel velocity along the trajectory of immigrant adaptation is much slower with respect to the other congregational leaders. Consequently, they begin to lag behind the other congregations. It is at this point of divergence in trajectories as a result of differing velocities that conflicts begin to emerge.

In this latter phase, Complex Systems Science would argue that the rise in conflict is not necessarily a result of "stress," as the traditional linear model of revitalization would suppose, but due to the response of leaders as the leadership structure transforms from a star to a ring network in tandem with increasing separation across the congregational immigrant trajectories. Again, it should be noted that such an explanation does not cast blame, but provides a greater understanding as to how the conflicts developed. In other words, as "... all of the roles are interrelated.... meaning emerges in the 'spaces between' people rather than in the acts of individual." (Lichtenstein 2007, 135) As such, the mitigation of conflict is not understood to occur from the elimination of one party or another party – for that would collapse the network, but understood to be by the process of re-aligning the relationships across leaders at the "nodes of the network" of the meso-level ring network.

More importantly, Complex Systems analysis offers a pathway toward resolution of the conflict; conflict mitigation is possible if the travel velocities are adjusted so that the locations across the immigrant adaptation trajectories are once again realigned and their distances reduced. Such moves would bring the ring network into balance. Either some leaders would have to accelerate adaptation or other leaders would have to decelerate adaptation. For the wellbeing of the church, church leaders must "submit one to another" in unity (Ephesians 5:21) to form "a new man in Christ." (Ephesians 2:15) As Johnson-Miller notes, "Diaspora tensions between faith and culture give birth to new 'multicultural' forms that bring new life to immigrant communities...." (2013, 167)

Indeed, as Complex Systems Science matures, it will not only provide the conceptual models and metaphors to recognize and describe the emergence of social movements, such as organizational revitalization, but may one day provide predictive tools, such as agent-base modeling (ABM) simulations, to help organizations discern the mazeways that future trajectories must travel. As computational power continues to grow, models will only become better able to mimic reality, "... to identify a wide range of active forces, and how they potentially intersect, evolve, and coincide with particular forms of revitalization" (Johnson-Miller 2011, 13) responding to the call of missiologists for tools that not only study past and ongoing phenomena, but as well to initiate and predict the trajectories of revitalization. If so, "While the Holy Spirit is *the* catalytic force, many other Spirit empowered forces exist. Forces coincide with revitalization goals and dimensions can be organized according to a variety of generative themes.... meta-themes associated with the breadth and complexity of revitalization forces." (Johnson-Miller 2011, 13).

In summary, as the global human contexts continue to become increasingly interconnected, missiologists must adapt and learn how to apply Complex systems analysis to overcome the limitations and bias of traditional models. Such a paradigm shift will not only help missiologists understand the process of responding to change, but as well, allow missiologists to aid the Church in the navigation, participation, and even the mediation of, change.

7.3 *Gestalting* Dimensional Integration

From the discussion in the last chapter, it is clear that Complex Systems Science can provide a more robust framework for analysis than the traditional Wallacian model. Rather than trying to argue whether or not a movement was a revitalization movement or not and trying to fit events into the five-phase pattern, a Complex Systems-enhanced revitalization model increases the dimensional approaches of analysis and creates a system perspective of the data collected that is more robust integratively, and more importantly, creates mazeways for missiologists and church leaders to mediate the organization such that it is better able to respond and adapt to changing realities. And because the foundation of Complex Systems analysis recognizes the bidirectional interaction between the environment, network, and collective constituents, Complex Systems analyses possess the potential for mediating the change process itself. As such, Complex Systems analysis does not merely evaluate a historical event, but provides a dynamic analysis that can be used to predict mazeways forward through change so that an organization may achieve its *telos*.

To validate the application of Complex Systems analysis, this section examines the case study data on the micro- and meso- levels. The macro-level analysis is not included because it is a theoretical construct and cannot be validated at this time. However, a discussion of possible avenues for future research of the macro-level is provided in Chapter 8.

7.3.1 Micro-level Agency

For the Chinese churches of the case study, the Christian journey of discipleship has been described as a liminal process of cultural and social adaptation to a new culture (Lee 2003, Adeney 2011). As such, it is not just an isolated event, but can also be a continuous, ongoing, process. Chinese Christians are "... placed at the edge of both worlds and thus not at the center of either – a situation that puts me betwixt and between those two worlds." (Lee 2003, 11) Hence, "revitalization" is not an isolated period in a Chinese Christian's immigrant life, but a lifelong process of cultural transformation.

If the conclusions of these missiologists are correct, supported by the concepts of micro-level agency from Complex Systems Science, then Chung's definition of Christian revitalization as praxis is correct. The data suggests that the churches that are able to maintain a vibrant organizational life defined by unity, generational relevance, and the assimilation of newcomers, are in the process of continual revitalization because of their intentional integration of the discipleship making process throughout their organizational network and across their ministries. Such an emphasis strengthens the "root programming" of the Christian identity, allowing micro-level agents to remain a part of the *status quo* as well adapt to changing cultural contexts. Steven O'Malley writes, that

> ... it is Christian memory which is largely responsible for Christianity to be constantly generating revitalization and reform movements. Remembering who is our God, and how God has acted redemptively in our past, chiefly in the saving work of Jesus Christ as witnessed in apostolic testimony, is basic to expecting and facilitating new manifestations of that redemptive life, in the ministry of the Holy Spirit, among the people of God." (2011, 197)

Complex Systems Science would define such a revitalization trajectory as the continuous process that sustains the delicate balance of keeping the organization in "Criticalization," on the "Cusp of Change," balancing stability on one side, and promoting adaptation to change on the other side.

One piece of evidence of this stabilization is the impact of the Cantonese and English-speaking congregations in the case study churches. As noted before, several church leaders had voiced that they are often the "glue" for the entire church (see Table 4); in other words, these members have an influence beyond their own congregations. Their ability to mediate conflicts and stabilize the church is generally believed to be a result of their longer history of discipleship. Most of the Cantonese and English congregation members are second-generation Christians, the majority having been raised in Christian homes. Consequently, Complex Systems Science would argue that their "memory" and "internal programming" are much more ingrained than other micro-level agents, for example, mainland Chinese Christians, most having converted within a ten year period. The Cantonese and English congregation members, ingrained with what Walls calls a "cross-generational salvation," serve as the glue, as arbiters for "real Christianity." It is this "glue" that in turn stabilizes the entire church and ameliorates the influences of the environment.

As well, because most children's and youth ministries are run by the English congregation, Chinese churches which have an English congregation, equipped with a means of cross-generational discipleship, are empowered to adapt to change such that the entire church is able to maintain the forward direction toward the church's *telos*. In many ways, because they are already well adapted in their immigrant journey, they serve as positive deviants that are "reprogramming" the emerging generations of the church.

Hence, Complexity Systems Science revisions Christian revitalization away from solely relying on the Wallacian model that channels culture reformulation through a discrete visionary leader, and expands the possible trajectories of change to include micr-level agents. Complexity Systems Science redefines revitalization such that it embraces the multiplexity of Christian revitalization trajectories that are observed in global realities. Many of these trajectories are through an incremental, continuous process toward a specific *telos* through discipleship, the sustaining of the internal memory of existing micro-level agents and the provision of an assimilation avenue to "root program" newcomers. Such shared memories and programming allow for resonance that can propagate the adaptations of positive deviants across the entire organizational network.

7.3.2 Meso-level Role of Leadership

In the same manner, meso-level concepts of Complex Systems Science regarding the role of leaders add a level of robustness to the traditional Wallacian model. While Wallace's original revitalization model may have been able to explain the role of founding pastors when each Chinese church was founded, it may not sufficiently robust to describe how churches adapted, or were unable to adapt, in the contemporary multiethnic, multigenerational, multicongregational contexts of each church. In contrast, Complex Systems Science, through the concepts from Systems Intelligence, well explain the roles and interactions of church leaders, both the senior leader and/or the leadership team, in sustaining a revitalizing community through the concepts of generative leadership.

Of significance from the data is the critical impact of leaders who possess Systems Intelligence, that is, they have a broad understanding of the cultures and of the church organization. From Table 6, one notes growing, less conflicted churches when their leaders are bicultural and have a systemic view of the church (see churches D, E, and F) This is in contrast to churches where leaders are monocultural and the senior leadership position is seen as administrative (churches A, B and C). In other words, these leaders see their primary role as coordinators and focus on reducing points of conflict instead of recognizing conflict as a manifestation of emerging positive deviancy.

The leadership transitions of the churches also hint at the importance of Systems Intelligence. Of note is church D which continues to grow rapidly. Among the six churches, the senior leader has perhaps the strongest understanding of the church organization as an integrated whole. More importantly, from interviews with his leadership team, the senior leader in church D is perceived as being intentional and working hard to ensure every leader and every congregation understands their role in the entire church organization and are equipped and supported to fulfill their unique ministries. The senior leader of church D is seen to have a working, open leadership culture in contrast to the other churches where open leadership is more an ideal rather than actual practice; one of the church D leaders commented that "he 'walks the walk' as well as 'talks the talk'."

In contrast, leaders in other churches may talk about unity, but in reality lean more toward a hierarchical, managerial mindset which seeks to suppress conflict; in other words, unity is defined as the absence of conflict. Again, this example validates Complexity Leadership Theory's concept of generative leadership.

Undoubtedly, the leader in church D has a charismatic quality, and proponents of the traditional revitalization model could argue that it is the leader's vision and charisma that is driving the church's revitalization. But it is important to recognize that the leader in church D works primarily in the Mandarin-speaking congregation; he has only infrequent relationships with the other congregations. Hence, the senior leader of church D must by necessity rely on other leaders in the other congregations to lead the entire church. If so, then Complexity Leadership Theory could more easily explain the overall church health as a network phenomenon in contrast to the more traditional revitalization model which seeks to make direct connections with the leader himself. In fact, Wallace himself, contra Weber, did not believe such a transfer of power to be part of the revitalization model. To Wallace, Weber was only "... discussing a quality of leadership, and one which is found in contexts other than that of revitalization movements." (1956, 274)

Yet one of the key characteristics is the willingness of church D's senior leader to grant freedom to the other leaders to respond to environmental change as they saw fit; this is particularly manifested in the church's continued willingness for church planting. More than merely sending off a church plant, the senior leader willingly sacrifices the stability of the church by mobilizing the entire church to support the church plant. In terms of Complexity Theory, the senior leader allows positive deviants to undergo the process of adapting to environmental changes. Hence, while other churches have planted churches in the past, many have stopped doing so as church growth slowed (see Table 2), seeking to conserve resources. In contrast, church D continues to plant churches – and continues to grow rapidly.

The actions of church D's senior leader are all characteristics of generative leadership as he enables the emergence of positive deviants in his leadership team and in new church plants. According to Goldstein *et al*, generative leadership

> . . . appreciates the "nucleation" process of emergence: the see of novelty represents on the first step in an iterative sequence of dissemination. Once the new structure takes hold in one place, it has a much greater likelihood of spreading to additional areas, potentially reconfiguring the entire attractor. Here again, by going against the typical response of reinforcing current stabilizing order, generative leadership facilitates subtle emergence processes such as reducing the number of parts in the new organizational entity while increasing its functionality. In both cases the key is to balance the top-down urge to facilitate emergence with the bottom-up messiness and uncertainty that are inherent in recombinations that work. (2010, 186)

The process of church planting is, in essence, what Goldstein *et al* describe as nucleation. This is most likely why church D continues to grow rapidly in contrast to the other churches which, in some ways, are seeking to stabilize the trajectories around existing attractors, but in actuality creating imbalance between stabilization and change.

Churches which seek to stabilize and conserve resources are, in fact, destabilizing their organization from the continuous revitalization in the Cusp of Change. For these churches, they are moving from the Cusp of Change at the edge of Chaos and moving toward conservation; the consequence is stagnation as they are no longer willing to risk adapting to change. As one of the Mandarin congregation leaders of church B commented, "We need to take care of our founding generation and maintain the roots of our church as a Mandarin-speaking church." Consequently, the Mandarin-speaking service continues to sing traditional hymns, but, as well, is graying and has decreased ten percent in attendance between 2007 and 2013. As a consequence, the other congregations, particularly the English-speaking congregation, has also suffered. Without a growing Mandarin-speaking congregation, the influx of second generation Chinese has also stunted the English-speaking congregation. Without Systems Intelligence and only a singularly-driven perspective, church B is on its way to, if not already, falling out of the Cusp of Change.

Hence, the focus of Complex Systems Science on sustaining the Cusp of Change appears more compatible with the observed data, and provides more insight into how to "revitalize." Revitalization is seen as the normative state, stagnation the aberrant state.

In contrast, the traditional model considers revitalization only as a discontinuous, isolated event; if so, one wonders what might such an event look like in the real world? Several possibilities come to mind.

First, such an event could be a "revival." There could be an outworking of the Holy Spirit that revitalizes a church. But if such a revitalization movement enters a steady state, would it not imply that the church is once again stagnant in a homeostatic state that is outside the Cusp of Change?

Another manifestation of the traditional model of revitalization could be a church split or the formation of a new denomination in which a group follows a new paradigm. One might then wonder why any church would want to be "re-vitalized?"

An alternative manifestation for a discontinuous paradigm shift would be the removal of an existing leader for a new leader or the hiring of a new visionary leader. But again, the observations from the case studies suggest that the installation of a new leader does not necessarily revitalize a church (see Table 6). A revitalization – or lack of revitalization, instead, appears to be dependent on whether or not the new leader possesses a broader cultural perspective, a Systems Intelligence, and whether s/he possesses the flexibility and willingness to adapt to change.

Hence, while Complex Systems Science-framed models can account for Wallacian revitalization, it allows for an infinite number of other revitalization trajectories. Like the trajectories of Oracle and IBM described in Chapter 3, trajectories that are micro-level, incremental, and guided by generative leadership may in the end be the more preferred and beneficial path for most churches.

In summary, one finds the concepts of generative leadership from Complexity Leadership Theory much more consistent in explaining differences among the case study churches in contrast to the traditional revitalization model. As such, this section argues that re-visioning the existing revitalization model through the lens of Complex Systems Science results in more robust and inclusive models of revitalization that can more realistically describe the diverse phenomena found in multiethnic, multigenerational, networked contexts of twenty-first century realities.

7.4 Model Integration

Figure 26 illustrates what an integrated Complex Systems Science-framed model of a CIC on the Cusp of Change may look like. In the top right hand corner, the Lorenz pattern shows the perspective of the leaders for reference. It reveals some leaders as marginalized and inflexible, but other leaders with are centrist and flexible. The diagram shows that even when a senior leader is inflexible and marginalized, the change process can still occur.

190 Revitalizing Missions on the Cusp of Change

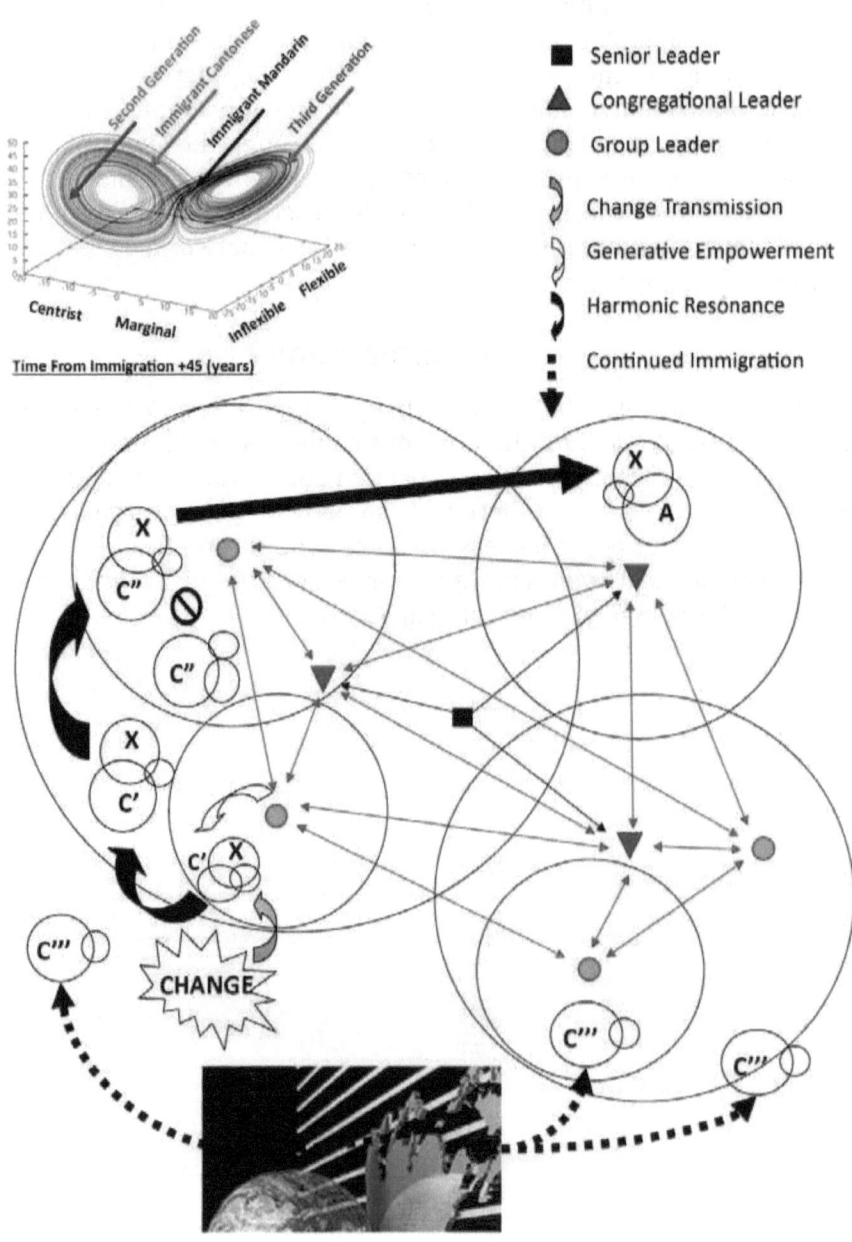

Figure 26 - CIC Church on the Cusp of Change

At the bottom of the page, the dashed lines show that the flow of immigration continues and that new immigrants continue to enter the CIC context and some begin to attend the church. Immigrants are labeled C', C", and C"' to differentiate the period of time each immigrant enters the context.

In the lower left hand corner, a change in the context has taken place. The change is noticed, not by any leader, but by a positive deviant, a micro-level agent who, through a particular relationship illustrated by the gray arrow, notices the change.

A generative leader recognizes that there is a beneficial change in the positive deviant and, illustrated by the white arrow, mentors and encourages him/her. The positive deviant then communicates this new behavior via harmonic resonance to others in the CIC, illustrated by the black arrow. One should note that the "X" circle, implying that the level of spiritual formation are similar, suggesting harmonic resonance. It should be noted that the cultural identity is not the primary factor of the resonance, but the "X" circle, the diameter defined by the level of Christian identity, a measure of spiritual formation. The diagram illustrates this by the black arrows impinging on C', C", and A members; this is intended to show the transcultural transformation nature of harmonic resonance achieved through a shared Christian identity.

Not all members can resonate with the positive deviant. If one looks at the second member of the resonant chain, there is a failure to transmit the change to a dissonant member, illustrated by a smaller "X" circle.

This is obviously a highly simplified representation of a Complex Systems Science-framed Cusp of Change model. Nevertheless, it illustrates the gist of the Christian revitalization process in a CIC on the Cusp of Change.

Most readers will still find this "simplified" model rather complex. But that is the intended purpose of a Complex Systems Science-framed model – to help researchers avoid biases toward reductionist solutions. A Complex Systems Science-framed model is intended to force researchers to step back and take in the entire system perspective, then consider all the potential possibilities to describe what is observed in complex realities (see Byrne 1998 and Castellani and Hafferty 2009).

But as well, Complex Systems analysis can aid researchers to visualize interactions and understand the roles of every agent and their interactions on multiple levels. In actual Complex Systems analysis, the entire model could be analyzed using Multiple Analysis of Variance methods (MANOVA) across the system in the simplest, static form of analysis. And in the most sophisticated form, the model would be represented in an Agent-based Model (ABM) computer simulation. Once the model conforms to actual data, one can then alter the network structure and associated variables of leaders and micro-level agents to understand how the change process permeates through the entire system. As well, one can alter macro-level, internal memory, and root programming variables to account for the work of the Holy Spirit, and observe how the model responds to such changes.

Many computational tools are already available and can be modified for missiological research. If a missiologist has access to a smartphone, iPad or other table, not to mention a computer, s/he already has within one's hands, the necessary tool to initiate a Complex Systems-framed paradigm for study. It is merely a matter of making the paradigm shift to Complex Systems Science and embracing its metaphors, methods, and models for missiological research applications.

7.5 Chapter Summary: Formulating a New Mazeway through Rapid, Complex Change

The context of the multicultural, multicongregational Chinese church in North America is changing. Environmentally, immigration patterns are shifting in composition and complexity. As well, the North American social and cultural realities are continuously changing. Internally, the composition of the congregations are shifting - old leaders are retiring and new leaders emerging; people from new immigrant groups are joining churches, and new generations are rising with their own distinctive cultural worldview. In such a context, as the organizational network grows, relationships and their interactions are becoming increasingly complex, potentially increasing conflicts with the breakdown of resonance and equilibria.

In such a context of rapid, complex change, how can Chinese churches maintain an continuous process of revitalization, that is, adaptation, in the Cusp of Change?

From the discussion, Complex Systems analysis offers insights that allow for the formulation of new mazeways through the rapidly and continuously changing context. Five critical factors, though not inclusive of all factors, emerge from the observed phenomena.

First, churches must understand their historical context and recognize that change does not necessarily lead to discontinuity, but that continuous, ongoing processes are alternate, even desirable, trajectories for revitalization. As such, churches do not need to fear change. They must, however, develop a process of adaptation that will allow them to remain in the Cusp of Change. Revitalization should be seen as the normative state the Church, not a transitory period.

Second, churches must recognize that the hiring a new visionary leader or adopting trendy programs are not necessarily the means of revitalization. They may be helpful, but only in a supportive capacity. Rather, churches should strengthen their internal memory and root programming. The mazeway through change is discipleship, the strengthening of the collective identity, *imago Dei*, that will enable resonance to occur throughout the entire church (John 13:34-38). Christian revitalization is Christian practice; it is the fulfillment of the Great Commission to "make disciples of all nations" (Matthew 28:19). Christian revitalization revolves around "loving God and love one another," (Matthew 22:36-40) that is, to understand the macro-level perspective and the micro-level perspective.

Third, churches must see diversity as the foundation of unity, not its enemy. It is in diversity that positive deviants emerge who will guide the entire church through change. Church unity is not one of control, but one of empowering "the priesthood of all believers" to exercise their spiritual gifts for the welfare of the entire Church (1 Corinthians 12, Romans 12:5-8)

Fourth, churches should look for generative leaders with System Intelligence. Their task is not to *gestalt* a new mazeway, but to help the church network *gestalt* the mazeway. As such, leadership entails the equipping and empowerment the collective constituency, the identification, mobilization, and support of positive deviants, and to guide network formation such that resonance can be achieved across the entire church (Ephesians 4:11-12). Another aspect of the generative leader's responsibility is to guide, not reduce, conflict, for conflict is oftentimes part of the pathway to change. Conflict is the manifestation of positive deviancy which needs to be heard, evaluated, and if found to be a necessary behavior to respond to change, released to resonate through the network (Acts 1:8, 1 Corinthians 11:1-2, Philippians 3:17).

Fifth, generative leaders must hold in focus the *telos* of the Church (Hebrews 10:24-25). The purpose of the church is not to survive change (Romans 12:2), but to formulate mazeways and trajectories through the wave fronts of change that ensure the Church's macro-level *telos*, the Kingdom-oriented *missio Dei*, is able to be achieved.

As churches follow these principles gained from Complex System Science-framed analyses, they will be able to remain in the Cusp of Change, they will be able to sustain the ongoing, continuous process of revitalization, continuously adapting to the twenty-first century of rapid, complex change. For "... if any should be able to survive such cataclysmic changes, it should be those who claim to be heirs to the faith of the psalmist who long ago sang: 'God is our refuge and strength, a very present help in trouble. Therefore we will not fear, though the earth should change, though the mountains shake in the heart of the sea.' (Psalm 46:1-2)" (Gonzalez 2002, 46)

Chapter 8

Missiology on the Cusp of Change – The Creation of New Mazeways to *Shalom* Via Complex Systems Science

8.1 Physician, Heal Thyself

As the twenty-first century comes of age, rapid, complex change is occurring, requiring new research paradigms to understand the realities of this new context. Missiology, the study of, and participation in, *misso Dei*, is no exception. Research in this field must travel the new mazeways forged by its hard science and soft science siblings into the new realities – or be left behind and marginalized (Shenk 2002, Jorgenson 2011, Paas 2011, Rynkiewich 2011, Baker 2014).

In this book, I have argued that missiology must engage in a research paradigm shift more in line with Complex Systems Science, a step that most of the other sciences *have already taken.* Though the distances traveled in the expanded universe of complexity vary substantially, the transition is inevitable; for like all new paradigms, this one poses new and interesting questions that will probe the nature of stasis and change. As has been described in Chapter 3, the disciplines that have taken the shift have experienced profound revitalization and have experienced an explosion of new research mazeways.

Using Wallace's traditional model of revitalization, this book has illustrated how a shift in paradigms through a comparison with the Cusp of Change model provides a more robust, efficacious and comprehensive model that can represent, study, and systematize the diverse contexts of Christian revitalizations that are occurring through the globally networked system of cultures and societies as observed by the contemporary consultations sponsored by the Center for the Study of World Christian Revitalization Movements. Moreover, as the scales of research expand, Complex Systems Science-framed approaches can provide new mazeways the expanding network of interconnecting contexts that are our twenty-first century realities.

Again, it does not mean that traditional approaches are invalid; rather, as the boundaries of reality expand, traditional approaches will be inadequate in the ever increasing and diverse realities. That is, "...we need to develop both the ability to recognize the extent to which our mental models are correct and the ability to use different models simultaneously. This is not a case about making value judgements about simplicity or complexity, but instead to see the world as it really is: to have new eyes." (Ramalingam 2013, 234)-09-28).

With this said, the adaptation of new paradigms creates is not without problems. Indeed, as there are concerns with traditional, linear methods, Complex Systems Science, its methods and metaphors, like all human endeavors, have limitations and caveats as well. As Roth notes, it is inherently reductionist as it distills complex data into comparatively simplistic (comprehensible) terms. He writes, "As Fogelin observes, 'Many metaphors are lame, misleading, overblown, inaccurate.' Many nonlinear natural metaphors will be too." (1992: 238) Nevertheless, if one is mindful of its limitations, Complex Systems Science offers significant benefits for missiology.

As well, there are concerns as to issues of collecting complex data (Abbott 1988, 183; Harkin 2004, xxxii); but as much as methodologies become more complex, Complex Systems Science is not "rocket science," a fear raised during the "Question and Answer" session after this paper's presentation at the 2013 American Society of Missiology meeting when an attendee asked, "So how smart do I have to be to use this?" In response, it has already been noted that many social science disciplines have already undergone revitalization merely by embracing the metaphors of Complex Systems Science.

As missiology is once again playing catch up, there are already an abundance of texts to draw from (see also Battram, 2002; Goldstein et al, 2011). Missiology, especially those areas with origins in anthropology and sociology, will find that mazeways have already been developed that can be readily adapted, like Hiebert's bounded/centered set theory of conversion, Shaw's contextualization model, and in this book, the Cusp of Change Christian revitalization model. And if computational methods and models are to be pursued, missiologists also need not start from scratch. Missiologists have available to them a host of developed programs and software by social scientists, the vast majority of them in the public domain (i.e.

free) (Wilensky, 1999; Nikolai and Madey, 2009; Railsback and Grimm, 2012).

But on the flip side, it does challenge missiology-related programs to prepare a new generation of researchers to travel in these new realities of complexity and change (Joregenen 2011, Paas 2011, Rynkiewich 2011). If future missiologists do not become adept and familiar with Complex Systems Science, it really will be "rocket science" and they will be left in the solar system of general linear reality in the universe of complex realities.

Some may also question whether or not Complex Systems Science is compatible with the biblical worldview. To this, one should be reminded of Romans 1:20 which informs us that "since the creation of the world, His invisible attributes, His eternal power and divine nature, have been clearly seen, being understood through what has been made." As Complex Systems Science is a systemic perspective, more holistic in nature, it is ideally compatible with the biblical worldview (Clayton and Davies 2009). As has been noted earlier, because Complex Systems understands that all are within a grand network, it restores the nodes and connections between religion and science that the Enlightenment removed. And with regard to the discussion on revitalization, it has been shown that Complex Systems Science is more compatible with the biblical worldview because it begins with systems perspective and acknowledges mystery as opposed to a positivist, logical empiricist perspective. As such, Complex Systems Science should be seen as a mediator that rebuilds interdisciplinary bridges.

Hence, missiologists should be mindful of the limitations of Complex Systems Science, but the potential advantages far outweigh not harnessing what it offers. Because of the increased complexities resulting from global networks and its consequential impact on change processes to rapid and complex, metaphors, models and methodologies must now be released into a much larger reality, a global, networked, rapidly changing complex systems perspective, to avoid lethal results due to short-sightedness of long-term consequences. General linear reality is just no longer adequate for the twenty-first century *realities* (Abbott 1988). It is crucial for missiology to rapidly make the transition.

In fact, many missiologists have voiced concerns over the lack of adequate foresight in missions due to the lack of appropriate training as well as adequate models for the twenty-first century context (Jorgensen 2011, Paas 2011, Rynkiewich 2011). Whether it be a "hole in the gospel" (Stearns 2010) or "when helping hurts (Corbett and Fickkert 2009) or creating "split-level Christians" (Hiebert *et al* 1999, 90), traditional, linear thinking and linear approaches have resulted in less than desired results and more often than not, are accompanied with unanticipated deleterious consequences (Abbott 1988).

This is why many missiologists have called for a more holistic approach to missions, one step toward a Complex Systems Science world view. For example, Bruce Bradshaw writes that the concept of holism

> ... seeks to restore the harmony of creation that reflects the glory of God. To this extent, distinctions between evangelism and development, or the physical and the spiritual aspects of creation are detrimental to our understanding and fulfilling the call of Christians to ministry. The visible, physical aspects of creation as well as the invisible, spiritual aspects must be harmonized to support the abundant life we have in Christ. (1993, 16)

Bradshaw terms this holism *shalom*, ". . . the state of wholeness and holiness possessed by individuals and communities as they become part of the greater community of faith. . . . It does not see [things] as contradictory or competitive, but seeks their roles redemptively" (18). If one compares this with the understanding of the Cusp of Change, one might concluded that the Cusp of Change is the communal process in which *shalom* is achieved.

In the same vein, Tetsunao Yamamori uses the term "contextual holism."

> To effectively reach top-end and bottom end population groups, 'contextual holism' is necessary. This is a holistic ministry strategy that takes into account the needs, problems, opportunities, receptivity, and available resources of a particular area to determine which aspect of holistic ministry should be underscored at any given time to fully accomplish God's work. The principle of contextual holism is sensible, practical, necessary and most important, biblical. (1996, 8)

Although Complexity Theory is not mentioned in the case studies in *Serving with the Poor in Africa,* it is interesting to note that Complexity Leadership terminology, metaphors, and models are used throughout. For example, in his case study on community participation and holistic development, Samuel Voorhies writes about capacity building.

> Sustaining participation as well as project benefits will often depend on the community's capacity. Building the basic organizational capacity of communities must be an intentional part of the program strategy. This capacity should include the capability to forge links with other

organizations, design and continue ways for local residents to participate in decision-making, collect information from local persons for decision-making and develop processes for solving problems and implementing decisions. (1996, 134)

Contextualized to the terminology and metaphors of Complexity Leadership Theory, Voorhies is essentially describing the identification and empowerment of positive deviants and enabling network resonance in order to sustain an organization in the Cusp of Change, what this book argues as the steady-state of ongoing revitalization.

Interestingly, a "chaos-vision paradigm" is mentioned in Kweku Hutchful's case study. But instead of referring to Complexity Theory, he is referring to Genesis 1:2.

> While it is important to start with a clear description and understanding of chaos confronting communities, it is even more important that there is a crossover from chaos to vision, from a problem focus to a solution focus. Many communities in Africa are stuck in the problem analysis stage, needing help to move on to creative formulations of solutions.
>
> Holistic ministries should demonstrate the processes of creative thinking, envisioning and crossing over from problem to solution, and these ministries should train community leaders to do that for themselves. This will ensure a future and hope for the communities when they are finally left on their own to implement their own solutions to the problems confronting them. (152)

Again, Hutchful's description can be easily contextualized as a Complex Systems processes to sustain the Cusp of Change.

The similarities are not coincidental, but are manifestations of concurrently emerging process. In his study of aid development, Ben Ramalingam's makes the same arguments.

> As a result of the dominance of single-loop learning, which has only been reinforced by the formal movement, I would argue that an epidemic of 'bestpracticitis' is afflicting aid agencies. This may seem like a facetious framing, but my intention is a serious one: aid is suffering from a non-trivial ailment. The symptoms include the following: organizations spend all their time looking for the single right answer rather than diverse solutions; people spend more time trying to do things right than doing the right things; there is much more focus on knowledge transfer than on knowledge creation; the whole enterprise is underpinned by a search for efficiency and cost-based value-for-money measures that assume that what is known is needed (and should be cheap, although that is another issue). (2013, 26)

Ramalingams offers numerous case studies of how short-sighted practices have only compounded problems, such as the result of pesticide-resistant mosquitos now furthering the spread of malaria in the twenty-first century as a consequence of efforts to eradicate malaria in the 1950s (2013, 30). Reaching the same conclusions as Corbett and Fikkert (2009), helping hurts.

Similarly, Walls argues the exact same observation with regard to twentieth century missions, particularly American mission efforts. He writes, "Here we see again the characteristically American problem-solving approach at work: identify the problem, apply the right tools, and a solution will appear. Then move on to the next problem." (1996, 234)

In response to the failure of aid organizations to fulfill their mission, Ramalingam's argues for the critical need to shift from traditional approaches to Complex Systems Science approaches (see Table 9). In order to restore a clear vision in the twenty-first context of globally networked, rapid, complex change, ". . . four lenses of system, behaviours , networks, and dynamics have direct relevance for the challenges in aid— learning and knowledge, strategies and policies, organizations and relationships, performance, and accountability. (2013, xviii) (see Figure 27) These are very similar to the lenses that were highlighted in Chapter 6.

	Conventional aid thinking	New Perspectives
Systems and problems	Systems and problems are closed, static, linear systems; reductionist—parts would reveal the whole	Systems are open, dynamic, non-linear systems far from equilibrium. Macro patterns emerge from micro behaviours and interactions
Human agency	Individuals use rational deduction; behaviour and action can be specified from top-down; perfect knowledge of future outcomes is possible	Heterogeneous agents that mix deductive/inductive decisions, are subject to errors and biases, and which learn, adapt, self-organize and co-evolve over time
Social structures	Formal relations between actors are most important; relationships are ahistorical and can be designed; actors can be treated as independent and atomized	Interpersonal relationships and interactions matter in form of culture, ties, values, beliefs, peers. Informal matters, relationships are path dependent and historical
The nature of change	Change is direct result of actions; proportional, additive and predictable; can hold things constant; simple cause and effect	Change is non-linear, unpredictable, with phase transitions

Table 9 - Conventional and Complex Systems Science-framed Approaches to Aid (from Ramalingam 2013, 142)

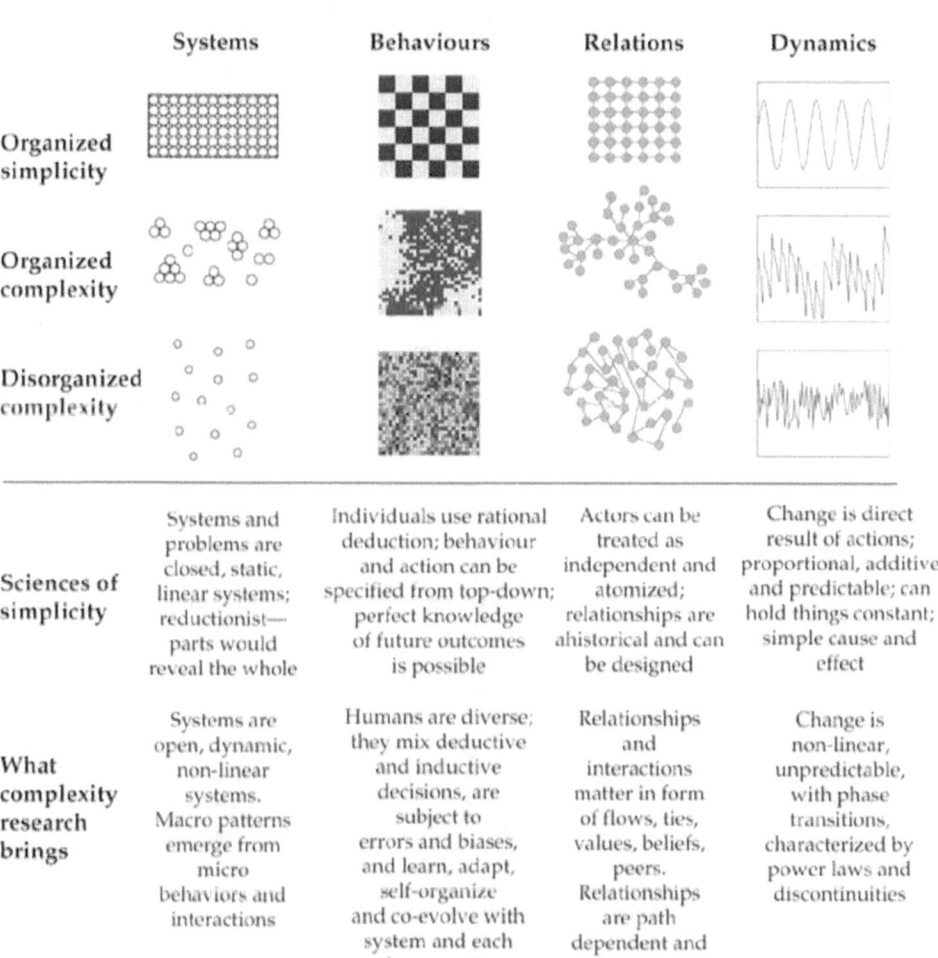

Figure 27 - Visual Signatures and Contribution of Complexity Research (from Ramalingam 2013, 232)

Hence, the evidence is concurrent and emerging that traditional methodologies are reaching their limits of validity and useful without a paradigm shift. It is why so many fields are transitioning to Complex Systems Science. Missiology must join this paradigm shift.

This paradigm shift to Complexity Systems Science in missiological analysis is even more critically necessary now as many mission agencies seek new mazeways for the twenty-first century context such as business missions, development models, and the increasing use of short-term missions in place of career missionaries. The concern is that without adequate supporting terminology, metaphors, models and methodologies for analyses of networked, rapidly changing complex systems, missiologists will be unprepared and unable to provide the necessary guidance for success, and worse, provide short-sighted, inaccurate, and detrimental guidance.

Alternatively, beyond the revitalization, development and aid, the application of Complex Systems Science to the host of missiological issues holds great potential.

> Stuart Kauffman [one of the founders of Complex Systems Science] has described complex systems research as helping reconnect us to the immense and unknowable cosmos of which we are a part. Because of the ubiquity of the patterns revealed in complexity research— from our own backyard to the formation of galaxies— he says that understanding these patterns can make us feel more "at home in the universe." On a somewhat smaller scale, I think these ideas can help make sense of our existing realities, enable more open conversations about the challenges we face, and generate new ways of thinking about problems. Complex interconnections , behaviours, relationships, and dynamics are everywhere around us, if we are willing to change how we see the world: to not just discover new landscapes but to also see through new eyes. To my mind, this transformation can contribute to a form of familiarity just as important as Kauffman's grander vision. Acknowledging rather than denying complexity can make us feel more at home in our own world. It can help us understand the world better than we do, in some key areas where our understanding, ways of thinking, and ways of acting are lacking. It can help us ask the right kinds of questions, it can serve as an engine for intuition, and it can help us critically engage with the answers. It can point to possibilities we might not have otherwise considered, ideas we may have discarded, approaches that could be more relevant and appropriate. (Ramalingam 2013, 361 – 362)

Some, like Hiebert and Shaw, have shown the way as has already been noted.

And despite the sparseness of direct use of Complex Systems Science, it does not mean that missiologists are not trying to address complexity. In a review of three primary mission journals, *Missiology, International Bulletin of Missionary Research,* and *Mission Studies,* over a five year period from 2010 to 2014, it was found that of 284 articles, two-thirds, 189 article, were "complex" in nature (see Table 10). By complex,

Missiology articles from January 2010 to Oct 2014 categorized

TOTAL: 121	Qualitative: 109	Quantitative: 12
Historical	14	
	Linear: 9 (1 dualistic tension) Complex: 5	
Theological	20	1
	Linear: 8 (5 dualistic tension) Complex: 12 (5 chart/diagram)	0 1
Methodological	75	11
	Linear: 41 (10 dualistic tension) Complex: 34 (9 charts/diagrams)	1 10 (7 charts/diagrams)

Mission Studies articles from January 2010 to Oct 2014 categorized

TOTAL: 52	Qualitative: 41	Quantitative: 1
Historical	10	0
	Linear: 6 (1 dualistic) Complex: 4	
Theological	14	0
	Linear: 2 (1 dualistic) Complex:12 (2 charts/diagrams)	
Methodological	27	1
	Linear: 6 (2 multimodal, rdtcn) Complex: 21 (1 chart/diagram)	0 1 (1 chart/diagram)

IBMR articles from January 2010 to July 2014 categorized

TOTAL: 111	Qualitative: 100	Quantitative: 11
Historical	41	2
	Linear: 13 Complex: 28	0 2 (1 chart/diagram)
Theological	9	0
	Linear: 1 (multi-modal,	

	redctn) Complex: 8	
Methodological	50	4
	Linear: 8 Complex: 42 (2 charts/diagrams)	0 4 (2 charts/diagrams)

Combined Tally of Articles

TOTAL: 284	Qualitative: 260	Quantitative: 24
Historical	65	2
	Linear: 28 (2 dualistic tension) Complex: 37	0 2 (1 chart/diagram)
Theological	43	1
	Linear: 11 (7 dualistic tension) Complex: 32 (7 chart/diagram)	0 1
Methodological	152	21
	Linear: 55 (12 that CSS can help) Complex: 97 (12 charts/diagrams)	1 20 (10 charts/diagrams)

Table 10. Tabulation by Category of Missiology Journals from 2010 – 2014

articles had to consider their subject matter systemically, multi-modally, multi-directionally, dynamically, and draw "open-ended" conclusions; that is, they offered multiple possibilities, yet with the realization that their conclusions were bound to certain contexts and realities.

An example of an article categorized as complex is written by Nathan D. Showalter and Yichao Tu, entitled, "Billy Graham, American Evangelicals, and Sino-American Relations." (2010) They conclude, writing

> There is no simple way to parse the relationship between the United States and China in its political, diplomatic, and military manifestations during the past half-century. When we introduce the irreducible complexity of religion into this discussion of Sino-US relations, we can be sure that analyzing the influence of one man and the organizations and networks he represents will not yield incontrovertible conclusions. (2010, 455)

Showalter and Tu acknowledge complexity and the limits of their conclusions. Nevertheless, it did not deter them from attempting to describe the complex nature of topic. The article is well balanced by including a systemic overview, multiple perspectives at different levels, multiple modalities of influence, and a description of interactions and their results, all encapsulated in epistemological humility. Framing their topic in Complex Systems Science terminology and metaphors however, would have been beneficial to help readers better visualize the relationships and would most likely have enhanced the breadth of their conclusions.

It is also interesting to note that many articles that were categorized as complex were in response to linearity in other works. One example is the article written by Lamin Sanneh, entitled "The Last Great Frontier: Currents in Resurgence, Convergence, and Divergence of Religion," (2013) in response to Samuel Huntington's *Clash of Civilizations and the Remaking of World Order* (1996). In his article, Sanneh paints a broad picture of the complexities of religion across the world to counter Huntington's general linear reality. If one googles Huntington, his book, and "linear," one will hit on hundreds of articles and blogs in support of Sanneh's contention.[14] One hit was the op-ed article by *New York Times* columnist David Brooks who concludes

> I'd say Huntington misunderstood the nature of historical change. In his book, he describes transformations that move along linear, projectable trajectories. But that's not how things work in times of tumult. Instead, one person moves a step. Then the next person moves a step. Pretty soon, millions are caught up in a contagion, activating passions they had but dimly perceived just weeks before. They get swept up in momentums that have no central authority and that, nonetheless, exercise a sweeping influence on those caught up in their tides. (2011)

If one notes Brooks' language, it draws directly from Complex Systems Science. Hence, had Huntington used Complex Systems Science as his framework, he could have avoided becoming a major attractor where complex articles gravitate.

In contrast, articles which were considered "linear" tended to be reductionist, unilateral, and with the intent to draw a single conclusion, that is, seeing reality as generally linear (Abbott 1988). An example of what was categorized as linear is an article written by Auli Vähäkangas, entitled "African Feminist Contributions to Missiologi-

---

14

https://www.google.com/search?q=samuel+huntington+clash+of+civilizations+linear&rls=com.microsoft:en-us:IE-Address&ie=UTF-8&oe=UTF-8&sourceid=ie7&gws_rd=ssl. accessed October 9, 2014 cal Anthropology."[15] (2011) It is well-written with many insights and substantive observations. Nevertheless, it was singularly focused on the contributions of African feminists. In fact, Vähäkangas herself acknowledges this, writing

> Until now I have been summarizing the contribution of African feminist theologians to missiological anthropology. But what has missiological anthropology contributed to African feminist theologians? What could be the contribution of missiological anthropology to African feminist theology and to the wider community of African missiology and to the Christian church in Africa? (2011, 183)

In essence, Vähäkangas recognizes her own linearity and acknowledges the need to be more bilateral and systemic. But despite acknowledging the fact, it is only a token gesture to complexity and, as such, the article is categorized as linear.

Other examples of linearity can be seen in the biographies found in each issue of the *International Bulletin of Missionary Research*. Biographies which were categorized as linear tended to singularly present the contributions of each person, what essentially amounts to hagiography. In contrast, biographies which were considered complex included how the context of the mission field changed the person. Such biographies tended to look not merely at the contributions, but at different aspects of the person and how s/he changed over the course of life. A complex biography made for a richer understanding of the person than a linear biography focused on a person's achievements.

Finally, it should be noted that of the 95 articles categorized as "linear," 21 had discussions that were either multimodal or dualistic in nature. This again suggests that the application of Complex Systems Science-framed approaches could have been beneficial had they incorporated this framework.

The journal review confirms that missiologists are seeing complexity; however, they have yet to adopt the metaphors, models, and methods that may enhance their ability to describe and analyze the realities of our twenty-first century context. As well, without adaptation to Complex Systems Science-framed approaches, lacking a corresponding framework and terminology, missiologists will be severely limited in their dialogue with their hard and soft science colleagues (Jorgensen 2011, Paas 2011) and as such, reduces the inter-

---

[15] I chose this article as an example because Vähäkangas herself noted that the article was not bilateral

disciplinary nature of missiology (Van Engen 1996, Escobar 2003, Rynkiewich 2011, Baker 2014)

So much more work can be done. So much more needs to be done. Mission theory, ecclesiology, and mission theology and history all abound with a plethora of topics that can find greater illumination or solution through Complex Systems Science. Some that come to mind are: the hermeneutical circle in biblical interpretation; resolving the polarities of the global and local, movement and institution, centripetal and centrifugal, evangelism and social justice, and church growth and the missional church; the art of preaching between two worlds; Bevans and Schoeder's constants and contexts; missions from everywhere to everywhere formed around multiple centers; inter-religious dialogue; the quest to better understand the C1 – C6 spectrum; and of course, explaining the Trinity as three-in-one. In this author's reflections, there are ready-made parallels found in Complex Systems Science. Hence, whether it be new theological models of the Trinity or missional models of *missio Dei* using attractors, historiographic integration of world Christianities using Chaos Theory, inter-religious dialogue using dimensional integration, or re-examining conversion as a resonant interaction process, Complex Systems Science can offer new insights, new questions, and new mazeways for the twenty-first century context.

Much of this work will be, and must be, done by missiologists.

8.2 Integrating Complex Systems Analysis into Existing Missiological Mazeways

As mentioned earlier, while there may be an initial learning and adoption curve, the mazeway to integrating Complex Systems Analysis need not be difficult. It can be executed in three stages, with metaphors, models, and methods. The Sociology and Complexity Science (SACS) toolkit provides numerous examples of this process (Byrne 1998, Castellani and Hafferty 2009).

First, missiologists need to understand Complex System Science metaphors, then reflectively compare them with established missiological metaphors. Once potential pairs are found, missiologists can then analyze whether or not new insights are gained from overlaying Complex System Science metaphors to the existing metaphors. For example, consider the Missional Helix proposed by Gailyn Van Rheenan in his study of the Church Growth Movement. Van Rheenan developed the Missional Helix based on his observed limitations of the

Church Growth model, writing, "The four limitations of Church Growth that we have discussed – anthropocentric focus, pragmatics and the segmentation of theology and praxis, theological level of inquiry, and focus on growth – suggest the need for a new model of missions." In response, the "*missional helix* visualizes such an 'interdisciplinary and interactive' approach to the practice of ministry and provides a corrective to traditional Church Growth perspectives." (2004, 186) The missional helix is shown in Figure 28.

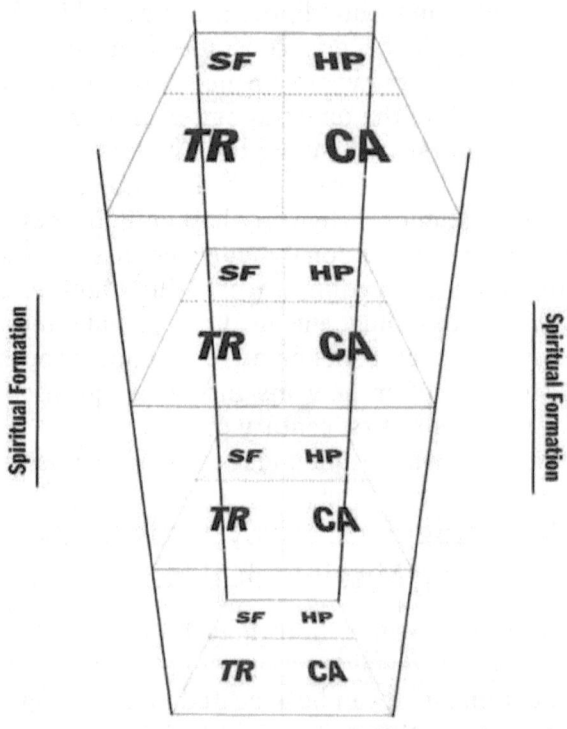

Figure 28 - The Missional Helix (Van Rheenan 2004, 188)

Van Rheenan argues that "Church Growth determines effective practice and then seeks to validate this practice by the use of Scripture. The movement emphasizes growth rather than faithful proclamation of the gospel and faithful living of the gospel. A missional model, on the other hand, begins with theological reflection (TR), while taking seriously [historical perspective (HP),] cultural analysis (CA) and strategy formation (SF)." (2004, 189) Unlike Church Growth with is linear, discrete and static, only requiring scriptural validation, Van Rheenan's proposal is a fluid process. The process is continuous and is a spiral because all elements must interact with one all the other elements and cyclical, with each cycle building on the previous cycle.

If one reviews Complex Systems literature, one finds a very similar metaphor in the Nonaka SECI model of Knowledge Creation illustrated in Figure 29. This Complex Systems Science-framed model was developed for Japanese companies to bring the entire organization into the innovation process. The SECI model is also helical with multiple iterations in response to the continuously changing market environments.

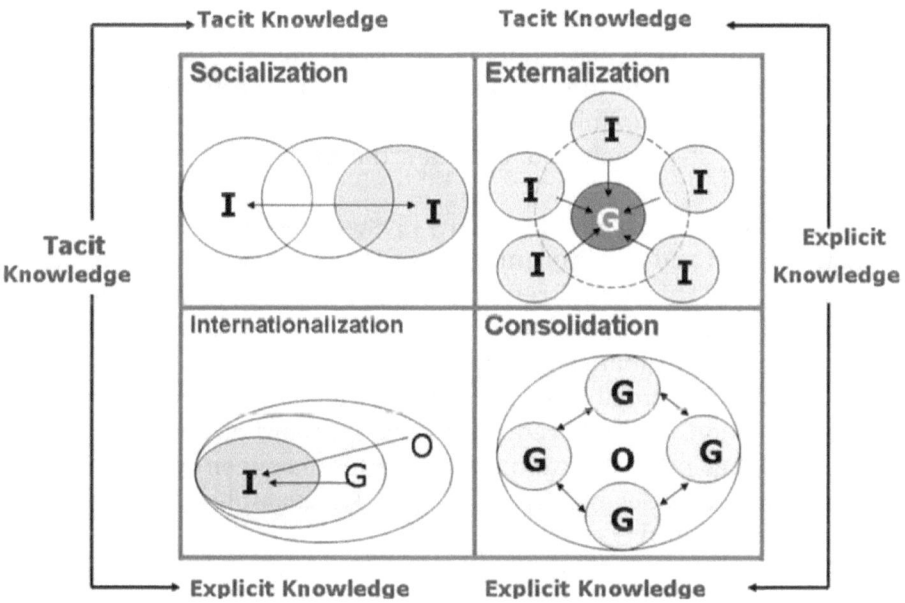

Figure 29 – Nonaka SECI model of Knowledge Creation (Wierzbicki and Nakamori 2006, 69)

Here, Tacit Knowledge, derived through the more abstract avenues of personal experience and relationships are similar to Van Rheenan's Theological Reflection and Cultural Analysis, and Explicit Knowledge, derived through tangible communication avenues, are similar to Van Rheenan's Historical Perspective and Strategy Formation. If one reviews the literature, one will find close parallels in the proceses.

However, Nonaka took the metaphor further by defining a model the contexts in which the processes should occur, whether it be the individual (I), a small group (G), or the entire organization. This is generally that case as the intent of Complexity Systems Science is to move beyond the metaphor phase to create a model that can be implemented as a method.

After a metaphor is identified, the next step is to integrate the models. This process would be similar to that described in Chapter 5. Observed data would need to be analyzed to discern corresponding variables. At this point, observed data can be qualitative, following traditional social science data collection methods. And for many missiological research studies, this may be all that is sufficient if the context is relatively complex. Even in complex contexts, if the intent is one of discovery, ascertaining the right metaphors and models may prove sufficient to provide illumination to the study. Reaching this level would minimize the reductionist bias, empowering the researcher to step back and consider the system as an integrated whole.

But the strength of Complexity Systems analysis would be in methodology and the implementation of the model using computational tools. This would require researchers to add the additional aspect of obtaining quantitative data. Quantitative data is necessary to develop and validate any proposed model.

It should be noted that even qualitative data can be quantified post-collection. It would require a valid, standard protocol for quantification, but post-collection quantification has been performed on data that is decades old (Abbott 2000; for examples, see Eve *et al* 1997, Byrne 1998).

The final step in developing a computational model requires entering the data into an appropriate software program. Missiologists need not develop their own independently, but can draw on a host of readily available programs from the hard and soft sciences.[16] Once a program is selected, a dataset are assigned as program variables and simulations are run. Complex Systems computational are all statistical and heuristic in nature; that is, they become more realistic through an iterative learning process that reduces the margin of error between simulations and observed data. The computation is valid once an acceptable margin of error is attained. The researcher can

---

[16] For example, http://www2.econ.iastate.edu/tesfatsi/acecode.htm contains hundreds of web-accessible programs. accessed August 25, 2014. See also Castellani and Hafferty 2009

then manipulate data and variables to analyze how change would affect the entire system.

8.3 The Role of Missiologists in the Twenty-First Century Context of Globally Networked, Rapid, Complex Change.

In the twenty-first century context of rapid, complex change, as pathfinders across boundaries, cultural, geographic, and now temporal, missiologists play a critical role in helping the church develop mazeways across the globalized, networks through the rapid, complex change that is our twenty-first century context. Being interdisciplinary in nature, among the academy, missiologists are those best able to ascertain the emerging patterns of change. As Alan R. Tippett, the first editor of *Missiology*, writes, missiology is to be a "synthesis of material that speaks to an entirely new world situation." (Scherer 1994, 177)

As well, missiologists are those best able to discern emerging patterns because they are both transcultural and intracultural. Hiebert argues that missiologists are what P.S. Adler would call multicultural, described as the following

> Multicultural man is the person who is intellectually and emotionally committed to the fundamental unity of all human beings while at the same time he recognizes, legitimizes, accepts, and appreciates the fundamental differences that lie between people of different cultures. . . . multicultural man is recognized by the configuration of his outlooks and worldviews, by the way he incorporates the universe as a dynamically moving process, by the way he reflects on the interconnectedness of life in his thoughts and his actions, and by the way he remains open to the imminence of experience (quoted in Hiebert 2006, 301)

This trait allows missiologists to be more able to recognize change through reflecting the interconnections across boundaries, whether cultural or disciplines.

Hence, in the midst of complexity overload, missiologists can provide generative leadership to help the Church with Systems Intelligence that is grounded in the universal hermeneutic of *missio Dei*, enabling the Church to identify positive deviants and assist in conforming networks so that resonance is made possible and maintained to sustain the Church in the Cusp of Change and continuously revitalize in the onslaught of global changes. Only with the Systems

Intelligent metanarrative of *missio Dei* can churches revitalize by remaining in the Cusp of Change by balancing between incremental local changes and remaining fixed on the global Kingdom *telos* of the Church, that is, holding the tension between the historical and eschatological as humanity crosses successive temporal the rapid and continuous waves of complex change (Costas, 1994: 7). Hence, missiologists are call to remind the Church, that despite the complexities of the twenty-first century, "... our belief [is] that there is a real future for us and for the world and that there are therefore solid grounds for hope." (Scherer, 1994: 24)

In conclusion, missiologists, as the pathfinders of the Church, play a critical role in helping the Church to anticipate, participate in and mediate the shaping of the wave fronts of rapid, complex changes and trajectories across global networks that is our twenty-first century context. As Costas writes,

> The new order of life is seen most concretely in the small and large transformations that occur within history. To be sure, these historical signs are not easy to discern. Just as wheat and chaff grow together, so signs of the new order appear in the middle of contradictory situations and thus make it very difficult at times to distinguish clearly between a real signal and a short circuit. Nevertheless it is possible to discern the "signs of the times" through the Holy Spirit's guidance and by the orientation of the Word of God. The church, as the community nourished by the Spirit and the Word, has the privilege and the responsibility to interpret history, distinguishing the signs of the kingdom of God from the antisigns produced by the kingdoms of this world." (1994: 8).

As such, we would do well to heed Gordon Aeschliman's challenge,

> We need the courage to adapt to a new jungle, a new uncharted world in which the accomplishments of the past have produced a global society that desperately needs a new visitation from the people of Jesus. If we're brave enough to let go of the security that old ways of thinking allow, we will have the honor of entering the new territories of the coming century – and of serving the broken and needy inhabitants. (2010, 11)

Embracing Complex Systems Science, its methods and metaphors, has the potential to revitalize missiology in the same way it has for the hard sciences and missiology's soft science siblings. As well, a revitalized missiology will only equip missiologists to be generative leaders for the Church to sustain it in the Cusp of Change. In doing so, the Church, sustained in ongoing, steady-state process of continuous revitalization, serves as a beacon of simplicity that is *missio Dei*, drawing people to the peaceful still waters of Christ in the chaos of humanity.

Bibliography

Abbott, Andrew. "Reflections on the Future of Sociology." *Contemporary Sociology*, 29 (2) (March 2000): 296-300
_____ . *Chaos of Disciplines.* Chicago: University of Chicago Press, 2001
_____ . *Methods of Discovery: Heuristics for the Social Sciences.* New York: W.W. Norton and Company, 2004
_____ . "Transcending General Linear Reality," *Sociological Theory*, 6 (2) (Autumn 1998): 169-186
Adeney, Miriam. "Colorful Initiatives: North American Diasporas in Mission," *Missiology* 39 (1) (2011): 5 - 23
Aeschliman, Gordon. *Global Trends: Ten Changes Affecting Christians Everywhere.* Downers Grove (IL): Intervarsity Press, 1990
Allen, Roland. *Missionary Methods: St. Paul's or Ours?*(American edition). Grand Rapids (MI): Eerdmans, 1962
Augsburger, David W. *Conflict Mediation Across Cultures: Pathways and Patterns.* Louisville: Westminster John Knox Press, 1992
Aula, Pekka and Kalle Siira. "Towards Social Complexity View on Conflict, Communication, and Leadership," in *Complex Systems Leadership Theory: New Perspectives from Complexity Science on Social and Organizational Effectiveness.* edited by in James K. Hazy, Jeffery A. Goldstein, and Benyamin B. Lichtenstein, 367 - 384, Mansfield (MA): ISCE Publishing, 2007
Axelrod, Robert. "Agent-based Modeling as a Bridge Between Disciplines," in *Handbook of Computational Economics. Volume 2: Agent-based Computational Economics.* edited by Leigh Tesfatsion and Kenneth L. Judd, 1565-1584. Amsterdam: North Holland, 2006
_____. "Appendix A: A Guide for Newcomers to Agent-based Modeling in the Social Sciences." in *Handbook of Computational Economics. Volume 2: Agent-based Computational Economics.* edited by Leigh Tesfatsion and Kenneth L. Judd, 1647-1659. Amsterdam: North Holland, 2006

Baker, Dwight P. "Missiology as an Interested Discipline – and Where Is It Happening?" *International Bulletin of Missionary Research.* 38 (1) (January 2014): 17 - 20

Bales, Brian. *An Assessment of Pastors' Moral Development Stage Related to Conflict Management Styles.* Ed.D. dissertation, Southern Baptist Theological Seminary, 2005

Bandy, Thomas. *Christian chaos: revolutionizing the congregation.* Nashville: Abingdon Press, 1999

Barnes, Jessica and Claudette Bennett. *The Asian Population: 2000: Census 2000 Brief.* Washington, DC: US Census Bureau, 2002

Bedford, Olwen and Kwang-Kuo Hwang. "Guilt and Shame in Chinese Culture: A Cross-cultural Framework from the Perspective of Morality and Identity," *Journal for the Theory of Social Behaviour* 33(2) (2003): 127 – 144

Benkirane, Reda. "The Alchemy of Revolution: The Role of Social Networks and New Media in the Arab Spring." Policy paper of the *"Revolution and Reform" Project of the Middle East and North Africa Programme at the Geneva Centre for Security Policy.* (7)2012 1-4.http://www.gcsp.ch/RegionalDevelopment/Publications/GCSP-Publications/Policy-Papers/The-Alchemy-of-Revolution-The-Role-of-Social-Networks-and-New-Media-in-the-Arab-Spring. accessed June 10, 2014

Bonk, Jonathan J., with Erika Stalcup, Wendy Jennings, and Dwight P. Baker. "Missiological Journals: A Checklist," *International Bulletin of Missionary Research.* 37 (1) (2013): 42-49

Bevans Stephen B. and Roger P. Schroeder. *Constants In Context: A Theology of Mission Today.* Maryknoll (NY): Orbis Books, 2004

Bradshaw, Bruce. *Bridging the Gap: Evangelism, Development and Shalom.* Monrovia (CA): MARC, 1993

Brooks, David. "Opinion Page: Huntington's Clash Revisited," *New YorkTimes.*March3,2011.
http://www.nytimes.com/2011/03/04/opinion/04brooks.html. accessed October 9, 2014

Browning, Robert L. and Roy A. Reed. *Forgiveness, Reconciliation, and Moral Courage: Motives and Designs for Ministry in a Troubled World.* Grand Rapids (MI): Eerdmans, 2004

Byrne, David. *Complexity Theory and the Social Sciences: An Introduction.* New York: Routledge, 1998

Cannell, Fenella (ed). *The Anthropology of Christianity.* Durham (NC): Duke University Press, 2006

Castellani, Brian and Frederic W. Hafferty. *Sociology and Complexity Science: A New Field of Inquiry.* Berlin: Springer-Verlag, 2009.

Chang, Myong-hun and Joseph E. Harrington Jr. "Agent-Based Models of Organizations," in *Handbook of Computational Economics. Volume 2: Agent-based Computational Economics.* edited by Leigh Tesfatsion and Kenneth L. Judd, 1273 - 1338. Amsterdam: North Holland, 2006

Chen, Guo-Ming and William J. Starosta. "Chinese Conflict Management and Resolution: Overview and Implications," *Intercultural Communication Studies* 7(1) (1997-8): 1 - 17

Chung, Paul S., Veli-Matti Karkkaninen, and Kyoung-Jae Kim. *Asian Contextual Theology for the Third Millennium: a Theology for of Minjung in Fourth-Eye Formation.* Eugene (OR): Wipf and Stock Publishers, 2007

_____ . "Mosaic Cultural Ministry in the Interface of Korean and Southeast Asian Communities: Reflections from Table Two," in *Revitalization Amid Diaspora: Consultation Three: Explorations in World Christian Movements.* edited by J. Stephen O'Malley, 129 – 140. Lexington (KY): Emeth Press 2013

Clayton, Philip. *Adventures in the Spirit: God, World, Divine Action.* Minneapolis: Fortress Press, 2008

Clayton, Philip and Paul Davies, (eds). *The Re-Emergence of Emergence: The Emergenist Hypothesis from Science to Religion.* New York: Oxford University Press, 2006

Costa, Rebecca D. *The Watchmen's Rattle: Thinking Our Way Out of Extinction.* Philadelphia: Vanguard Press, 2010

Covell, Ralph R. *Confucius, the Buddha and Christ: A History of the Gospel in Chinese.* Eugene (OR): Wipf and Stock Publishers, 1986

de Gruchy, John W. *Reconciliation: Restoring Justice.* London: SCM Press, 2002

Dent, Eric B. "Reconciling Complexity Theory in Organizations and Christian Spirituality," *Emergence: Complexity and Organization.* 5(4):2003, 124-140

Donovan, Vincent J. *Christianity Rediscovered.* Second edition. Maryknoll (NY): Orbis Books, 1982

Dooley, Kevin, Patti Hamilton, Mona Cherri, Bruce West, and Paul Fisher. "Chaotic Behavior in Society: Adolescent Childbearing in Texas, 1964 – 1990. in *Chaos, Complexity, and Sociology: Myths, Models, and Theories.* edited by Ramond A. Eve, Sara Harsfall, and Mary E. Lee, 243-268. Thousand Oaks (CA): Sage Publications. 1997

Duffy, John. "Agent-based Models and Human Subject Experiments." in *Handbook of Computational Economics. Volume 2: Agent-based Computational Economics.* edited by Leigh Tesfatsion and Kenneth L. Judd, 949-1011. Amsterdam: North Holland, 2006

Dyrness, William and Veli-Matti Karkkainen. *Global Dictionary of Theology: a resource for the Worldwide Church.* Downers Grove (IL): Intervarsity Press, 2008

Ebaugh, Helen Rose and Janet Saltzman Chafetz. *Religion and the New Immigrants: Continuities and Adaptations in Immigrant Congregation (abridged student edition).* New York: Altamira Press, 2000.

Elmer, Duane. *Cross-Cultural Conflict: Building Relationships for Effective Ministry.* Downers Grove (IL): Intervarsity Press, 1993

Endicott, Leilani, Tania Bock, and Darcia Navarrez. "Moral reasoning, intercultural development, and multicultural experiences: relations and cognitive underpinnings," *International Journal of Intercultural Relations* 27:2003, 403-419

Epstein, Joshua M. *Generative Social Science: Studies in Agent-Based Computational Modeling.* Princeton (NJ): Princeton University Press 2006

Escobar, Samuel. *The New Global Mission: The Gospel from Everywhere to Everyone.* Downers Grove (IL): Intervarsity Press Academic, 2003

Eve, Raymond A., Sara Harsfall, and Mary E. Lee (eds). *Chaos, Complexity, and Sociology: Myths, Models, and Theories.* Thousand Oaks (CA): Sage Publications. 1997

Fiske, Alan. "Relativity within Moose ("Mossi") Culture: Four Incommensurable Models for Social Relationships. *Ethos* 18(2):1990, 180 – 204

Flake, Gary William. *The Computational Beauty of Nature: Computer Explorations of Fractals, Chaos, Complex Systems, and Adaptation.* Cambridge (MA): MIT Press, 1999

Flanders, Christopher L. "About Face: Reorienting Thai Face For Soteriology and Mission." Ph.D. Dissertation, Fuller Theological Seminary (Los Angeles, CA), June 2005

Fong, Ken. *Pursuing the Pearl.* Valley Forge (PA): Judson Press, 1999

Fortosis, Steve. "A Model for Understanding Cross-Cultural Morality," *Missiology* 18(2) (April 1990): 163 – 176

Fowler, Floyd J. *Survey Research Methods (rev. ed.).* Thousand Oaks (CA): 1988

Fowler, Jeaneanne and Merv Fowler. *Chinese Religions: Beliefs and Practices.* Portland (OR): Sussex Academic Press, 2008

Friedman, Thomas L. *The World is Flat: A Brief History of the 21st Century.* New York: Farrar, Straus and Giroux, 2005

Fritz, David A. and Nabil A. Ibrahim. "The Impact of Leader Tenure on Proactiveness in Religious Organizations," 2011

Froehle, Bryan T. "Theological and Missional Perspectives in Light of World Christian Revitalization in Asia: Reflections from Table Three," in *Revitalization Amid Diaspora: Consultation Three: Explorations in World Christian Movements.* edited by J. Stephen O'Malley, 141 – 160. Lexington (KY): Emeth Press 2013

Gaventa, Beverly Roberts. *From Darkness to Light: Aspects of Conversion in the New Testament.* Philadelphia: Fortress Press, 1986

Gow, Peter. "Forgetting Conversion: The Summer Institute of Linguistics Mission in the Piro Lived World" in *The Anthropology of Christianity.* edited by Fenella Cannell, 211 – 239, Durham (NC): Duke University Press, 2006

Gleick, James. *Chaos: Making a New Science.* New York: Viking Press, 1987

Goldstein, Jeffrey. "Conceptual Foundations of Complexity Science," in *Complexity Leadership, Part I: Conceptual Foundations*, edited by Mary Uhl-Bien and Russ Marion, 17 - 48, Charlotte (NC): Information Age Publishing, 2008

Goldstein, Jeffrey, James K. Hazy, and Benyamin B. Lichtenstein. *Complexity and the Nexus of Leadership: Leveraging Nonlinear Science to Create Ecologies of Innovation.* New York: Palgrave Macmillan, 2010

Gonzalez, Justo L. *The Changing Shape of Church History.* St. Louis: Chalice Press, 2002

Grant, Beth. "Comparative Leadership Development: The Cultural Variable of Self in Spiritual Transformation," *Missiology*, 39 (2) (April 2011): 191 – 203.

Grumet, Robert S. "Preface" in *Revitalizations and Mazeways: Essays on Culture Change, Volume 1,* Anthony F.C. Wallace and edited by Robert S. Grumet, vii – xvi, Lincoln (NE): University of Nebraska Press, 2003

Guder, Darrell L., ed. *Missional Church: A Vision for the sending of the Church in North America.* Grand Rapids: Eerdmans, 1998

Guthrie, George H. *NIV Application Commentary, New Testament: Hebrews.* Grand Rapids (MI): Zondervan, 1998

Hamalainen, Raimo P. and Esa Saarinen (eds). *Systems Intelligence in Leadership and Everyday Life,* Espo (Finland): Helsinki University of Technology, 2007

_____ . "Systems Intelligence Leadership," in *Systems Intelligence in Leadership and Everyday Life,* edited by Raimo P. Hamalainen and Esa Saarinen, 3 – 39, Espo (Finland): Helsinki University of Technology, 2007

Haak, Cornelius. "The Missional Approach: Reconsidering Elenctics (Part I). *Calvin Theological Journal* 44(1):2009, 37 – 48

Hall, Douglas A. *The Cat and the Toaster: Living System Ministry in a Technological Age.* Eugene (OR): Wipf and Stock, 2010

Harkin, Michael E. *Reassessing Revitalization Movements: Perspectives from North American and the Pacific Islands.* Lincoln (NE): University of Nebraska Press, 2004.

Harter, Nathan. "Leadership as the Promise of Simplification," in *Complex Systems Leadership Theory: New Perspectives from Complexity Science on Social and Organizational Effectiveness.* edited by in James K. Hazy, Jeffery A. Goldstein, and Benyamin B. Lichtenstein, 333 - 347, Mansfield (MA): ISCE Publishing, 2007

Hazy James K., Jeffrey A. Goldstein, and Benyamin B. Lichtenstein (eds). *Complex Systems Leadership Theory: New Perspectives from Complexity Science on Social and Organizational Effectiveness.* Mansfield (MA): ISCE Publishing, 2007

Heckscher, C. "Defining the post-bureaucratic type," in *The Post-Bureaucratic Organization: New Perspectives on Organizational Change.* edited by Anne Connellon and Charles Hecksher, 14 – 63, Thousand Oaks (CA): Sage Publications, 1994

Herrington, Jim, Mike Bonem, and James H. Furr. *Leading Congregational Change: A Practical Guide for the Transformational Journey.* San Francisco: Jossey-Bass, 2000

Hesselgrave, David. "Missionary Elenctics," *Missiology* 11(4): 1983, 461 - 483

Hiebert, Paul G. *Anthropological Reflections on Missiological Issues.* Grand Rapids (MI): Baker Books, 1991

_____ . *Missiological Implications of Epistemological Shifts: Affirming Truth in a Modern/Postmodern World.* Harrisburg (PA): Trinity Press International, 1999

_____ . *Transforming Worldviews: An Anthropological Understanding of How People Change.* Grand Rapids (MI): Baker Academic, 2008

Hiebert, Paul G., R. Daniel Shaw, and Tite Tienou. *Understanding Folk Religion.* Grand Rapids (MI): Baker Books, 1999

Hirsch, Alan. *The forgotten ways: reactivating the missional church.* Grand Rapids (MI): Brazos Press, 2006

Ho, David Yau-fai. "The Concept of Face," *The American Journal of Sociology* 81(4) (January 1976): 867 - 884

Hofstede, Geert. *Culture's Consequences (second edition).* Thousand Oaks (CA): Sage Publications, 2001

Hofstede, Geert, Jan Hofstede, and Michael Minkov. *Cultures and Organizations: Software of the Mind.* New York: McGraw-Hill, 2010

Howard, Philip N. and Muzammil M. Hussain. *Democracy's Fourth Wave?: Digital Media and the Arab Spring.* London: Oxford University Press, 2013

Hwang, Kwang-kuo. "Face and Favor: The Chinese Power Game," *The American Journal of Sociology* 92(4) (January 1987), 944 – 974

_____. "Two moralities: Reinterpreting the finds of empirical research on moral reasoning in Taiwan," *Asian Journal of Social Psychology* 1(1998): 211-238

Iggers, Georg G., Q. Edward Wang, with contributions from Supriya Mukherjee. *A Global History of Modern Historiography.* Harlow (UK): Pearson Education Limited, 2008

Irwin, Eunice. "How Do You Spell Revitalization?" Definitions, Defining Characteristics, Language," in *Interpretive Trends in Christian Revitalization for the Early Twenty First Century.* edited by J. Steven O'Malley, 229-243. Lexington (KY): Emeth Press 2011

Jandt, Fred and Paul Pedersen (eds). *Constructive Conflict Management: Asia-Pacific Cases.* Thousand Oaks (CA): SAGE Publications, 1996

Johnson, Stephen. *Emergence: The Connected Lives of Ants, Brains, Cities, and Software.* New York: Scribner. 1991

Johnson-Miller, Beverly. "Dancing with God: The Forms and Forces of Revitalization," in *Interpretive Trends in Christian Revitalization for the Early Twenty First Century.* edited by J. Steven O'Malley, 9 - 19. Lexington (KY): Emeth Press 2011

_____. "Revitalization in the Crucible of Discussion: The Mosaic of God in Motion," in *Revitalization Amid Diaspora: Consultation Three: Explorations in World Christian Movements.* edited by J. Stephen O'Malley, 162 - 169. Lexington (KY): Emeth Press 2013

Jorgensen, Jonas A. "Anthropology of Christianity and Missiology: Disciplinary Contexts, Converging Themes, and Future Tasks of Mission Studies. *Mission Studies,* 28(2) (2011):186-208

Karkkainen, Veli-Matti. "Lessons for Revitalization from the Broader, Missional Phenomenology of the Holy Spirit as Found in the Data," in *Interpretive Trends in Christian Revitalization for the Early Twenty First Century.* edited by J. Steven O'Malley, 101-108. Lexington (KY): Emeth Press 2011

Keener, Craig S. *Miracles: the credibility of the New Testament accounts.* Grand Rapids (MI): Baker Academic, 2011.

Kellert, Stephen H. *In the Wake of Chaos.* Chicago: University of Chicago Press, 1993

King, Roberta R. "Music, Liturgy, and Culture Driving Revitalization," in *Interpretive Trends in Christian Revitalization for the Early Twenty First Century.* edited by J. Steven O'Malley, 81 - 90. Lexington (KY): Emeth Press 2011

Kluger, Jeffrey. *Simplexity: Why Simple Things Become Complex (and How Complex Things Can be Made Simple).* New York: Hyperion Press, 2008

Kuhn, Thomas S. *The Structure of Scientific Revolutions* (3rd edition). Chicago: University of Chicago Press, 1996

Kim, Young-Gwan. "The Confucian-Christian Context in Korean Christianity." *B.C. Asian Review* 13 (Spring 2002): 79 - 91

Kohlberg, Lawrence. *Essays on Moral Development, Volume 2: The Psychology of Moral Development.* San Francisco: Harper and Row, 1984

Konior, Jan. "Confession rituals and the philosophy of forgiveness in Asian religions and Christianity," *Forum Philosophicum* 15 (2010): 91 - 102

Kreiser, Patrick M., Louis D. Marino, Pat Dickson, and K. Mark Weaver. "Cultural Influences on Entrepreneurial Orientation: The Impact of National Culture on Risk Taking and Proactiveness in SMEs." *Entrepreneurship Theory and Practice* (2010): 959 - 983

Kuhn, Thomas S. *The Structure of Scientific Revolutions* (3rd edition). Chicago: University of Chicago Press, 1996

Law, Eric H.F. *The Wolfe Shall Dwell with the Lamb: A Spirituality for Leadership in a Multicultural Community.* St Louis (MO): Chalice Press, 1993

Law, Samuel K. "Spline Generated Surface Laplacian Estimates for Improving Spatial Resolution in Electroencephalography," Ph.D. Dissertation, Tulane University (New Orleans, LA), 1991

_____. "Anticipating Change: Missions and Paradigm Shifts in Emergence," *The Asbury Journal.* 67(1)(2012): 4 – 26

Law, Samuel K, Paul L. Nunez, and Ranjith S. Wijesinghe. "High-Resolution EEG Using Spline Generated Surface Lapacians on Spherical and Ellipsoidal Surfaces," *IEEE Transactions on Biomedical Engineering.* 40(2)(1993): 145-153

Lee, Sung Hyun, "Marginality as Coerced Liminality," in Fumitaka Matsuoka and Eleazar S. Fernandez (eds), *Realizing the America of Our Hearts: Theological Voices of Asian Americans* (St. Louis: Chalice Press, 2003), 11-28

Lewellen, Ted C. *The Anthropology of Globalization: Cultural Anthropology Enters the 21st Century.* Westport (CT): Bergin and Garvey, 2002

Lien, Pei-Te. "Tansnational Homeland Concerns and Participation in US Politics: A Comparison among Immigrants from China, Taiwan, and Hong Kong," *Journal of Chinese Overseas.* 2(1)(2006): 56-78

Lichtenstein Benyamin B, Mary Ulh-Bien, Russ Marion, Anson Seers, James Douglas Orton, and Craig Schreiber. "Complexity Leadership Theory: An Interactive Perspective on Leading in Complex Adaptive Systems," in *Complex Systems Leadership Theory: New Perspectives from Complexity Science on Social and Organizational Effectiveness.* edited by in James K. Hazy, Jeffery A. Goldstein, and Benyamin B. Lichtenstein, 129 - 141, Mansfield (MA): ISCE Publishing, 2007

Lindgren, Alvin J. and Norman Shawchuck. *Management for Your Church: How to Revitalize Your Church's Potential Through a Systems Approach.* Nashville: Abingdon Press, 1977

Lingenfelter, Sherwood G. *Leading Cross-Culturally: Covenant Relationships for Effective Christian Leadership.* Grand Rapids (MI): Baker Book House, 2008

Liu, Tong S. "Dual Personality and Truthfulness – On the issue of dual personality encountered in the Ministry for Mainlanders in North American." *Behold* (3) (2003):8 - 12

Liu, Yu. "The Intricacies of Accommodation: The Proselytizing Strategy of Matteo Ricci." *Journal of World History* 19(4) (2008): 465 - 487

Loder, James. *The Logic of the Spirit: Human Development in Theological Perspective.* San Francisco: Jossey-Bass, 1998

Loder, James and W. Jim Neidhardt. *Knight's Move: The Relational Logic of the Spirit in Theology and Science.* Colorado Springs (CO): Helmers and Howard, 1992

Marion, Russ. *The Edge of Organization: Chaos and Complexity Theories of Formal Social Systems.* Thousand Oaks (CA): Sage Publications, 1998

_____. "Complexity Theory for Organizations and Organizational Leadership," in *Complexity Leadership, Part I: Conceptual Foundations,* edited by Mary Uhl-Bien and Russ Marion, 1 - 15, Charlotte (NC): Information Age Publishing, 2008

Marsella, Anthony J., "Culture and conflict: Understanding, negotiating, and reconciling conflicting constructions of reality." *International Journal of Intercultural Relations.* 29 (2005): 651-673

Mehn, John W. "Leaders Reproducing Churches: Research from Japan," in *Missionary Methods: Research, Reflections, and Realities.* Edited by Craig Ott and J.D. Payne, 157 - 174. Pasadena (CA): William Carey Library 2013

Miller, John H. and Scott E. Page. *Complex Adaptive Systems: An Introduction to Computational Models of Social Life.* Princeton: Princeton University Press, 2007

Mitchell, Melanie. *Complexity: A Guided Tour.* New York: Oxford University Press, 2009

Mosko, Mark S. and Frederick H. Damon (eds). *On the Order of Chaos: Social Anthropology and the Science of Chaos.* New York: Berhahn Books, 2005

Muck, Terry and Frances S. Adeney. *Christianity Encountering World Religions: The Practice of Mission in the Twenty-first Century.* Grand Rapids (MI): Baker Academic, 2009

Mungello, David. *The Great Encounter of China and the West, 1500 – 1800.* New York: Rowman & Littlefiled Publishers, Inc., 2005

Nehrbass, Kenneth. "The Half-life of Missiological Facts," *Missiology* 42(3)(2014):384-294

Nicholls, Bruce. "The Role of Shame and Guilt in a Theology of Cross-Cultural Mission" *Evangelical Review of Theology* 25(3): 1998, 231 - 241

Nortey, Jacob. *Acculturation in Moral Development.* Ed.D. dissertation, La Sierra University, 2005

O'Malley, J. Steven (ed). *Interpretive Trends in Christian Revitalization for the Early Twenty First Century.* Lexington (KY): Emeth Press 2011

_____. "What Is It About Christianity That is Ever Generating Revitalization and Reform Movements?" in in *Interpretive Trends in Christian Revitalization for the Early Twenty First Century.* edited by J. Steven O'Malley, 197 - 204. Lexington (KY): Emeth Press 2011

_____ . (ed). *Revitalization Amid Diaspora: Consultation Three: Explorations in World Christian Movements.* Lexington (KY): Emeth Press 2013

Osgood, Charles; William May, and Murray Miron. *Cross-Cultural Universals of Affective Meaning.* Urbana (IL): University of Illinois Press, 1975

Ott, Craig and J.D. Payne (eds). *Missionary Methods: Research, Reflections, and Realities.* Pasadena (CA): William Carey Library 2013

Pachuau, Lalsangkima. "Ethnic Identity and the Gospel of Reconciliation," *Mission Studies* 26 (2009):49-63

Page, Scott E. *Diversity and Complexity.* Princeton (NJ): Princeton University Press, 2011

Pasquarello, Michael. "B. Advancing Christian Revitalization by Following the Spirit: A Summary and Projection" in *Revitalization Amid Diaspora: Consultation Three: Explorations in World Christian Movements.* edited by J. Stephen O'Malley, 170 – 175. Lexington (KY): Emeth Press 2013

Payne, J.D., "Introduction: Methodological Stewardship: Always Evaluating, Always Adjusting," in *Missionary Methods: Research, Reflections, and Realities.* edited by Craig Ott and J.D. Payne, xv – xxii. Pasadena (CA): William Carey Library 2013

Paz, Regina, Feliz Neto, and Etienne Mullet. "Forgiveness: A China-Western Europe Comparison," *Journal of Psychology.* 142(2) (2008): 147-157

_____ . "Forgivingness: Similarities and Differences Between Buddhist and Christians Living in China." *International Journal for the Psychology of Religion.* 17(4) (2007):289-301

Pike, Kenneth L. "Christianity and Culture 1. Conscience and Culture," *Journal of the American Scientific Affiliation* 31(March 1979): 8 – 12

_____ . "Christianity and Culture III. Biblical Absolutes and Certain Cultural Relativisms" *Journal of the American Scientific Affiliation* 31:1979, 139 - 145

Postman, Neil. *Technopoly: The Surrender of Culture to Technology.* New York: Alfred A. Knopf, 1992

Priest, Robert. "Missionary Elenctics: Consicence and Culture," *Missiology* 22(3): 1994, 291 – 315

Purzycki, Benjamin G., Omar S. Haque, and Richard Sosis. "Extending Evolutionary Accounts of Religion beyond the Mind: Religions as

Adaptive Systems." in *The Evolution, Religion and Cognitive Science: Critical and Constructive Essays,* edited by Fraser Watts and Léon Turner, 74 – 91. New York: Oxford University Press, 2014

Quan, Derek. "Finding Ministry Success for American-Born Chinese Pastors in the Overseas-Born Dominant Chinese Bi-cultural Church." D.Min. Dissertation, Phoenix Seminary (Phoenix, AZ), 2004

Railsback, Steven F. and Volker Grimm. *Agent-Based and Individual-Based Modeling: A Practical Introduction.* Princeton (NJ): Princeton University Press, 2012

Ramalingam, Ben. *Aid on the Edge of Chaos: Rethinking International Cooperation in a Complex World.* London: Oxford University Press.

Reese, William L. *Dictionary of Philosophy and Religion: Eastern and Western Thought* (expanded edition). Amherst (NY): Humanity Books, 1996

Reyna, Stephen P. *Connections: Brain, Mind and Culture in a Social Anthropology.* New York: Routledge, 2002

Rogers, Everett M. *Diffusion of Innovations (5th edition).* New York: Free Press, 2003

Roxburgh, Alan with Mike Regele. *Crossing the Bridge: Church Leadership in a Time of Change.* Rancho Santa Margarita (CA): The Percept Group, 2000

Rynkiewich, Michael A. "The World in My Parish: Rethinking the Standard Missiological Model," *Missiology* 30(3) (2002):301-321

_____ . *Soul, Self, and Society: A Postmodern Anthropology for Mission in a Postcolonial World.* Eugene (OR): Cascade Books, 2011

_____ . "Models and Myths of Revitalization: Wallace's Theory of a Half Century On." in *Interpretive Trends in Christian Revitalization for the Early Twenty First Century.* edited by J. Steven O'Malley, 39 - 45. Lexington (KY): Emeth Press 2011

Saarinen, Martin F. *The Life Cycle of A Congregation.* Bethesda (MD): The Alban Institute, 2001

Saarinen, Esa and Raimo P. Hamalinen. " Systems Intelligence: A Key Competence in Human Action and Organizational Life," in *Systems Intelligence in Leadership and Everyday Life,* edited by Raimo P. Hamalainen and Esa Saarinen, 39 – 50, Espo (Finland): Helsinki University of Technology, 2007

Sanneh, Lamin. "The Last Great Frontier: Currents in Resurgence, Convergence, and Divergence of Religion," *International Bulletin of Missionary Research.* 37 (2) (2013): 67 - 72

Scherer, James A. *Gospel, Church, and Kingdom: Comparative Studies in World Mission Theology.* Minneapolis: Augsburg Publishing, 1987

Schneider, Marguerite and Mark Somers. "Organizations as complex adaptive systems: Implications of Complexity Theory for leadership research." *The Leadership Quarterly,* 17(2006):351-356

Schreiter, Robert J. *The New Catholicity: Theology between the Global and the Local.* Maryknowll (NY): Orbis Books, 1997

Schwandt, David R. "Individual and Collective Coevolution: Leadership[as Emergent Social Structuring," in *Complexity Leadership, Part I: Conceptual Foundations,* edited by Mary Uhl-Bien and Russ Marion, 101 - 127, Charlotte (NC): Information Age Publishing, 2008

Schwandt, David R. and David B. Szabla. "Systems and Leadership: Coevolution or Mutual Evolution Towards Complexity?" in *Complex Systems Leadership Theory: New Perspectives from Complexity Science on Social and Organizational Effectiveness.* edited by in James K. Hazy, Jeffery A. Goldstein, and Benyamin B. Lichtenstein, 35 - 60, Mansfield (MA): ISCE Publishing, 2007

Shaw, Mark. "Revivalism, Revivals," in *Global Dictionary of Theology: a resource for the Worldwide Church.* edited by William Dyrness and Veli-Matti Karkkainen, 767 - 771, Downers Grove (IL): Intervarsity Press, 2008

Shaw, R. Daniel. "Beyond Contextualization: Toward a Twenty-first Century Model for Enabling Mission." *International Review of Missionary Research.* 34(4)(2010): 208-2014

Shenk, Wilbert R. *Enlarging the Story: Perspectives on Writing World Christian History.* Maryknoll (NY): Orbis Books, 2002.

Showalter, Nathan D. and Yichao Tu. "Billy Graham, American Evangelicals, and Sino-American Relations." *Missiology* 38 (4) (2012): 444 - 459

Skreslet, Stanley H. *Comprehending Mission: The Questions, Methods, Themes, Problems, and Prospects of Missiology.* Maryknoll (NY): Orbis Books, 2012

Snyder, Howard. *The Radical Wesley and Patterns for Church Renewal.* Grand Rapids (MI): Francis Asbury Press, 1980

_____. *Earth Currents: The Struggle for the World's Soul.* Nashville: Abingdon Press, 1995

Spickard, James V. "Simulating Sects: A Computer Model of the Stark-Finke-Bainbridge-Iannoccone Theory of Religious Markets," presented at the Society for the Scientific Study of Religion, October 2004. http://newton.uor.edu/FacultyFolder/Spickard/OnlinePubs/ReligSim.htm. accessed 12/13/2012

Stevens, R. Paul and Phil Collins. *The Equipping Pastor: A Systems Approach to Congregational Leadership.* Washington (DC): The Alban Institute, 1993

Su, Shan-Yun and Kwang-Kuo Hwang. "Face and Relation in Different Domains of Life: A Comparison Between Senior Citizens and University Students." *Chinese Journal of Psychology* 45(3) (2003): 295 – 311

Surie, Gita and James K. Hazy. "Generative Leadership: Nurturing Innovation in Complex Systems," in *Complex Systems Leadership Theory: New Perspectives from Complexity Science on Social and Organizational Effectiveness.* edited by in James K. Hazy, Jeffery A. Goldstein, and Benyamin B. Lichtenstein, 349 - 365, Mansfield (MA): ISCE Publishing, 2007

Tamney, Joseph B. and Linda Hseuh-Ling Chiang. *Modernization, Globalization, and Confucianism in Chinese Societies.* Westport (CT): Praeger Publishers, 2002

Taylor, John V. *The Go-Between God.* Surrey (UK): SCM Press, 2004

Tennent, Timothy C. *Theology in the Context of World Christianity: How the Global Church Is Influencing the Way We Think about and Discuss Theology.* Grand Rapids (MI): Zondervan, 2007

Tesfatsion, Leigh and Kenneth L. Judd (eds). *Handbook of Computational Economics. Volume 2: Agent-based Computational Economics.* Amsterdam: North Holland, 2006

Thompson Jr., George B. *Treasures in Clay Jars: New Ways to Understand Your Church.* Cleveland: Pilgrim Press, 2003

Turner, Victor. *The Ritual Process: Structure and Anti-Structure.* New Brunswick (NJ): Aldine Transaction, 1977

Uhl-Bien, Mary and Russ Marion (eds). *Complexity Leadership, Part I: Conceptual Foundations.* Charlotte (NC): Information Age Publishing, 2008

Uhl-Bien, Mary and Russ Marion. "Complexity Leadership – A Framework for Leadership in the Twenty-First Century," in *Complexity Leadership, Part I: Conceptual Foundations*, edited by Mary Uhl-Bien and Russ Marion, xi – xxiv, Charlotte (NC): Information Age Publishing, 2008

US Census Bureau, "Asian Community Survey, 2006." http://factfinder.census.gov/servlet/IPTable? bm=y&-geo id=01000US&-qr name=ACS 2007 1YR G00 S0201&-

qr name=ACS_2007_1YR_G00_S0201PR&-
qr name=ACS_2007_1YR_G00_S0201T&-
qr name=ACS_2007_1YR_G00_S0201TPR&-
ds_name=ACS_2007_1YR_G00_&-
reg=ACS_2007_1YR_G00_S0201:035;ACS_2007_1YR_G00_S0201P R:035;ACS_2007_1YR_G00_S0201T:035;ACS_2007_1YR_G00_S020 1TPR:035&- lang=en&-redoLog=false&-format=. (accessed October 1, 2010)

United States. Department of Homeland Security. *Yearbook of Immigration Statistics: 2009*. Washington, D.C.: U.S. Department of Homeland Security, Office of Immigration Statistics, 2010.

Vähäkangas, Auli. "African Feminist Contributions to Missiological Anthropology," *Mission Studies*. 28 (2) (2011): 170 - 185

Van Engen, Charles. *God's Missionary People: Rethinking the Purpose of the Local Church*. Grand Rapids (MI): Baker Books, 1991

_____ . *Mission on the Way: Issues in Mission Theology*. Grand Rapids (MI): Baker Books, 1996

Van Gelder, Craig. "The future of the discipline of Missiology: Framing current realities and future possibilities," *Missiology* 42 (1) (2014): 39 - 56

Volf, Miroslav. *Exclusion and Embrace*. Nashville: Abingdon Press, 1996

Vriend, Nicolaas J. "ACE Models of Endogenous Interactions" in *Handbook of Computational Economics. Volume 2: Agent-based Computational Economics.* edited by Leigh Tesfatsion and Kenneth L. Judd, 1047 - 1079. Amsterdam: North Holland, 2006

Walby, Sylvia. "Complexity Theory, Systems Theory, and Multiple Intersecting Social Inequalities," *Philosophy of the Social Sciences*. 37 (2007):449-470

Waldrop, Mitchell M. *Complexity: The Emerging Science at the Edge of Order and Chaos*. New York: Simon and Schuster, 1992.

Wallace, Anthony F.C. "Revitalization Movements: Some Theoretical Considerations for their Comparative Study," *American Anthropologist* 58 (1956):264-281

Wallace, Anthony F.C. and Robert S. Grumet (eds). *Revitalizations and Mazeways: Essays on Culture Change, Volume 1.* Lincoln (NE): University of Nebraska Press, 2003

_____ . *Modernity and Mind: Essays on Culture Change, Volume 2.* Lincoln (NE): University of Nebraska Press, 2004

Walls, Andrew. *The Cross Culture Process in Christian History: Studies in the Transmission and Appropriation of Faith.* Maryknoll (NY): Orbis Books, 2002

_____ . *The Missionary Movement in Christian History.* Maryknoll (NY): Orbis Books, 1996

Wan, Enoch. "Mission among the Chinese Diaspora: A Case Study of Migration and Mission," *Missiology* 31(1) (January 2003):35 – 43

Wang, Paul C. "A Study of Cross-Cultural Conflict Patterns and Intervention Between Two Generations of Leaders in Two Chinese Churches in Vancouver: Toward a Vibrant Intergenerational Partnership in Ministry." D.Min. Dissertation, Trinity Evangelical Divinity School (Chicago, IL), 2003

Ward, Kevin. "The East African Revival and the Revitalization of Christianity," in *Revitalization Amid Diaspora: Consultation Three: Explorations in World Christian Movements.* edited by J. Stephen O'Malley, 9 - 26. Lexington (KY): Emeth Press 2013

Wierzbicki, Andrzej P. and Yoshiteru Nakamori. *Creative Space: Models of Creative Processes for the Knowledge Civilization Age.* New York: Springer 2006

Wilensky, U. 1999. NetLogo. http://ccl.northwestern.edu/netlogo/. Center for Connected Learning and Computer-Based Modeling, Northwestern University. Evanston, IL.

Wilhite, Allen. "Economic Activity on Fixed Networks." in *Handbook of Computational Economics. Volume 2: Agent-based Computational Economics.* edited by Leigh Tesfatsion and Kenneth L. Judd, 1013-1045. Amsterdam: North Holland, 2006

Willard, Dallas. *Renovation of the Heart.* Colorado Springs: Navigator Press, 2002

Wilson, Carmen R., Van Vorrhis, and Betsy L. Morgan. "Understanding Power and Rules of Thumb for Determining Sample Sizes." *Tutorials in Quantitative Methods for Psychology.* 3(2) (2007): 43 – 50

Wright, Dana and John Kuentzel. *Redemptive Transformation in Practical Theology.* Grand Rapids (MI): Eerdmans, 2004

Worthington, Everett L. *Forgiveness and Reconciliation: Theory and Application.* New York: Routledge, 2006

Yep, Jeanette, Peter Cha, Susan Cho Van Riesen, Greg Jao, and Paul Tokunaga. *Following Jesus Without Dishonoring Your Parents.* Downers Grove (IL): Intervarsity Press, 1998

Yang, Fengang. *Chinese Christians in America: Conversion, Assimilation and Adhesive Identities.* University Park (PA): The Pennsylvania State University Press, 1999

Yin, Robert K. *Case Study Research: Design and methods (2nd ed.).* Thousand Oaks (CA): Sage, 1994

Yin, Xiao-Huang. "Diverse and Transnational: Chinese (PRC) Immigrants in the United States," *Journal of Chinese Overseas.* 3(1)(2007): 122-145

Yong, Amos. *Beyond the Impasse: Toward a Pneumatological Theology of Religions.* Grand Rapids (MI): Baker Academic, 2003

Yong, Amos. *The Spirit Poured Out on All Flesh: Pentecostalism and the Possibility of Global Theology.* Grand Rapids (MI): Baker Academic, 2005

Zhang, Jianxin and Michael H. Bond. "Personality and Filial Piety among College Students in Two Chinese Societies," *Journal of Cross-Cultural Psychology* 29(3) (1998): 402-417

Zhao, Xiaojian. *The New Chinese America: Class, Economy, and Social Harmony.* New Brunswick (NJ): Rutgers University Press, 2010

Zhou, Min. *Contemporary Chinese America: Immigration, Ethnicity, and Community Transformation.* Philadelphia: Temple University Press, 2009

Appendix 1
Definition of Terms

Definition of Terms

Systems

Simple System: a closed system comprised of two units whose interactions can be explained by discrete, linear relationships (Mosko and Damon 2005, 8)

Complicated System: when various elements that make up the system maintain a degree of independence from one another. Thus removing one such element (which reduces the level of complication) does not fundamentally alter the system's behavior apart from that which directly resulted from the piece that was removed. (Page and Miller 2007, 9)

Complex System: "... a system in which large networks of components with no central control and simple rules of operation give rise to complex collective behavior, sophisticated information processing, and adaptation via learning or evolution." (Mitchell 2009, 13) Page and Miller further define it as "... a system when the dependencies among the elements become important. In such a system, removing one such element destroys system behavior to an extent that goes well beyond what is embodied by the particular element that is removed. Complexity is a deep property of a system, whereas complication is not. A complex system dies when an element is removed, but complicated ones continue to live on, albeit slightly compromised." (Page and Miller 2007, 9)

Complex Adaptive System (CAS): A non-reductionist model that looks at the interactions between agents. In other words, the model does not assume "... that by perfectly understanding the behavior of each component part of a system we will then understand the system as a whole" but recognizes there the possibility of global or emergent explanations (Miller and Page 2007, 3). CAS are homeostatic, that is, dynamically stable, possessing both Chaotic and stable characteristics. As such, CAS are able to drift over a fairly wide range of structures and behaviors without threatening its relative stability; yet it is also capable of changing dramatically if needed. Homeostatic systems can be represented as Complex attractors in that they are relatively small, moderately coupled to other systems, and relatively isolated. (Marion 1999, 82)

Dynamic system: "a simplified model for the time-varying behavior of an actual system." It includes both a "mathematical description of the instantaneous state of a physical system and a rule for transforming the current state description into a description for some future, or perhaps past, time." (Kellert 1993, 2)

Complex Systems Subdisciplines and Characteristics

Chaos Theory: the qualitative study of unstable aperiodic behavior in deterministic nonlinear dynamical systems (Kellert 1993, 2) Marion adds that that chaotic systems carry only a limited memory of their past (1999, 6)

Complexity Theory: similar to Chaos Theory, and bordering on Chaos, Complexity Theory includes the characteristic of memories and the ability to process information. As such, it is not merely mechanical in nature, but has the ability to reproduce, to self-organize or emerge without intervention (Marion 1999, 7)

Emergence Theory: when a system may transcend its components so that the whole is greater than the sum of its parts (Mosko and Damon 2005, 35) Because the understanding of downward causation is critical, it is also important to understand the difference between "strong" and "weak" emergence.

- Strong Emergence: when genuinely new causal agents or causal processes come into existence over the course of evolutionary history. Strong emergence is sometimes called "ontological emergence," implying that the explanation of emergence phenomena cannot be fully deduced from study of the physical world and constituent material units.
- Weak Emergence: as new patterns emerge, the fundamental causal processes remain, ultimately, physical.

Weak emergence is sometimes called "epistemological emergence" implying that the explanation of emergence phenomena can be deduced through understanding the material. (Clayton and Davies 2006, 7)
- Lorenz Attractor: a set of points such that all trajectories nearby converge to (Kellert 1993, 13). This is also called a "Strange Attractor" because one can see the results but not the cause.
- Nonlinear: when the whole is different from the sum of the parts or cannot be fully be explained by an understanding of the component parts (Mitchell 2009, 23)
- Reductionism: when all properties of a system are reducible to the properties of its parts, where the reduction may be spelled out in terms of logical equivalence, supervenience, or the like (Kellert 1993, 89-90)

Modeling

Abstraction-based Modeling: a "top-down" approach to modeling where we impose high-level rules on the system. "Thus, in top-down modeling we abstract broadly over the entire behavior of the system." (Miller and Page 2007, 66)

Agent-Base Modeling: a "bottom-up" approach in with the model is ". . . generated from the bottom of the system by the direct interactions of the entities that form the basis of the model. . . . in bottom-up modeling we focus our abstractions over the lower-level individual entities that make up the system." (Miller and Page 2007, 66)

Appendix 2

Lilly Endowment Interview Questions

Pastors overseeing each of the different congregations in each church were interviewed. The following questions were asked for each population group:

- **General Questions Regarding the Church**

G1. Please share with us what makes your church's unique characteristics which God has used to bring people into your church community.
G2. Please describe the demographic changes in your target population and what changes have you made to your church's ministry in the past two years to adjust to these changes?
G3. Please share with us what you consider to be the strengths of your church?
G4. Please share with us what you consider to be the ministry challenges of your church?

- **Questions Regarding Spiritual Formation Practices for the Church**

S1. What ways have you found most effective to help a person move from seeker to believer?
S2. What ways have you found most effective to help a member move from a "baby" Christian to mature and committed disciple (self – growing)?
S3. What ways have you found most effective to help your members develop a missionary mindset?
S4. What role does your youth and children's ministry play in your overall church ministry?

- **Specific Questions for Chinese congregation pastors (Mandarin and Cantonese):**

  C1. What do you see as some of the greatest challenges facing Chinese churches in the next decade?
  C2. What are you doing to prepare for those challenges?
  C3. Describe how you have helped to build unity between overseas (Taiwan, Hong Kong, etc.) Chinese and mainland Chinese (the reason for this question is that many Chinese congregations face these issues and some churches have planted purely mainland Chinese churches)?
  C4. Describe how you have worked to build unity between the Chinese and English congregations.

- **These questions are for English congregation pastors:**

  E1. How have you addressed the challenges of being an English pastor in a Chinese church?
  E2. What ways have the Chinese pastoral staff helped you to bridge those challenges?
  E3. Describe how you have helped to build unity between the English and Chinese congregations.
  E4. Describe what ways you are using to continue to minister to Chinese beyond the second generation (the reason for this questions trends show that few immigrant Chinese churches have been able to retain these generations and many have moved on to Asian American churches)?

Appendix 3

Second Time Point Follow Up Survey

Thank you for your willingness to complete the survey. Your participation will help me in my journey to understand the challenges facing North American Chinese churches and it is my hope that the findings, should you desire the final report, may also be of benefit to you in your ministry.

The purpose of this study is intended to determine what changes are facing the original thirteen churches I visited in 2006-2007 in order to help North American Chinese churches better understand and prepare for the future shifts in immigration, demographics and cultural identity. The focus of the study, due to unique issues, are on churches which are all multilingual, multi-congregational and have an average attendance over 800 members as opposed to smaller single dialect Chinese churches. Out of the roughly 1000-plus Chinese churches in the US, these have been the fastest growing churches and are considered exemplars for the Chinese Christian community.

All answers will be strictly confidential. No individual names or church names will be mentioned in the dissertation or subsequent reports. Survey responses will only be used in aggregate to determine ongoing trends among North American Chinese churches. If you have any concerns about privacy issues, please feel free to e-mail me for clarification.

Please include any personal comments or identification only in the e-mail, not in your completed survey form.

Once again, your assistance is greatly appreciated!

Sam Law
Sam.law@asburyseminary.edu or samlaw@eccseattle.org.
859-536-4827

Ph.D. candidate, Intercultural Studies
Asbury Theological Seminary

Lexington, Kentucky

Senior Pastor
Lexington Chinese Christian Church

Pastor-at-Large
Evangelical Chinese Church of Seattle

Instructions

Please place an "X" next to the answer that best corresponds to your church. For example:

    - declined   **X** - remained the same   - grown slowly (<10%)   - grown rapidly (>10%)

You may add any clarification in the "Comments" line.

SECTION 1: DEMOGRAPHICS: *IN THE PAST 5 YEARS...*

The Chinese population in the metropolitan area my church serves has:
    - declined   - remained the same   - grown slowly (<10%)   - grown rapidly (>10%)

- The mainland Chinese Mandarin-speaking population in the metropolitan area my church serves has:
    - declined   - remained the same   - grown slowly (<10%)   - grown rapidly (>10%)

- The overseas Mandarin-speaking Chinese population in the metropolitan area my church serves has:
    - declined   - remained the same   - grown slowly (<10%)   - grown rapidly (>10%)

- The Cantonese-speaking Chinese population in the metropolitan area my church serves has:
    - declined   - remained the same   - grown slowly (<10%)   - grown rapidly (>10%)

- The English-speaking Chinese population in the metropolitan area my church serves has:
    - declined   - remained the same   - grown slowly (<10%)   - grown rapidly (>10%)

In the last five years, overall church attendance has:
    - declined   - remained the same   - grown slowly (<10%)   - grown rapidly (>10%)

- Attendance in the Mandarin-speaking congregation has:
  - declined   - remained the same   - grown slowly (<10%)   - grown rapidly (>10%)

*The percentage of mainland Chinese in the Mandarin-speaking congregation has
  - declined   - remained the same   - grown slowly (<10%)   - grown rapidly (>10%)

*The percentage of overseas Chinese in the Mandarin-speaking congregation has
  - declined   - remained the same   - grown slowly (<10%)   - grown rapidly (>10%)

- Attendance in the Cantonese-speaking congregation has:
  - declined   - remained the same   - grown slowly (<10%)   - grown rapidly (>10%)

- Attendance in the English-speaking congregation has:
  - declined   - remained the same   - grown slowly (<10%)   - grown rapidly (>10%)

- Non-Chinese attending my church has:
  - declined   - remained the same   - grown slowly (<10%)   - grown rapidly (>10%)

CHANGE FACTORS TO MINISTRY IN THE PAST 5 YEARS AFFECTING GROWTH RATE

- Church plant (independent)
- New campus (one church/multiple campus model)
- New congregation
- Church conflict
- Church split
- Changes in Leadership
- OTHER/COMMENTS:

SECTION 2: ISSUES FACED IN MINISTRY

Below are lists of issues mentioned by <u>at least two leaders</u> in previous interviews in 2006-07. Please mark whether or not this issue exists in your church. If it does exist, please mark any changes.

- Mainland/OBC (Overseas Born Chinese) immigrants to not mix well.
  - does not exist/not a major issue in my church
  - exists in my church →   - no change   - improving   - challenge increasing
- Mainland/OBC leaders often do not share same perspective or priorities
  - does not exist/not a major issue in my church
  - exists in my church →   - no change   - improving   - challenge increasing
- Mainland Chinese immigrants require greater support in marriage and family issues
  - does not exist/not a major issue in my church
  - exists in my church →   - no change   - improving   - deteriorating
- Increasing difficulty to reach newly immigrated mainland Chinese (including students)
  - does not exist/not a major issue in my church
  - exists in my church →   - no change   - improving   - challenge increasing
- Aging OBC members require increasing ministry resources
  - does not exist/not a major issue in my church
  - exists in my church →   - no change   - improving   - challenge increasing

- Non-Christian Overseas Chinese no longer willing to attend church activities due to higher percentage of mainland Chinese
  - does not exist/not a major issue in my church
  - exists in my church → - no change - improving - challenge increasing
- Increasing secularized society has impacted the faith/beliefs of youth and young adults
  - does not exist/not a major issue in my church
  - exists in my church → - no change - improving - challenge increasing
- Youth and young adults leaving church membership (attend other church)
  - does not exist/not a major issue in my church
  - exists in my church → - no change - improving - challenge increasing
- Youth and young adults leaving Christian faith
  - does not exist/not a major issue in my church
  - exists in my church → - no change - improving - challenge increasing
- Difficulty to maintain unity across congregations
  - does not exist/not a major issue in my church
  - exists in my church → - no change - improving - challenge increasing
- Lack of vision about future direction of church
  - does not exist/not a major issue in my church
  - exists in my church → - no change - improving - challenge increasing
- Lack of vision about role of Chinese church in American society
  - does not exist/not a major issue in my church
  - exists in my church → - no change - improving - challenge increasing
- Increased emphasis on efficiency/church growth has led to a deterioration of spiritual life of the church
  - does not exist/not a major issue in my church
  - exists in my church → - no change - improving - challenge increasing

Thinking about the _Next_ Five Years, other Significant Challenges you Feel Should Be Addressed In Chinese Churches:

1.

2.

3.

4.

5.

Thank You for Your Time!

If you would like a copy of the final report (hopefully to be completed December 2014), please make let me know *in the return e-mail.*

www.ingramcontent.com/pod-product-compliance
Lightning Source LLC
Chambersburg PA
CBHW021807220426
43662CB00006B/209